SCHIZOPHRENIC

A Diagnosis of the
Independent Baptist Movement

TOM BRENNAN

Xulon PRESS

Table of Contents

Introduction

The experience and behavior that gets labeled schizophrenic
is a special strategy that a person invents in order to
live in an unlivable situation.
-Dr. R. D. Lang

S chizophrenia is defined as a state characterized by the coexistence of contradictory or incompatible elements. Its presence brings pain not only to the afflicted person but to those who love that person. At times, the person they love is reasonable and delightful. At other times, the person they love is malicious and delusional. It is almost as if two radically different persons are to be found inhabiting the same body. No one knows which one will take precedence at any given moment – Dr. Jekyll or Mr. Hyde.

For over forty years, I have been an independent Baptist. I have attended independent Baptist schools and colleges. I have read independent Baptist periodicals. I have held membership in independent Baptist churches. I have read independent Baptist books. I have attended independent Baptist conferences. I was raised in an independent Baptist home. For over thirty-three years, my father was an independent Baptist pastor. For almost twenty years, I have pastored independent Baptist churches. Over the last ten years, I have increasingly felt like the family member of a schizophrenic individual.

I love the independent Baptist movement. It has a rich history, a wide impact, and tremendous strengths. Where it came from, where it is now, and where it is going – these concepts are dear to

vii

me. At the same time, I am driven to confess that there are aspects of the independent Baptist world that I loathe. It has a checkered past, a splintered present, and deep flaws. It is characterized by the co-existence of contradictory and incompatible elements. In short, it is schizophrenic.

Out of that love and loathing, I have been driven to write this book. On the one hand, I see much of what is right and good being abandoned in a pell-mell rush out of the ditch on one side of the road into the ditch on the other side. Many of my peers in ministry and in the generation behind mine see the same errors I see but have entirely overreacted to them. In so doing they have discarded much that is wise and good and right. This borderline hysterical stampede to the left will result in even deeper flaws in the succeeding generations if their course is not corrected. At the same time, many of my peers and those largely in the generations preceding mine have dug in their heels. They refuse to openly acknowledge few, if any, flaws. They cling with tenacity to questionable and unscriptural practices. With borderline bitterness, they view the alarm of others as treasonous, disrespectful, and dangerous. This dogged insistence on an unquestioning followship has fractured our movement, and if it is continued, it will result in the complete frittering away of what I genuinely believe is the world's last best hope for a real, warm, orthodox, committed, holy Christianity.

Please do not misunderstand me. I do not believe my book will fix everything. I do not even believe my book will be right about everything. As God knows my heart, I have worked diligently to ensure that I am correct in both position and spirit; but I labor under no illusions. I am exceedingly human. God did not give me all the light; I still see through a glass darkly. Consequently, I am wrong about something. But though the words you are about to read are not infallible, I still offer them to you. I am driven to do so out of a belief that they are right, that they are necessary, and that they are helpful.

I fear that some may see this book as an attempt by me to set myself up as the judge of fundamentalism. I have no such desire. Each Baptist who reads this book will answer to God alone. I have been called to pastor one church, and it is not your church. I deeply believe in individual soul liberty, and I do not think any Baptist

viii

wants me as pope. At the same time, though I will not answer for any other independent Baptist, I love each and every one. The publication of this book is simply the view of one concerned family member who sees a dangerous schizophrenia developing and wants to do his best to help to cure the afflictions that beset us.

There may be some as well who will simply take my words as the rantings of an ignorant critic. I have sought to balance this by including equal parts encouragement and admonishment. I am for just as much if not more of what we hold dear in the independent Baptist movement as I am against. I truly hope this book reflects that. In so doing, I realize I run the risk of being the soldier during the American Civil War who wore gray pants and a blue shirt. He did not bring unity; he was simply shot at by both sides. But from whichever side you hail, from whatever perspective, if you are my brother in Christ, I love you; and I want what is best for you, for me, for the next generation, for the lost world, and for the Lord. If you choose to shoot at me for something I have said here or for the very fact of daring to write this book, I hope I can receive it with a peaceful spirit. After all, you may be right, and the Lord may use you to teach me something I need to learn. You may be the instrument of my growth in grace. I hope in some small measure to be yours.

Let me speak a word about my approach. On the negative side, I have purposely chosen not to use the names of specific preachers, conferences, periodicals, and institutions. I do this for two reasons. First, I do not wish to unnecessarily alienate anyone from receiving what I believe to be the vital truth. I do not wish any preacher or group to think I believe they are completely wrong. The truth is I do not believe this to be the case even amongst those who hold deeply flawed positions. Second, I do not want to date this book. I have written to address the situations I have seen over the last four decades and those I see in the present. However, future generations have been much in my mind as I have written. You may certainly try to guess who I am talking about in any one particular illustration, but I would gently encourage you not to do so. It will simply distract from the point of the book. I have not written against any personality or place or group. I have written for what I believe is the right in an attempt to edify the brethren of our own and future generations.

I have divided this book into three sections. The first will discuss what I believe are the strengths of the independent Baptist movement historically and presently. The second will cover the opposite. I will delve into the weaknesses – where they come from and where they will take us if they are not corrected. The third section is my humble opinion as to the cures for what ails us.

I hope you will read this book with an open mind. I hope you will consider the experience, perspective, and spirit with which I write. I hope you will look past the personalities and look at the actual issues. I hope you will be encouraged to hold fast to that which is good. At the same time, I hope you will examine your positions. I hope you will hold them up to the light of Scripture. I hope you will consider again their impact on both the present and the future. There will continue to be disagreement and division until we stand together before Him at His return, but I hope this book will in some small way strengthen that which remains.

Tom Brennan
February 1, 2016
Chicago

Dedication

This book is warmly dedicated to the people of the First Baptist Church in McDonald, Ohio. For my first seventeen years they loved me, ministered to me, taught me the Word of God, and allowed me opportunity to serve Him. Their corporate labor of love in my life will leave me forever in their debt.

Acknowledgements

This book may have my name on the author page but the truth is many, many wonderful people contributed in bringing it to birth. I am grateful to my pastor friends across the country for their considered perspective on numbers of the subjects covered in these pages. At a crucial time of doubt in my mind two experienced men of ministry in particular encouraged me in this project, namely, my father, Pastor Tom Brennan of Port Huron, Michigan, and Pastor Ron Royalty of Poland, Ohio. Their counsel helped me immensely. Once again, Kasey Allen Steele provided her expert editorial advice. My lovely wife, Mandy, unselfishly gave me the time and space I needed for such a big project, and listened patiently as I talked my way through many of these thoughts first with her. She has a way of cutting through the chaff and getting straight to the heart of the matter. This book would not exist without her.

Most of all, I am thankful for the Lord Jesus Christ. What little light I have to shed about me and thus help others arises directly in Him. He is the source of anything good that comes from my life.

Forward

Are you a Baptist? Do you know why? Do you understand the sacrifices that have enabled you to attend a Baptist church? Are you an Independent Baptist? Have you recently considered walking away from that title? Do you understand the great sacrifice that was made a generation ago as many pastors were either forced out of large denominations or chose to leave over major differences in doctrine?

Are you an Independent Fundamental Baptist? Whether the answer is yes or no, I'm sure you feel strongly about it.

Schizophrenic will remind you that as an Independent Fundamental Baptist, you have a great heritage and a wonderful history of taking a strong doctrinal stand. The mainstream Christian churches of America are crumbling. Many are still attracting large crowds, but the foundations upon which they were built are disintegrating quickly. I believe this book will challenge you to continue standing for Christ as an Independent Fundamental Baptist.

I grew up in an Independent Baptist Church that pulled out of a denomination before I was born. My pastor truly had an independent spirit. When I left home for Bible college, I had never heard of most of the men who were considered the leaders of fundamentalism. I had never even heard of fundamentalism. In fact, during one of the first college chapel services of my freshman year, the preacher challenged all the students who were "fundamentalists" to stand up. Students stood all around us as my sister and I sat cautiously in our seats. We had never heard the term. We were just Baptists.

The more I learned what Fundamental Independent Baptists believed and stood for, the more I realized that this was the group I wanted to belong to. However, the more I learned what some Fundamental Independent Baptists actually did, and what types of sins seemed to be acceptable, the less I wanted to be labeled as one. One of the Bible's great attributes is that it tells us both the good and the bad. It doesn't hide the bad to make the good look better. Scripture describes King David as the sweet Psalmist of Israel, a man after God's own heart, and the greatest king of Israel; but It also documents that he had some dark times of deep sin and rebellion against God. God didn't hide the ugly facts when He gave us the history of His chosen people.

As you read this book, you will learn about the good and the bad of the Independent Fundamental Baptist movement through the years. You will also be presented with solutions to the problems we face right now. There is so much good! Yes, there is also some bad, but there are solutions!

In the West, we have wildfires nearly every summer. One year, we spent a week at junior camp choking on smoke and watching embers float over our cabins as a terrible fire burned several miles away. A small town near the camp was transformed into a tent city for firefighters that had come in from all over the country. The fire burned more than 840 square miles. Two years later, another fire claimed the lives of nineteen firefighters. While these fires may not have been completely preventable, their destructive impact may have been greatly limited if controlled burns had been implemented. A controlled burn is a fire that is started on purpose to remove the dense underbrush and dead timber that could lead to a wildfire. Controlled burning also releases seeds of some types of trees, bringing new life to the forest.

The Independent Fundamental Baptist movement needs a controlled burn.

The Independent Fundamental Baptist movement needs a controlled burn. Our churches compose a beautiful forest of godly people who desire to please God and reach our communities and the world with the Gospel of Jesus Christ. There are, however, problems that have been building up like dry tinder in our churches. If we never address these problems in a controlled-burn fashion, they will eventually ignite and hurt more people than we can imagine. I believe this book will help ignite a flame that has the potential to protect our churches from a great deal of damage. Many Christians have grown frustrated with the pride, arrogance, and sin that has marked many of our churches for decades. As a result, they are either leaving their Independent Baptist churches or trying to redefine what a Fundamental Independent Baptist is. If they leave, and if they are looking for a church that holds the same beliefs, the options of where to go are severely limited. If they stay, they face the possibility of being lumped together with the scoundrels that have caused great hurt to the name of Christ. I have felt that frustration. Too much has been sacrificed by men and women of previous generations to simply abandon our heritage. Yet, so many problems have been ignored for so long that sometimes it appears there isn't much left to save.

I believe this book will encourage you otherwise.

I challenge you to read this book and allow God to begin a controlled burn in your heart. You may not agree with everything presented in these pages. The author doesn't expect you to. There will be parts of this book that may re-ignite smoldering embers that have been recently blackened by a respected leader, a trusted friend, or even an entire group. While it is hard to address the problems Independent Fundamental Baptists face, I believe you will find the end result of this book to be refreshing.

You don't have to choose between ignoring the sins of Independent Baptist leaders or leaving behind the Independent Baptist movement that you love. You don't have to turn a blind eye to sin in the camp, but you don't have to hit the trail for a different camp either. You can keep the baby and not feel one bit guilty about throwing out the bathwater, but realize the baby still needs a good washing.

We don't need to quit being Independent Baptists, but we don't need a new brand of Independent Baptists either. We don't need to retire the title "Fundamental", but we don't need to ignore the grievous sins of those who have tarnished that name. We need a generation of Independent Fundamental Baptists who are Christians in both name and practice, who read, live, and preach the Word of God. We need a generation of Independent Fundamental Baptists who actually live out the meaning of those three important words. The author of this well researched book will walk you through the significance and the importance of that title, and then guide you through some challenges that, I believe, will help churches all across our country continue to bring glory to God.

Pastor David Reyes
New Heights Baptist Church
Albuquerque, New Mexico

Introduction of the Author

The deeply rooted love that Tom Brennan has for his Independent Baptist heritage is so clearly seen in his new book–*Schizophrenic*. Pride screams at us to sweep our shortcomings, sins, and even heresies under the proverbial rug, yet Brother Tom refuses to heed pride's cry in order to take us on an introspective journey so that we may examine who we truly are. He doesn't claim to have all the answers or even most of the answers; he simply divides this book into three incredibly well written yet simple sections–where we are right, where we are wrong, and ways to strengthen our shortcomings. Brother Tom has certainly done his homework from a scriptural as well as a historical standpoint. He's also knowingly embarked on a journey that could very easily put him in the crosshairs of criticism for his brutal honesty and opinion; I applaud his courage in this regard. Amidst the simultaneous throwing the baby out with the bath water on one side and an ostrich with his head in the sand on the other side, it's refreshing to see that someone has tackled the issues at hand in a loving, caring, and helpful way. As you finish this book you, like me, will most likely be both challenged and grateful for the help that this book has been to your life and ministry.

I don't know anyone more qualified to write a book of this nature than him as he was literally born into and spent his entire life in this movement. He's not a novice. He's young enough and tech savvy enough to relate to the younger generation, while being old enough and even stubborn enough to relate to the hoary heads of our movement.

Tom and I share an alma mater, and the parallel of two pastorates - one in a rural setting and one in a city setting. We both have four children (coincidentally two of our children share names, Abigail and Samuel), and many other similarities. In addition, we share a love for a heritage that we not only believe is Biblically right, but also the tool that God can use to bring a much needed revival to His people. For many years, however, I frustratingly looked at this great movement of ours and saw several elephants in the room. What could I do about the elephants? Nothing of course, because to ever share a concern would be deemed as disloyal and could be grounds for excommunication from a movement that has Independent in its name. Quite ironic indeed, I know! I also saw some people jumping ship to the new and shinier movements amongst Christianity and I knew that was certainly not the answer either. As I read this book I saw that many of the concerns that Tom addressed were also my concerns. He also conveyed some concerns that I had never thought of prior to him pointing them out. Finally, there were several areas that I had become lax in that this book has admonished me to retighten my belt in my own life.

This book is an absolute must read for all believers; especially those who have any connection on any level with the Independent Fundamental Baptist movement.

Pastor Justin Soto
River City Baptist Church
Sacramento, California

Book One–What is Right

Be sure you are right, then go ahead.
-Davy Crockett

We Are Baptists

We believe that the Baptists are the original Christians. We did not commence our existence at the Reformation, we were reformers before Luther and Calvin were born; we never came from the Church of Rome, for we were never in it, but we have an unbroken line up to the apostles themselves. We have always existed from the days of Christ, and our principles, sometimes veiled and forgotten, like a river which may travel underground for a little season, have always had honest and holy adherents. Persecuted alike by Romanists and Protestants of almost every sect, yet there has never existed a Government holding Baptist principles which persecuted others; nor, I believe, any body of Baptists ever held it to be right to put the consciences of others under the control of man. We have ever been ready to suffer, as our martyrologies will prove, but we are not ready to accept any help from the State, to prostitute the purity of the Bride of Christ to any alliance with Government, and we will never make the Church, although the Queen, the despot over the consciences of men.

-C. H. Spurgeon

The story is told that a man died and found himself standing in front of the pearly gates. Saint Peter ushered him inside and began to show him around his bright, shining new hometown. Peter explained to him that it was Bible conference time; various groups were gathered together for worship. They passed a large hall from which organ music flowed majestically. Saint Peter explained that this was where the Lutherans were meeting. Continuing on, they found themselves outside another large auditorium packed full of men and women reciting the Westminster Catechism. Peter did not need to explain that this was the Presbyterian assembly. A little further on was another group sitting spellbound as a white-haired John Wesley held forth. Of course, these were the Methodists. Shortly after leaving the Methodists, Saint Peter leaned over and quietly whispered in the ear of the man asking him to be quiet through this next stretch. They were coming up on the Baptists. Saint Peter did not want them disturbed, for they believed they were the only ones actually in Heaven.

I am not so parochial as to believe that only Baptists will enter Heaven. *What then? notwithstanding, every way, whether in pretence, or in truth, Christ is preached; and I therein do rejoice, yea, and will rejoice. (Philippians 1.18)* I am, however, very happy to be a Baptist. Without any apology, I assert that Baptist doctrine is the purest form of distilled scriptural ecclesiology on earth. Of course, this does not mean God loves us more than He loves those of His children who are not Baptist, let alone those who are not even His children. God loves the entire world – without exception. While that includes Baptists, it is not limited to Baptists. But that very love of God is not any proof or evidence of the correctness of a doctrinal position, nor is it indicative of the supposed fact that doctrinal positions do not matter. They most assuredly do, or else God would not have gone to such painstaking lengths of explaining and emphasizing them in such detail in Scripture. What you believe about the church – what it is, how it is structured, how it operates – is most assuredly important.

As Baptists, we hold to a core set of beliefs commonly labeled the Baptist distinctives. There are certainly other denominations that hold to some or other of these, but no other group holds to them all. These distinctives are often identified with an acrostic connected to the word Baptists. I realize this is not a book on Baptist history or theology, but let us briefly examine them in some detail.

Biblical Authority

The first Baptist distinctive is that the Bible is the sole authority of our faith and practice. For the past year, I have done an extensive study of various cults and false religions for a class I have been teaching. Without exception, they all embrace some authority other than or beyond the Word of God. For instance, Catholics accept the Bible as God's Word and authority, but they unashamedly mix that with church tradition. They appeal more often to church councils and papal encyclicals than they do the Scripture. Likewise, Charismatics accept the Bible, but their addition comes in the form of the continuing revelation of dreams, visions, and prophecies. Baptists, on the other hand, accept no other authority than the Word of God.

The Bible alone is the pure revelation of God. Christian Scientists are wrong about Mary Baker Eddy's *Science and Health with a Key to the Scriptures*. The Latter-day Saints are wrong about *The Book of Mormon*. The Hindus are wrong about the *Vedas* and the *Bhagavad Gita*. The Muslims are wrong about the *Quran*. The Jews are wrong about the *Talmud*. At the end of the New Testament, God placed a clear and significant full stop. *For I testify unto every man that heareth the words of the prophecy of this book, If any man shall add unto these things, God shall add unto him the plagues that are written in this book: And if any man shall take away from the words of the book of this prophecy, God shall take away his part out of the book of life, and out of the holy city, and from the things which are written in this book (Revelation 22.18-19)* God said, "That is it. It is finished. It is done. Do not add anything else and say it is from Me." Everything God has to reveal about Himself until the Second Coming is found in the pages of the Bible. *Every word of God is pure: he is a shield unto them that put their trust in him. Add thou not unto his words, lest he reprove thee, and thou be found a liar. (Proverbs 30.5-6)*

> *Baptists accept no other authority than the Word of God.*

Every other source of authority is fallible. Tradition quickly becomes obsolete. Confessions, catechisms, and creeds are not inerrant. Church councils are as often heretical as they are orthodox. Words of knowledge are not only doctrinally incorrect, but they are also incredibly prone to following the deceitful heart of the "prophet."

God's Word unaccompanied by anything else was authoritative for the Apostles and the Early Church. Paul, who made the statement *it is written* sixteen times in Romans alone, said it this way in *Galatians 4.30: Nevertheless what saith the scripture?*... The Bereans were commended as being better than the Thessalonian Christians *...in that they received the word with all readiness of mind, and searched the scriptures daily, whether those things were so. (Acts 17.11)* Peter plainly said that his authority came from *...a more sure word of prophecy;...(II Peter 1.19)* referencing the Word of God. It is the Scripture and only the Scripture that brings us to maturity and allows us to be *...thoroughly furnished unto all good works. (II Timothy 3.17)*

Autonomy of the Local Church

The second Baptist distinctive is the autonomy of the local church. I will speak about this at greater length in the next chapter, but the short version explains that Scripture teaches the only head of the church is Jesus Christ. The local church is to be under the authority of no higher governing power such as a denominational board. It is to govern itself directly under Jesus Christ.

Priesthood of the Believer

The third Baptist distinctive is the priesthood of the believer. In much of human history, religions have been structured in such a way that one person was a conduit for other people in their attempt to reach God. The Druid culture exemplified in Stonehenge represents this as does the Native American shaman and the African witchdoctor. Saul pursued the witch at Endor in an effort to contact God. In a similar albeit godly vein, God set up a system in the Old

Testament whereby access to God required a priest. *And it shall be, when he shall be guilty in one of these things, that he shall confess that he hath sinned in that thing: And he shall bring his trespass offering unto the LORD for his sin which he hath sinned, a female from the flock, a lamb or a kid of the goats, for a sin offering; and the priest shall make an atonement for him concerning his sin. (Leviticus 5.5-6)*

This concept of going through a priest to get to God was true in the matter of fixing what was wrong between you and God. It was also true if you simply wanted to hear from God. You did not access God directly; you went through His appointed mediator. *And they said unto Moses, Speak thou with us, and we will hear: but let not God speak with us, lest we die. And Moses said unto the people, Fear not: for God is come to prove you, and that his fear may be before your faces, that ye sin not. And the people stood afar off, and Moses drew near unto the thick darkness where God was. (Exodus 20.19-21)* For instance, when David was on the run from Saul and wanted to hear from God, he went to a shrine where Ahimelech the priest *...inquired of the Lord for him,... (1 Samuel 22.10)* This was done via the Urim and Thummim, as well as by other means.

At the death of Jesus Christ, this changed. Herod's Temple, an ornate complex eight decades in the making, was centered on the main building which contained the Holy Place and the Most Holy Place. Between those two rooms hung a curtain or veil. Edersheim, quoting the Mishnah, stated that this veil was enormous. Requiring hundreds of priests to move it, the veil was as thick as a man's hand. *Jesus, when he had cried again with a loud voice, yielded up the ghost. And, behold, the veil of the temple was rent in twain from the top to the bottom; and the earth did quake, and the rocks rent; (Matthew 27.50-51)* Hebrews explains that this veil represented the Messiah's flesh. *(Hebrews 10.19-22)* When that flesh was torn in half, a way was opened up for us to go to God directly without the necessity for an intermediary priest.

So it is that we as Baptists believe Scripture teaches that each of us is in actuality a priest; thus, we personally have direct access to God. *But ye are a chosen generation, a royal priesthood...*

*(I Peter 2.9) And hath made us kings and priests unto God...
(Revelation 1.6)*

My father was a Baptist pastor for thirty-eight years. Prior to his salvation at the age of twenty-five, he was a Roman Catholic. He attended Catholic schools and sang in their choirs through high school. When his marriage began to fall apart, my mother sought counsel from a Baptist preacher. That preacher gave my father Loraine Boettner's thorough treatise *Roman Catholicism*. In between throwing it across the room when it made him upset, he slowly read it. By God's grace, my father came to Christ soon afterward. Years later my father gave me a copy of the book. As I read it, I found my blood boiling like his did – except as a Baptist; I was hot at the Catholics. Their concept of religion is specifically designed to control people via the sacraments, confession, penance, purgatory, tradition, etc. But one of the more egregious heresies promulgated by Rome is the idea that the common person cannot get to God without the aid of a Catholic priest. He cannot be in communion with God without the priest. He cannot be forgiven of his sins without the priest. He cannot accomplish anything of spiritual value without the imprimatur of an ordained Roman clergyman.

I have news for the practically pagan Pontifex Maximus in Rome – I do not need his aid or the aid of his priests to get to God. I can go directly to God for myself. I reject the Roman Catholic model. It is deceptive, unfair, cruel, proud, and unscriptural for a church to teach that its clergy class of priests controls access to God and that if you do not come through those priests, you cannot get to God. Such an awful theology hamstrings a person. It makes them entirely dependent spiritually upon another human being and that person's ecclesiastical organization. There are no other words for it. It is just flat out wrong.

Two Ordinances

The fourth Baptist distinctive is our position on the ordinances. We do not believe they are sacraments because they convey no grace. Nothing conveys grace to the sinner except simple faith in Christ. *(Romans 5.2)* And we believe there are only two such ordinances – baptism by immersion after salvation and the observance of the Lord's Supper. Paul, in the context of a detailed explanation of the Lord's Supper, admonished the Corinthian church to *...keep the ordinances... (I Corinthians 11.2)* So although there must be at least two, there is no necessity for an additional number. Baptism is a public profession before men asserting that you have placed your faith in Jesus Christ alone for your salvation. It signifies by its manner of immersion that you hold to the Gospel – the death, burial, and resurrection of Jesus Christ. Because of this, it obviously cannot be entered into by infants. Indeed, it is this very belief that led to our moniker Baptist. Our forefathers in Europe were labeled as those who baptized people again, the Anabaptists, the again baptizers. After all, if an infant is baptized but only later places his faith in Christ and if baptism must follow salvation, then baptism must take place again. Just as the Christians in Antioch we did not name ourselves. Our opponents took care of that for us.

The Lord's Supper is not magical at all. The use of unleavened bread pictures the sinless body of Jesus Christ, and the use of the fruit of the vine pictures His blood. That body was broken, and that blood was shed on the cross for you and me. Many an institution soon forgets its founder and its purpose; Jesus wanted to ensure that this was not the case with the church. Hence, He instructed His children to periodically lay everything else in their lives aside and receive the elements *...in remembrance of me. (I Corinthians 11.24)* The Lord's Supper is designed to turn our minds toward Christ, to make sure we are in genuine communion with Him and thus each other, and to thank Him for His sacrifice on Calvary. It is not designed to make you receive a Christ who mysteriously turned into a wafer in the hands of a priest.

The early church in the New Testament obviously practiced both of these as *Acts* makes clear. As Baptists, we identify with each of these symbols and happily obey our orders to observe them.

Individual Soul Liberty

The fifth Baptist distinctive is individual soul liberty. The basic concept of this is that each human being has the right to worship

God according to the dictates of his own conscience. E. Y. Mullin, the president of the Southern Baptist Theological Seminary in 1908 said, "The great principle underlying religious liberty is this: God alone is the Lord of my conscience." As with the autonomy of the local church, I will speak more to this later.

Saved Church Membership

The sixth Baptist distinctive is a belief in the necessity of salvation as a requirement for church membership.

There are some who hold that the very idea of a limited church membership is foreign to the Bible. Usually, one finds this amongst the universal church crowd. Their motivation is often simply a desire to excuse themselves from the necessity of being a member of any particular local assembly. In so doing they could not be more wrong. *But now hath God set the members every one of them in the body, as it hath pleased him. (I Corinthians 12.18)* I realize the illustration here is of a human body, but every word in the Bible is included in it on purpose. *Body* is a clear type of the church *(Ephesians 1.23)*, and *member* is used in *I Corinthians 12* nine times. In other words, this passage clearly teaches that not every person is a member of a local assembly and that only some will be.

Additionally, the scriptural teaching of church discipline assumes the concept of membership. How can you kick someone "out" if there is not an "in"? No, Paul clearly establishes there are those *within* and those *without* in the church. *(I Corinthians 5.12)* Accordingly, realistic considerations practically force the idea of membership. Would you want just anyone wandering in off the street and voting to borrow millions of dollars for a new building? Would you want just anyone to vote on calling a pastor? Would you want any widow woman in general to be the responsibility of the assembly? No, beloved, there must be some sort of delineation of who belongs to the church and who does not.

Having established the doctrinal and practical philosophical foundation for membership, we must then ask ourselves what the guidelines are. Well, what saith the Scripture? *...the Lord added to the church daily such as should be saved. (Acts 2.47)* I am not against a church having additional requirements such as age and activity, but I am convinced it is wrong for a church to not have at least this requirement: without a clear profession of salvation through Jesus Christ there can be no church membership.

Without a clear profession of salvation through Jesus Christ there can be no church membership.

When the Puritans settled New England in the seventeenth century, their ecclesiastical setup was congregational. They believed in the necessity of the new birth, but they also practiced infant baptism. As the children of these saved church members grew to maturity, they were not allowed to partake of the Lord's Supper without a personal profession of faith in Christ. However, many grew up without any conversion experience, yet they were considered members of the church since they had been baptized into the church. This confusing situation was settled in 1622 with a notoriously (in a theological sense) bad compromise called the Halfway Covenant. This covenant formalized unconverted people as secondary but still quite genuine members of their church. In a relatively short period of time, the churches of New England became so filled with unbelievers that it took the Heaven-sent wind of the Great Awakening in the 1730s to shake New England for God. Not coincidentally, it was primarily the Congregationalist churches, filled with unconverted members and led by unconverted pastors that provided the most opposition to Jonathan Edward's and George Whitefield's calls to be born again. The great spiritual fervor of the Puritans in the seventeenth century became the spiritual opposition of the eighteenth century because the Puritans were wrong about the necessity for a saved church membership.

Two Offices

The seventh Baptist distinctive is our belief that there are only two formal positions in the church – pastor and deacon. *Paul and Timothy, the servants of Jesus Christ, to all the saints in Christ Jesus which are at Philippi, with the bishops and deacons: Grace be unto you, and peace, from God our Father, and from the Lord Jesus Christ. (Philippians 1.1-2)* We see here that Paul divided the church at Philippi into three groups – saints (all who are saved), bishops (pastors), and deacons. Of course, I do not believe Paul was setting up the pastors and deacons as a hierarchy over the saints. He was, however, differentiating for the sake of placing an emphasis upon these two offices. Paul would later do the same in his first epistle to Timothy when he used the phrase *office of a bishop (I Timothy 3.1)* and *office of a deacon. (I Timothy 3.10)* Peter would elsewhere equate pastors, bishops, and elders as being the same position. *(I Peter 5.1-4)* The simplicity of this is set in absolute contradistinction to the Roman Catholic position, for instance, with its multiplied layers of the hierarchal clergy.

Separation of Church and State

The eighth Baptist distinctive is separation of church and state. In truth, I almost wish we used another explanatory phrase. This phrase has been so hijacked as to be almost unrecognizable to the average American citizen. Negatively speaking, separation of church and state does not mean the church cannot hold or express an opinion on political, governmental, or public matters. Nor does it mean that public expressions of religion are inappropriate or illegal. Positively then, it does mean that the church and the state are fundamentally two separate organizations. The church does not run the state, and the state does not run the church. The church is not supported with public money, nor are the church's instructions and teachings legally the law of the land.

The longest day of Jesus' life was the time period between Tuesday morning and Wednesday afternoon when He died. Most of Tuesday morning was spent in the Temple. There Jesus engaged in several vigorous discussions with His enemies – the Pharisees, Sadducees, and Herodians. In one of those conversations *(Matthew 22.15-22)*, Jesus explains in the course of avoiding a verbal trap that the government and religion are two different spheres. ... *Render therefore unto Caesar the things which are Caesar's; and unto God the things that are God's.* Jesus had opportunity after opportunity to attempt to establish a theocracy on earth, and each time He patently refused. He will certainly do so at His Second Coming, but the church was established at His first coming. The church is His body in this dispensation. It was not established to be the overarching authority over humanity, no matter what the Council of Trent claimed for the pope. The church is only to be composed of saved people. Thus, all of society cannot be included within the bounds of the church. Other passages such as *Romans 13.1-7* and *Genesis 9* establish the purpose of human government. The church's work is conspicuously absent in those discussions.

Rulers of human societies have long known that there is great authority in combining the secular power of government with the religious power of popular worship. Egypt's pharaohs claimed to be divine as early as 3500 B.C. Greece's Alexander the Great ran with the idea when he encountered it in Egypt. Rome's caesars fashioned this to perfection. Not coincidentally, both Egypt and Rome established state-controlled religions, supporting a priestly class with tax dollars. They demanded religious adherence from their citizens and proclaimed their supreme rulers to be divine gods clothed in mortal flesh.

In the centuries immediately after Christ, paganism and Christianity fought for the soul of the Roman Empire. As paganism gradually declined and Christianity slowly ascended, Rome's emperors took notice. Politicians have always held one finger to the wind. By the early fourth century, we find the last and worst spasm of persecution under Diocletian. This persecution was almost immediately followed by the first openly Christian emperor Constantine. (I use the word "Christian" loosely in this context.) Over the succeeding years, Christianity came to exercise greater and greater control via Christian emperors. In A.D. 380, the Christian emperor Theodosius, in a fit of rage as a result of a riot, ordered the mass extermination of thousands of people during chariot races in Thessalonica. Sensing a great opportunity, Ambrose, the highly influential bishop of Milan, refused communion to Theodosius until he repented. Theodosius proved his repentance by declaring Christianity to be the only acceptable religion in the whole of the Roman Empire. The result was the famous Edict of Thessalonica:

"It is our desire that all the various nations which are subject to our Clemency and Moderation, should continue to profess that religion which was delivered to the Romans by the divine Apostle Peter, as it has been preserved by faithful tradition, and which is now professed by the Pontiff Damasus and by Peter, Bishop of Alexandria, a man of apostolic holiness. According to the apostolic teaching and the doctrine of the Gospel, let us believe in the one deity of the Father, the Son and the Holy Spirit, in equal majesty and in a holy Trinity. We authorize the followers of this law to assume the title of Catholic Christians; but as for the others, since, in our judgment they are foolish madmen, we decree that they shall be branded with the ignominious name of heretics, and shall not presume to give to their conventicles the name of churches. They will suffer in the first place the chastisement of the divine condemnation and in the second the punishment of our authority which in accordance with the will of Heaven we shall decide to inflict."

On the surface, this seems like a smashing success for Christianity. But what was on the surface eventually paved the way for the horror history knows as the Dark Ages. As the Roman Empire was thrown down in the West and decamped for Constantinople in the East, it fell to the bishops of Rome to attempt to hold Western civilization together. They wrapped themselves in the mantle of the caesars and attempted to build a society in which the pope was the be-all and end- all. The church and the state were entwined so tightly that they became practically synonymous. For all intents and purposes, more than a millennium would pass before any real attempt to split them up would take root and grow to fruition.

Even after the Protestant Reformation, the errors of this held sway. Often, as each particular ruler chose to be Roman Catholic or Protestant, he chose the religion for his entire region. His government financed that religion, enforced the edicts of that religion, and persecuted other religions. In fact, the great error of the Reformers was that they kept so much of the

> *The great error of the Reformers was that they kept so much of the system of the Roman Catholic Church.*

system of the Roman Catholic Church while at the same seeking to fix a large percentage of her doctrinal heresies.

This model – a state and church union – is the historic model of England. Henry VIII created the Anglican church out of the whole cloth of the Roman church in 1534 for the dubiously spiritual purpose of dissolving a marriage. To this day, the current queen of England still holds the title "Defender of the Faith." To this day, the Anglican church in England is still financed by tax dollars.

It was this Protestant model copied from the Roman Catholic Church which was in turn copied from the Roman Empire that came to America during the colonial period. In Massachusetts, the Puritans sought to erect a shining city on a hill. I applaud much of their theology, practice, and motives; but the end result was a spiritual disaster. Our Pilgrim forefathers in Plymouth Colony were no better in this regard. Both the Puritans and the Pilgrims established governments married to the church and persecuted those who held differing religious views. In both of these colonies, people were forced to attend the state church and forced to subsidize its ministry with their taxes.

As the sixteenth century progressed and colonial America grew, increasing numbers of Baptists began to emigrate from Europe. If it were not so sad, I would label it ironic that the non-conformists in America who fled the religious persecution of Europe turned right around and persecuted those who followed them to the New World for the same reason.

In 1636, the Baptist Roger Williams, after being hounded out of New England by the Puritan and Pilgrim Congregationalists, founded the haven of Rhode Island. He called its first city Providence and wrote into its first governing documents the concept that government ruled "only in civil things." This model, though, failed to take hold. Even up until the Revolutionary War period, the most influential American colony, Virginia, still had an established state church. This state church, the Episcopal church, united with the government of Virginia to jail Baptist preachers who refused to obtain a license to preach the Gospel.

You may thank these early American Baptists for taking Thomas Jefferson and James Madison in hand and teaching them the importance of complete freedom of religion and the necessity for a wall of separation between the state and the church. In 1773, a twenty-seven-year-old Baptist preacher named Jeremiah Moore was thrown in jail for preaching without a license. In our modern day vernacular, he became highly motivated. In 1776, he brought a petition before the Virginia Assembly demanding a revocation of the established state church. His petition for complete religious liberty was signed by ten thousand Baptists. Thomas Jefferson, just weeks removed from writing the Declaration of Independence, became the primary supporter for that petition. It finally passed into Virginia law in 1786.

In 1788, James Madison was trying to get Virginia to ratify the new United States Constitution. John Leland, an influential Baptist leader, sent Madison a letter explaining that Baptists could not back the Constitution because of its glaring lack of religious liberty. Madison asked to meet with Leland to discuss the matter. The place they met in Orange County, Virginia is now called Leland-Madison Memorial Park. There Leland explained the Baptist position on the separation of church and state to Madison. Leland pressed him to include in the Constitution religious liberty for all. Madison promised Leland that if he would urge the Baptists of Virginia to support ratification of the new Constitution, Madison would press for a Bill of Rights at the first opportunity. That Bill of Rights would include the distinctive Baptist belief of separation of church and state with its corresponding religious liberty. The rest is history. Baptists brought it to America, and America brought it to the world.

It would be wrong for us to have control over the levers of government. But it is not wrong for us to lobby, to vote, to persuade, to march, to proclaim, or otherwise to seek to influence our government and our society for the right. We hold no man's conscience hostage against his will. In turn, we refuse to accept any man, movement, council, court, or legislative body holding our conscience hostage, either.

In holding these eight distinctives, we assume the moniker Baptist. And it warms my heart that in this day of marked compromise with the world on every hand, so many of our brethren hold firmly to both their beliefs and their name. This name is important.

The term Baptist is important because it identifies us. It is truth in labeling. If you have ever purchased a mislabeled can in the grocery store, you know how aggravating it can be. Integrity drives us to be open about what we believe to those who seek us out. After all, there are only two reasons why churches refuse an identifying moniker: either they do not believe anything or they do not want people to know what they believe. Thank God that is not true of independent Baptists.

The term Baptist is also important because it connects us. It does so in two ways. First, it connects us to a rich and honored past. It ties us to our forefathers who were imprisoned, whipped, and even martyred as a result of clinging to these Baptist distinctives. Their sacrificial stand deserves our deep respect, and I am delighted that we as a group are happy to give it.

Second, it connects us explicitly with these eight Baptist distinctives. It is not unusual at all for a Baptist church in our generation to quietly remove the term Baptist from their name. They generally do so out of a sincere desire to eliminate what they believe could be a hindrance in reaching their community. Over and over again I have had people in such churches tell me that nothing about their doctrine is going to change by simply removing a term from their name. This is a self-deceptive and patently false position. For when you remove the term, you remove the necessity for constant emphasis and explanation of that term. In relatively short order, the distinctives behind that name cease to be important.

Take the Baptist General Conference, for example. Formed in the mid-nineteenth century by Swedish immigrants to America, it currently encompasses nearly thirteen hundred churches with 300,000 members. As they entered the twenty-first century, however, they began to see the term *Baptist* as an obstacle to further growth. Their website uses two short paragraphs to explain it.

"Toward the end of the 20th century, the Baptist General Conference name began to lose its cultural currency. More than a fifth of all BGC churches had been planted within the prior 15 years, and a scant few wanted to identify themselves by the name Baptist. They held to Baptist convictions, but didn't want to spend precious time refuting stereotypes of other Baptist leaders or groups. Meanwhile, the Baptist name put valuable missionaries and their national partners at risk in several countries overseas. Converge leaders saw the need to make a change.

In 2008 the board of overseers approved a new missional name, Converge Worldwide, while retaining the historic name Baptist General Conference in some settings and for legal purposes. The Converge name captures the strategy of starting and strengthening churches through the collaboration of 11 districts, approximately 1250 Converge churches and national and international ministries."

Sounds good, right? Yet every week of my life I have members of a local Converge church attend our church here in Chicago. They do so because their church does not have Sunday night or Wednesday night services. Recently, I asked them if their church was Baptist. Their puzzled looks were the only answer I needed. The Baptist General Conference chose to abandon the term Baptist while keeping an adherence to Baptist doctrine. While this may seem logical to its leadership, the man in the pew is now losing his hold on the importance of Baptist doctrine.

The term means something. It represents necessary doctrines worth holding and emphasizing. Our religion is about Jesus. In all things He must have the preeminence. But the doctrine He and the Apostles taught was sound Baptist doctrine. One of the best ways to accomplish a continual emphasis on these doctrines is to use and teach the name Baptist.

What are we right about? This first – we are Baptists. And we are not afraid to say it.

We Are Independent

The battle is hard but compromising with the enemy isn't one of my failings so I keep on. However, I am through cleaning up the denomination. Hereafter the Convention meetings will neither be adorned or marred by my presence. I have become a come-outer. I am through with the Northern Baptist Convention. I write this with regret but I see no other way for me but that. My church here is with me. We are free from convention control and will remain so. I have no place to hang my hat, ecclesiastically speaking, for I stand practically alone here. But I am going to hang in mid air awhile I suppose. Outside the camp alone is preferable to the camp.
-Chester Tulga of North Platte, Nebraska, letter to Oliver Van Osdel, Grand Rapids, Michigan, April, 1930

To study church history is to grind your teeth in frustration. I have dozens of books on the subject in my office, and often as I read them, I find myself practically howling in frustration as the same ecclesiastical errors are repeated generation after generation. We saw these illustrated in the last chapter with the error of the state church. It was promulgated by the Roman Empire, perfected by the Roman Catholic Church, and carried over by our well-meaning Protestant brethren. It took Baptist blood, to paraphrase the Welsh poet Dylan Thomas, to send it not so gently into that good night.

Baptists, however, are not immune from the same failing. We so often imitate the failings of our own forefathers. I suppose this is because our frail human nature is the common inheritance of all men. We are all weak. We are all short of the glory of God.

As with other denominational groupings, Baptists in America have long desired unity and cooperation. The Pilgrims landed at Plymouth Rock in 1620, and the Puritans established the Massachusetts Bay Colony in 1629. In spite of their concerted efforts, the first Baptist church was established in New England by 1637. Throughout the rest of the seventeenth century, men would plant Baptist churches up and down the Eastern seaboard. By the dawn of the eighteenth century, those Baptist churches began to gather in an organized way into local associations.

These associations did much good and grew exponentially. The most influential of the early ones was the Philadelphia Association. In 1742, it led in adopting the Philadelphia Confession of Faith. It began in 1707 with five Baptist churches; by 1791, it had grown to include fifty-three distinct assemblies.

Such growth was not limited exclusively to the North. The first Baptist church in South Carolina was founded in 1683. By the 1760s, the largest social, political, or religious meeting of any kind in America was the annual meeting of the Baptist Sandy Creek Association. It consisted of scores of churches in three states and gathered tens of thousands of people into its embrace. All of this was done in the face of governmental opposition, taxation, and occasional imprisonment.

By 1784, one historian estimates there were 471 Baptist churches in the newly forming United States. William Cathcart, who published *The Baptist Encyclopedia* in 1881, had this to say regarding the rapid growth of Baptists in the eighteenth century: "In 1774, according to Howison, the Baptists increased on every side; if one preacher was imprisoned, ten arose to take his place; if one congregation was dispersed, a larger assembled on the next opportunity. The influence of the denomination was strong among the

In two points they were distinguished: first, in their love of freedom; and, secondly, in their hatred of the church establishment.

-William Cathcart

common people and was beginning to be felt in high places. In two points they were distinguished: first, in their love of freedom; and, secondly, in their hatred of the church establishment."

As America turned increasingly to the West, Baptists were planting churches all along the way. Kentucky, that dark and bloody ground first settled by the Baptist Boone family, had three associations with forty-two member churches by 1790. That is one Baptist church for every two thousand people in the territory. Similar church planting efforts followed as Ohio, Illinois, Mississippi, Tennessee, Indiana, Missouri, Louisiana, and Arkansas were settled. In each of these territories, local Baptist churches gathered into associations. In 1792, Baptist churches nationwide increased from 892 to a staggering 2,164 just twenty years later.

In a group so clearly marked with a priority on church planting and evangelism, it is not strange at all that they would soon turn their eyes to the foreign field. The first national Baptist conference was formed for just such a purpose on May 18, 1814, in Philadelphia. Initially known as simply the Triennial Convention, its purpose was to recruit and finance Baptist missionary work. By the mid-1830s, it had become a loosely structured nationwide denominational organization.

Along the way, this evangelism had not bypassed African-Americans. In 1793, approximately one fourth of all Baptists were black. In the South and the North, this often took the form of separate black Baptist churches. Increasingly over time, Baptist leaders in the North began to speak out against the evils of slavery and to push for increased racial unity. This did not sit well at all in the South, and gradually a split developed amongst Baptists. By 1845, the Triennial Convention was dead. In its place were formed two separate organizations: the Southern Baptist Convention and the American Baptist Missionary Union (later the Northern Baptist Convention and now the American Baptist Convention).

In this short summation of Baptist history in America, we see a pattern developing. Churches do not like to be by themselves. They want to be part of something bigger. In very real ways, such associations lent the encouragement that comes with strength in numbers. They also furnished the forms for larger joint endeavors that were not thought possible on the scale of an individual church. Seminaries, Bible societies, printing and colportage societies, young people's societies, and mission boards became the hallmark of national Baptist organizations. Little thought was apparently given to either the scriptural support for such organizations or their inevitable future. It was exciting. It worked. Full steam ahead.

In the Fundamentalist-Modernist controversies of the early twentieth century (which I will speak to a bit more in the next chapter), we see the exact same thing take place. Over time, the group deteriorated spiritually. Reasons to separate emerged, and an association was severed. The group that left then formed another association to replace the one they left. They again formed the seminaries, mission boards, Bible societies, and national organizations that had marked the old group. Over time, the group deteriorated spiritually. Reasons to separate emerged; an association was severed, and so on. The cycles simply kept repeating.

Just as the Protestants made the mistake of copying the ecclesiastical forms of Roman Catholicism, so the Baptists made the mistake of copying the ecclesiastical forms of the associations and conventions. Each generation finds compromise, if not apostasy. Each generation splits and begins anew. Each generation vows to build a structure that will finally get it right. Each generation is wrong.

Thus, in the early to mid-twentieth century, a new form of Baptist church union developed. This one was marked not by formal partnership – whether termed association, convention, union, or fellowship – but by informal communion. Strong men who led their churches out of compromising, formal associations began to resist the urge to form new ones. Instead, they simply enjoyed each other's company.

Birds of a feather have long flocked together, but in my father's generation, a large group of Baptists began to do that flocking together in an unofficial manner. Instead of being gathered around associations, they began to assemble around newspapers and conferences. Large churches – which in our day are termed megachurches – increasingly marked out spheres of influence in the wider Baptist community.

This evolution had now come full circle. Initially, the first Baptist churches in America were entirely independent. Then they grouped themselves into associations. Those associations matured into conventions. The conventions split into fellowships. And for many men, even fellowships were too constricting. They demanded and obtained complete independence.

History, however, was not the only driving force in the birth of what is genuinely an independent Baptist movement. Along with this history of associational failure, three doctrinal concepts became increasingly clear and more widely embraced. These doctrinal concepts built our approach as independent Baptists – an emphasis on the local church, the autonomy of the church, and the perpetuity of the church.

The Church as Local

In the summer before His death, Jesus started the very first church in the mountains north of Galilee around Caesarea Philippi. I freely admit that the vast majority of Christians believe the church started in *Acts 2* when the Holy Spirit came at Pentecost, Peter preached, and three thousand people were saved and baptized. What both Catholics and Protestants miss is the context of the first mention of the church in the Bible. *And I say also unto thee, That thou art Peter, and upon this rock I will build my church... (Matthew 16.18)* To assert that there is a play-on-words between *Peter* and *rock* and to then point to *Acts 2* as the occasion in which Peter became the rock on which the church is built is to completely ignore when Jesus said it. Just prior to *Matthew 16.18* we find Peter's great confession of faith in Jesus. *...But whom say ye that I am? And Simon Peter answered and said, Thou art the Christ, the Son of the living God. (Matthew 16.15-16)* The rock upon which Jesus built His church was not Peter but rather Peter's confession of faith. The fact that Peter happened to preach the message at Pentecost has nothing to do with it.

The rock upon which Jesus built His church was not Peter but rather Peter's confession of faith.

43

The truth is that the word *church* is first found in *Matthew 16*, not in *Acts 2*. The truth is that *Acts 2* specifically tells us that at Pentecost three thousand believers were saved and baptized and *...added to the church. (Acts 2.41, 47)* In order to be added to something, that something had to be in existence prior to that addition. The truth is that two chapters later in *Matthew* we find Jesus giving instructions to His Apostles about how to deal with problems amongst the brethren, and He tells them to *...tell it unto the church... (Matthew 18.17)* You cannot take present problems fourteen months forward in time to some future church that is not yet in existence. *(Acts 2)*

No, beloved, Peter did not found the church. Jesus did in the beautiful mountainous region around Caesarea Philippi in the summer before His death.

From this fact – that the church predates *Acts 2* – we find some helpful truth. One of the primary supports for a universal church model is in *Acts 2*. People were gathered together temporarily from all around the Mediterranean world. So if the church started then, its genesis was as a regional organization, not a local one. From regional to universal is but a short step.

A universal (or invisible as it is sometimes called) church model logically leads to a desire for formal association. After all, if all Christians are united into one universal church now, then unity should prevail. The resulting organization of visible churches must needs have a hierarchy of bureaucrats to manage it, and separation from this organization is labeled schism in the body of Christ.

On the other hand, if the church was founded as local by Jesus and not regional by Peter, then the visible church is the church. It is not just a physical representation of a slice of the universal, invisible church. While there may be fellowship and companionship between individual churches, there is no compelling theological demand for a formal, visible organization of churches.

When we take the scriptural position that the church is now not universal in aspect but rather local, we see that there is no necessity for an overarching hierarchy. In other words, an emphasis on the church as local instead of universal leads directly to our emphasis on the autonomy of each individual local church.

The Autonomy of the Local Church

Jesus is unquestionably the head of the church. After all, the church is His body. *And he is the head of the body, the church:... (Colossians 1.18) ...Fill up that which is behind of the afflictions of Christ in my flesh for his body's sake, which is the church: (Colossians 1.24)* Just as my head controls my body, so the church's head, Jesus Christ, is to control His body, the church. *For the husband is the head of the wife, even as Christ is the head of the church: and he is the savior of the body. (Ephesians 5.23)*

In contradistinction, the Roman Catholic model between the church and Jesus Christ portrays a veritable plethora of authorities. The church is told what to do by the priest. The priest is told what to do by the bishop. The bishop is told what to do by the archbishop. The archbishop is told what to do by the cardinal. The cardinal is told what to do by the pope. The pope is apparently the stand-in for Jesus on Earth.

This system works – well, it really does not, but let us set aside the numerous Roman Catholic heresies and practical disasters for the moment, provided the church is universal. After all, a universal church must have some organization above the local level if it is to function intelligently and wisely. In point of fact, this concept is at the very heart of the Roman system. The word *catholic* means universal.

Theologically speaking, though, a catholic approach to church completely violates the spirit and practice of a local church being organized directly under the headship of Jesus Christ. He designed the church to function independently without any layers of control between Himself and His churches.

Those who hold a universal church position – even orthodox believers – point to passages such as *I Corinthians 12.13* in response. *For by one Spirit are we all baptized into one body, whether we be Jews or Gentiles, whether we be bond or free; and have been all made to drink into one Spirit.* What they fail to appreciate about this passage is its point, namely unity. I will speak more to this later, but there is no place for racial conflict or ethnic divisions within a church. In our vernacular, there is no place for a

45

distinction between the boss and the employee. In that time-worn wonderful statement, the ground is level at the foot of the cross. *I Corinthians 12.13* teaches unity; it does not teach anything like a universal church position.

Contrarily, there are several good reasons to hold a local church position. For instance, the word *church* comes from the original language word *ecclesia*. *Ecclesia* is defined as a "called-out assembly" meaning a group of believers called out of the world and assembled together. That happens at the church I pastor each time we hold a church service. But it has never happened with all of Christianity, and it will not happen until the Rapture. Only in Heaven at the Marriage Supper of the Lamb will the entire church be called out of the world and assembled together. From this perspective, I do believe the Scripture teaches a universal church position – after the Rapture. *To the general assembly and church of the firstborn, which are written in heaven, and to God the Judge of all... (Hebrews 12.23)* That general assembly will happen, and it will be grand! *Revelation 4* and *5* give us a precious glimpse of this, but it has not yet happened.

Additionally, most of the time when the Bible mentions the church, it does so in a local context *...the church of God which is at Corinth... (II Corinthians 1.1)* There is a church (one of God's churches), and it is located at Corinth. There are others 750 miles away in Macedonia, *...the churches of Macedonia; (II Corinthians 8.1)* In fact, that word *churches* is used repeatedly in the Word of God. Between specific geographical placements and the use of the plural, the clear New Testament emphasis is local, visible assemblies of the saints.

The Perpetuity of the Local Church

Not only does the concept of the local church beget the practical practice of autonomy directly under the headship of Christ, so also the doctrine of the perpetuity of the church strengthens this autonomy. I use the word *perpetuity* here in the sense that God has guaranteed the church perpetual protection from the devil's attack. Jesus promised this perpetual protection in the same conversation that was the springboard for the birth of the very first church. *...upon this rock I will build my church; and the gates of hell shall not prevail against it. (Matthew 16.18)*

The devil mentioned earlier full well understands that the most important human institution on Earth is the church. Jesus loves the church. *(Ephesians 5.25)* The church is the pillar and ground

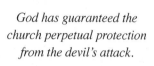

God has guaranteed the church perpetual protection from the devil's attack.

of the truth. *(I Timothy 3.15)* The church is the primary instrument for world evangelism. *(Acts 2.47, 13.1-3)* The church is the main source of strength for God's people. *(Hebrews 10.25)* So it is that the devil devotes a massive amount of thought and energy to attack it.

The devil has historically attacked the church via persecution. For the American church, that has largely not been true since the establishment of the Constitution. Many of God's discerning people see that day returning again and returning soon. Howsoever that may be, persecution has never stopped the church, whether under the Jewish Sanhedrin, the Roman emperor Diocletian, or the Communist Chinese. The second century Carthaginian Tertullian, who lived through great pressure from the pagan Roman Empire, said it best, "The blood of the martyrs is the seed of the church." Persecution drives the nominal Christian out of the church. This purifies the church in holiness, making it both more powerful and more attractive to the lost world around it.

The devil has also attacked the church via materialism. Contrary to popularly accepted wisdom, this is not an American sin alone. John said to a first-century church, *So then because thou art lukewarm, and neither cold nor hot, I will spue thee out of my mouth. Because thou sayest, I am rich, and increased with goods, and have need of nothing; ...(Revelation 3.16-17)* Yet in our generation, in spite of the highest standard of living any human society has ever enjoyed, there are large swaths of American Christianity that are strong and vibrant.

The devil attacks the church with false doctrine. Concepts such as the social gospel and the prosperity gospel completely minimize the actual gospel. Aberrant branches of Christianity such as the emerging church or the liberal mainline (historically) Protestant denominations know next to nothing of adhering to God's Word. However, these theological debacles have not destroyed orthodox Christianity. Thousands and thousands of good churches populate my country alone, not to mention tens of thousands of others across the world in Asia, Africa, and elsewhere. *...when the Son of man cometh, shall he find faith on the earth? (Luke 18.8)* If He were to return today, the answer would be a resounding yes.

What does this encouraging truth have to do with being an independent Baptist? Precisely this: Christ's promise of perpetual protection was never given to a fellowship, association, convention, or denomination. It was given to churches.

> *Christ's promise of perpetual protection was never given to a fellowship, association, convention, or denomination. It was given to churches.*

Christian history is absolutely littered with spiritually defunct denominations and their accompanying rubbish. Seminaries that were once bastions of the faith are now occupied by professors who advocate foul unbelief. Missionary societies that once started churches by the hundreds now exist solely to send mosquito nets to Africa. Bible societies that once shipped thousands of copies of God's Word to countries hither and yon now devote their energy to combatting spousal abuse. Denominations which once shone fierce and bright for the cause of Christ now fritter away their remaining energy advocating for homosexual marriage.

Such facts do not violate *Matthew 16.18* at all; they enforce it. The devil is after the church. Jesus promised the church His protection. Jesus has done an excellent job of protecting His church with the emphasis being on the word *church*.

It is for this reason that the independent church approach is not only doctrinally correct but practically wise. For the past seventy years, the independent Baptist movement has housed what would otherwise be a denomination's ancillary ministries completely inside the local church. Bible colleges and seminaries have become ministries of a local church. Periodicals have become ministries of the local church. Camps and Bible societies have become ministries of the local church.

Why? Associations, conventions, and their corresponding parachurch ministries have no guarantee of available protection. At some point, no matter how orthodox, they inevitably succumb to the devil's attack. Churches can succumb to this attack, of course, if they absent themselves from God's protecting hand; but they do not have to do so. Protection for them and their ministries is available for the asking. And even in cases where individual churches have dried up, their contagion did not reach an entire denomination. The fallout was limited, so to speak.

I can hear what some of you are muttering. "Yes, but I know an independent Baptist church in my city that closed. How does that fit into your neat little theory?" I sadly admit this happens. What I do not admit is that the happening of it invalidates the doctrine of the perpetuity of the local church.

Let me illustrate. *Ephesians 6* discusses in detail the spiritual protection offered to us by the armor of God. Yet the fact of the matter is that even though that protection is available to us, many a Christian succumbs to the attack of the devil. Is that because God has not provided protection? No. Does the existence of a backslidden Christian indicate that the whole armor of God was not good enough? No. The protection was promised and provided, but the Christian in question foolishly refused to avail themselves of it.

In the same sense, an individual church may become a spiritual casualty. John references this explicitly in his letter to the church at Ephesus. *Remember therefore from whence thou art fallen, and repent, and do the first works; or else I will come unto thee quickly, and will remove thy candlestick out of his place, except thou repent. (Revelation 2.5)* John was warning this particular local church that it was running the risk of losing its franchise – its right to be a church. God has promised each church perpetual protection, but that protection is not a magic force field. To borrow another analogy, churches must stay within the lines God has drawn if they are to avail themselves of the protection He offers. Every church that has ever closed its doors has only done so after a period of violating one or more of God's restrictions.

No church has to close; no church ministry has to fail. Perpetual protection is available to the church if it stays via obedience under the umbrella of God's protection.

The doctrine of the perpetuity of the individual church thus brings the wonderful shield of God's promise over each ministry in its embrace. I can think of few better reasons to embrace an autonomous, ecclesiological position.

We see thus the doctrinal reasons to establish and maintain a Baptist church in complete independence. Likewise, we see the historical evidence that leads us to such an important conclusion. I am an independent Baptist not by birth but by conviction. Yes, I came to it as a child, but I am held in it by a carefully considered understanding. I am utterly convinced that independent Baptist ecclesiology is not only the most scriptural model on Earth today but also categorically practical in the long term.

Where are we right? We are independent Baptist.

We Are Fundamentalists

A fundamentalist is just an evangelical
who is angry about something.
-Jerry Falwell

Go ahead. Cringe. I have studied our history too much to dislike this word. I embrace it. If you do not, this chapter will either aggravate you or enlighten you. Hopefully, it will be the latter.

Before I proceed, let me say that there are reasons many cringe at the label *Fundamentalist*. For the lost world, it often conveys the image of a wild-eyed Islamic revolutionary blowing himself up on a bus somewhere. For much of the saved world, it communicates the appearance of a buttoned-up, King-James-Bible-toting, short-hair-bristling fanatic with a pocketful of tracts, yelling on a street corner somewhere. Both of these extreme and extremely inaccurate portraits – terrorist and fundie – are no reason, in my view, to abandon a perfectly good adjective. That is especially true when you understand where the term comes from and why it is so very, very important.

I have divided this chapter into two basic sections. In the first section, I will walk you through some of the basics of the doctrinal foundation underlying fundamentalism. Namely, to be a Fundamentalist is to be orthodox, militant, and separatist.

To be a Fundamentalist is to be orthodox, militant, and separatist.

In this section, I will include

many scripture references that you are welcome to examine at your leisure. In the second section, I will lay out a brief overview of the birth of Fundamentalism. In this section too you will find much profit from further study. Laying these two sections side by side will reveal the too often forgotten reasons behind our under-appreciated appellation.

Orthodox

The truths the Bible teaches are known as doctrine. In many Christian circles, it is rather de-emphasized in the modern day. The truth is, however, that Jesus emphasized doctrine very much. People were astonished not at His love – though that was tremendous – but at His doctrine. *(Matthew 7.28)* Jesus told His Apostles to be wary of false doctrine. *(Matthew 16.12)* His doctrine was important enough that it formed part of the basis for His interrogation before the Sanhedrin. *(John 18.19)*

Along with Jesus in Christian history comes the towering figure of the Apostle Paul. He also emphasized doctrine in his ministry. He worked to ensure that correct doctrine was being taught in the church. *(I Timothy 1.3)* Paul said that preachers are to prioritize it. *(I Timothy 4.13-16)* In Paul's mind as well as the Holy Spirit's mind, doctrine was and is the first thing for which the Scripture is profitable. *(II Timothy 3.16)* In all, Paul used the word *doctrine* sixteen times in the Pastoral Epistles alone.

Over the course of the past two millennia of church history, the commonly accepted body of major doctrines the Scripture teaches has come to be called orthodoxy. To be orthodox in a scriptural sense is to hold to the major doctrines that the Bible teaches. This is not a book on systematic theology by any means, but every mature child of God needs a solid grasp on these doctrines. Broadly speaking, orthodox doctrine covers three major areas.

The first one (and the one on which all the others rests) is Bibliology. What does the Bible teach doctrinally about itself? It teaches us that the Bible is the Word of God. It is inspired. *(II Timothy 3.16)* It was not written by men but by God. It is verbally inspired. Not only are the thoughts behind the words inspired, but the very words themselves are inspired. *(Proverbs 30.5)* That inspiration is plenary, meaning the entirety of the Bible is God's Word. John is neither more nor less inspired than Genesis. Thus, as God's Word, the Bible is completely right about everything and wrong about nothing. The Word of God is inerrant.

The second major orthodox doctrine is Christology. What does the Bible teach us doctrinally about Jesus? He was eternally pre-existent. *(John 1.1-2)* Two thousand years ago He took upon Himself human flesh in the incarnation. *(John 1.14)* He was born of a virgin. *(Isaiah 7.14)* Jesus was not just a prophet or some avatar of exalted humanity. He was and is God Himself. *(John 1.1)* He lived a sinless life *(Hebrews 4.15)*, performed miracles to authenticate His claims *(John 2.23)*, and died an atoning death on the cross. His shed blood on the cross is what paid for our sin. *(John 1.29)* Three days later He walked away from His own tomb as the final and greatest proof that He was Who He said He was. *(John 2.19-22)* He is coming to Earth a second time to rule and reign for all eternity. *(Acts 1.11)*

The third major orthodox doctrine is Soteriology. What does the Bible teach us doctrinally about salvation? It teaches us that man is a sinner *(Romans 3.10)* and deserves hell for his sin. *(Revelation 21.8)* It teaches us that man has no hope of paying for his sins himself. *(Ephesians 2.8-9)* The Word of God reveals that our only hope of forgiveness and redemption lies in placing our faith in Jesus. *(Romans 3.23-28)* There is nothing we can humanly do to earn God's forgiveness or to pay for our salvation. It is solely the gift of God's grace. *(Romans 6.23)*

Each of these last three paragraphs could be greatly expanded, of course. Beyond that, as an independent Baptist, I hold to other doctrines that I think the Bible clearly teaches and that are also important. But at the bare minimum, the man who holds the last three paragraphs is my brother in Christ. We shall share Heaven someday. He is not my enemy though I may differ with him on a veritable plethora of other things. He is an orthodox Christian, not in a denominational sense, but in a doctrinal sense. This is the first and most foundational step in being a Fundamentalist.

Militant

To be orthodox is critical, but many an orthodox Christian is no kind of Fundamentalist. From time to time, I come across those who assert that Fundamentalism is simply an orthodox belief in the major doctrines of Scripture as I have outlined above. That is patently false. Fundamentalism carries within the seeds of its DNA a militant spirit. This militancy vigorously contends for the faith once delivered to the saints. *(Jude 3)* In other words, it is not enough for a man to believe the correct doctrine; he must also fight for those doctrines' acceptance and propagation.

I will lay this out more clearly in the second half of this chapter, but the idea of being a fighting Fundamentalist – of standing boldly and fiercely for the truth of orthodox doctrine – was present from the very beginning. In July 1920, the Christian paper *The Watchman Examiner* stated in an editorial, "We suggest that those who still cling to the great fundamentals and who mean to do battle royal for the fundamentals shall be called 'Fundamentalists'."

You are not a Fundamentalist if you are not willing to fight for the truth and earnestly contend for the faith. This is not my understanding alone. George Marsden used the word *militant* fifty-three times in his seminal work *Fundamentalism and American Culture*. Rolland McCune, late professor at Detroit Baptist Theological Seminary said, "Historic fundamentalism has always been characterized by militancy." David Beale in his excellent history of Fundamentalism, *In Pursuit of Purity*, asserts that militancy is the hallmark or identifying trait of Fundamentalism. Grant Wacker in his 1985 biography of Augustus Strong said, "Fundamentalism is used in a still more restricted fashion to designate the militant emphasis on the inerrancy of the Bible and the deity and miracles of Jesus Christ that emerged in the early twentieth century in opposition to theological modernism." Robert Delnay, historian and professor at Clearwater Christian College, gave nine marks of distinctive Fundamentalism. Militancy was number four. Larry Pettegrew, then dean of Central Baptist Theological Seminary stated in "Will the Real Fundamentalist Please Stand Up?" that one of the identifying characteristics of Fundamentalism is militancy.

My friend Fred Moritz, former mission board president and current professor at Maranatha Baptist University, said in one of his books, "Militance in opposing religious liberalism (that movement that denies the divine inspiration, authority, and doctrines of the Bible) is a second distinguishing mark." Kevin Bauder, the GARBC's resident theologian said in his book on Baptist history *One in Hope and Doctrine,* "The common factor among Fundamentalists was militancy or separatism." I could point to similar quotes from historians and professors such as Robert Handy, David Doran, and George Dollar.

I emphasize this point because I am weary with the notion that the fighting aspect of Fundamentalism is mistaken or that fighting Fundamentalism is passé. Fighting is who we are and rightly so. It was not enough for our fathers to believe the truth. It is not enough for us. We must hold the truth militantly.

Many a man reading this will say in response, "Yes, and that is exactly why I no longer wish to be a Fundamentalist. I have no more desire to fight. I am weary with the constant, never-ending bickering and attacks." If you stay with me in this book, I will speak to such things and to a wrong application of militancy, but it is worth pointing out that if you excise militancy from a religious approach and replace it with accommodationism, the eventual result is horrendous. Attempting to define the theology and practice of the modern emergent church is like trying to nail Jell-O to a tree. It cannot be done. They believe everything and nothing at once, and the only core emphasis is that of tolerance. Militancy and tolerance are mutually exclusive. Can militancy be misapplied? Yes. But the solution is not to carve it out of the body whole cloth as if it were a cancer. It is not. Instead, it is the very antibody we need to prevent the egregious spiritual sickness which has infected so many religious organizations of the modern day.

We are called to be soldiers. *(II Timothy 2.3-4)* Soldiers fight – no matter the odds – until the very end. *(II Timothy 4.7)* We are explicitly told to *Fight the good fight of faith... (I Timothy 6.12)* Fundamentalism does just that.

Separatist

Thus far, we have spoken much of sound doctrine. False doctrine, as well, is treated and treated very harshly in Scripture. *(I Timothy 4.1-6)* Such false doctrine ought to result in a dividing from or separation from those holding these false doctrines. ... *mark them which cause divisions and offences contrary to the doctrine which ye have learned; and avoid them. (Romans 16.17)* Elsewhere in *II Timothy 2* Paul tells us to shun such teachings and to purge ourselves from men who hold wrong positions. To this John agrees, stating in reference to those who hold wrong doctrine *...receive him not into your house, neither bid him God speed: (II John 1.9-11)*

Conversely, correct doctrine is supposed to be the only basis for true unity and fellowship. *Ephesians* reveals this. The epistle has two rather distinct sections. The first is primarily doctrinal. The second deals much with unity and harmony in the body of Christ, the church. The practical exhortation to unity flows out from an embrace of common doctrine. The *unity of the spirit* goes hand in hand with *the unity of the faith. (Ephesians 4.1-16)* David Martyn Lloyd-Jones said it this way in his excellent book on the Sermon on the Mount: "My contention is that the teaching of the New Testament is quite clear about this, that there is an absolute foundation, an irreducible minimum, without which the term 'Christian' is meaningless, and without subscribing to which a man is not a Christian. That is 'the foundation of the apostles and prophets' – the doctrine concerning 'Jesus Christ and him crucified,' and 'justification by faith only.' ...Apart from that there is no such thing as fellowship, no basis of unity at all."

No sooner had Christ established the church than the devil tried to corrupt it. He raised up false ministers *(II Corinthians 11.13)* to preach a false gospel *(Galatians 1.6-9)* in order to produce false disciples. *(Matthew 13.25)* This process waxes and wanes through church history, but it will eventually result in the great *falling away* of the church prior to the Rapture. *(II Thessalonians 2.3)* Transliterated into English, the original language word that underlies *falling away* is the word *apostasy*. It has the idea behind it of a revolt or a defection. It denotes a removal from or forsaking of a person or a system of thought. Such apostasy is epitomized in the devil. *(Ezekiel 28.11-19)*

Apostasy is progressive. What the Scripture has to say about this is critical, for it deals with the very heart of the refusal of so much of contemporary evangelical Christianity to hold to ecclesiastical separation. These brethren in Christ, sincere albeit misguided, are often just as against false doctrine as we Fundamentalists are. They just do not believe in separating from those who espouse it. Their preference is to love the erring one and to cleanse and purify the body of Christ (which they not coincidentally believe to be universal instead of local) rather than to separate from the body.

On several occasions, Jesus likened false doctrine to leaven. It quickly works its way through the entire mass until the whole is leavened. *(Matthew 13.33)* It has to be dealt with quickly and firmly, for once it gains a foothold, it is well-nigh impossible to eradicate. Indeed, once it has leavened the whole lump – whether you are talking of a denomination, a seminary, or a parachurch organization – the only solution left is to separate. Apostasy culminates in the world system known as Babylon during the Tribulation, and God's instructions in regards to Babylon are quite clear: ... *Come out of her, my people, that ye be not partakers of her sins, and that ye receive not her plagues. (Revelation 18.4)*

In the past several paragraphs, I have spoken several times of separation. After all, doctrine divides and rightly so. Holiness, which is simply being like God, has its foundation in separation.

For instance, this is true grammatically. Separation is implied in the very original language translated into English as *holiness*. In the Old Testament, holiness often comes from the Hebrew *qodesh*, which means apartness, holiness, sacredness, separateness. In the New Testament, the Greek word used most often for holiness is *hagios*, which means separation to God and the conduct of those who are separated. Vine's *Expository Dictionary of New Testament Words* explains that *hagios* "fundamentally signifies separated."

God's character is essentially one of holiness. God is not neutral regarding evil; He hates it. *(Psalm 45.7)* God is so thoroughly holy that He is actually unable to sin. *(Titus 1.2)* He is holy externally in what He does. He is holy intrinsically in what He is. Such a holy God cannot help but to demand holiness from others.

It is this very understanding of God's holiness that drives an understanding of our necessity for salvation. *(Romans 3.23)* Likewise, it forces us to come to terms with the fact that God definitively requires holiness of us. *(I Peter 1.16)* Consequently, we are supposed to be like the God who is *...of purer eyes than to behold evil. (Habakkuk 1.13)* God almost violently separates Himself from wickedness. *(Luke 13.27)* We are called to do the same. The psalmist used terms like *depart, cut off, not dwell, not tarry. (Psalm 101.2-5)* As the fundamentalist Bob Jones Sr. once said, "You cannot love flowers without hating weeds."

> *You cannot love flowers without hating weeds*
> *-Bob Jones, Sr.*

In response, our contemporary evangelical friends – orthodox in doctrine yet unwilling to ecclesiastically or personally separate from error – point to the overwhelming love of God as their answer. By implication, a loving God would not unkindly condemn those whose doctrine is beginning to err. By extension, His people, then, should forgive, extend mercy, think no evil, seek to befriend, etc.

I wholeheartedly agree that God is love. *(I John 4.8)* Fundamentalists and Evangelicals both believe in the holiness and love of God, but practically speaking, Fundamentalists believe God's holiness is pre-eminent among His attributes. The angels in Heaven do not thrice sing of God's love, but they

> *Fundamentalists believe God's holiness is pre-eminent among His attributes.*

do sing of His holiness. *(Isaiah 6.3, Revelation 4.8)* The seventeenth century Puritan divine Stephen Charnock said, "If any, this attribute has an excellency above his other perfections... Where do you find any other attribute trebled in praises of it, as this?" As well, holiness is the quality of God's that man is most notably commanded to incorporate. *(Leviticus 19.2, I Peter 1.15-16)* Holiness is the attribute by which God swears. *(Psalm 89.5)* Holiness is mentioned more often in the Bible than love is. Holiness is so essential to Him that it is the only attribute He specifically added to His name as a title.

Here then is where the rubber meets the road. God's holiness demands holy individuals, but it also demands holy congregations. Ernest Pickering in his essential book *The Tragedy of Compromise* says, "These things being true, it is mandatory for a congregation to maintain a separation from other congregations that deny the faith. It is simply the expected response of a holy people to their holy God."

When the church is presented as a bride to her husband, Jesus Christ, she is supposed to be holy. In my humble opinion, the following verse needs imprinted on the minds and hearts of churches of all kinds, for it has been sadly forgotten in our day: *That he might present it to himself a glorious church, not having spot, or wrinkle, or any such thing; but that it should be holy and without blemish. (Ephesians 5.27)* There are no glorious churches – regardless of their size, budget, sphere of influence, or national reputation – that are not holy churches.

Thus it is that holiness demands the doctrine of ecclesiastical separation. As we shall immediately see, the doctrine of ecclesiastical separation demands fundamentalism.

A Brief History of Fundamentalism

One of the most influential men in church history and probably the most famous Baptist in history was Charles Spurgeon. His impact, via a large church, printed sermons, books, an orphanage, a paper, and his Pastors' College was substantial in his lifetime all across the English speaking world. Since his death, his influence has not diminished but has grown.

Spurgeon was the nineteenth century's version of a Puritan. A thorough-going Calvinist, an eloquent preacher, and a man of impeccable morality, he referred often to Puritan writers and theologians in his own preaching and writing. He imbued from them not just his doctrine but his emphasis on personal and ecclesiastical purity.

With the coming of the Age of Enlightenment and rationalism, evolution and Darwin's *The Origin of the Species*, and higher

59

criticism in the nineteenth century also came a staggering increase in the number of clergy in Europe, England, and America who began to doubt, if not defy, historic orthodox doctrines. Spurgeon noticed this trend amongst some of the Baptist brethren of his day and sounded the alarm in the March and April 1887 editions of his paper, "The Sword and the Trowel." The particular issues at hand were a weakened view of the inspiration of Scripture, the atonement, and the reality of Hell.

Willis B. Glover in his 1954 book on the English separatist movement, *Evangelical Nonconformists and Higher Criticism in the Nineteenth Century,* explained in this way what would come to be known as the Downgrade Controversy: "The charges of Spurgeon put his evangelical contemporaries into a difficult position. It was impossible to deny that eternal punishment was no longer held by many evangelicals. On the other hand, they sincerely felt that the evangelical faith was held in all essentials as strongly as ever. That was the question: What are the essentials? Spurgeon saw very clearly that inspiration in its traditional sense meant inerrancy. To talk about the divine inspiration of an erring record was to use the term in an entirely different sense, and this simply bred confusion. But other evangelicals preferred to be confused."

The Baptist Union was the ecclesiastical organization in England to which almost all Baptists belonged, including Spurgeon. He urged the Union to draw up a clear, orthodox doctrinal position which its members must sign. Under the guise of individual soul liberty, the majority refused. This same argument was later recycled by liberals in the Northern Baptist Convention and Southern Baptist Convention in the twentieth century. Liberals and their defenders are ever the foes of clear doctrinal statements.

In response, Spurgeon felt he had no choice but to withdraw from the Baptist Union. In October of 1887 he wrote in "The Sword and the Trowel": "Believers in Christ's atonement are now in declared union with those who make light of it; believers in Holy Scripture are in confederacy with those who deny plenary inspiration; those who hold evangelical doctrine are in open alliance with those who call the fall a fable, who deny the personality of the Holy Ghost, who call justification by faith immoral, and hold that there is another probation after death…yes, we have before us the wretched spectacle of professedly orthodox Christians publicly avowing their union with those who deny the faith, and scarcely concealing their contempt for those who cannot be guilty of such gross disloyalty to Christ. To be very plain, we are unable to call these Christian Unions, they begin to look like Confederacies in Evil. It is our solemn conviction that where there can be no real spiritual communion there should be no pretense of fellowship. Fellowship with known and vital error is participation in sin."

Though the term *Fundamentalist* had not yet been invented, Spurgeon was a clear forerunner of the later movement. He was undoubtedly orthodox. He was fiercely militant. He was plainly separatist. He later said, "I have felt that no protest could be equal to that of distinct separation."

> *I have felt that no protest could be equal to that of distinct separation.*
> -C. H. Spurgeon

What Spurgeon discerned in the bud soon flowered into a truly noxious bloom. By the early part of the twentieth century, whole American denominations were filled with clergy whose belief system was no longer orthodox. Mostly younger men, they had been taught in seminaries that had been taken over in the preceding twenty years by theological liberals. These seminaries soon began turning out men who denied the inspiration of Scripture, the veracity of the miracles, the Creation account, the Resurrection, etc. They claimed that the Bible was a collection of edited legends collated long after the traditionally understood time frame.

Fundamentalism was the movement birthed in response by leading orthodox men. These men came from several different denominations and were willing to fight for and separate over the faith.

The term *fundamentalist* simply means someone who holds to and emphasizes the fundamental, foundational truths of anything. The term *evangelical* had long been used as synonymous with orthodox doctrine and was used to bridge denominational barriers in explaining men who largely agreed. To some extent, it is still used this way. When theological liberals (also called Modernists) who denied the basics of the Christian faith became prominent, the men who fought them did so by claiming there were certain truths that were absolutely fundamental to believe in order for a religion to be accurately called Christian. In the early twentieth century, some wealthy businessmen paid for 300,000 copies of a collection of articles to be sent to every preacher in the world. This collection, edited by R. A. Torrey, was entitled *The Fundamentals*. It is still sold today and is an excellent statement of orthodox Christianity written by a wide variety of learned preachers. As I mentioned earlier, *The Watchman Examiner* labeled those who were willing to fight for the truth as *Fundamentalists*, and the term became permanent.

In the seventeenth and eighteenth centuries, Presbyterians (though we would differ with them on many issues) were bastions of orthodox doctrine. As their seminaries came under the influence of liberals, their clergy began to reflect this. The remaining clergy who were still orthodox began a public fight to oust the liberal seminary professors and liberal pastors by way of heresy trials. Both of these methods, however, depended on votes, and the liberals already had the majority. For instance, a battle royal brewed over Princeton Theological Seminary.

In May 1922 Harry Emerson Fosdick, a Baptist pastor of a Presbyterian church in New York City, preached his famous sermon "Shall the Fundamentalists Win?" In it, he railed against the "intolerance" of Fundamentalists and called for "liberty" and "charity." Fosdick lost his church in the ensuing commotion, although Rockefeller soon built him the famous Riverside Church where he preached for many years.

Probably the most influential early Presbyterian Fundamentalist was J. Gresham Machen. Although he disavowed the term *Fundamentalist,* he clearly was one by belief and practice of the three positions cited above. His book *Christianity and Liberalism*, written in 1923, is still considered a classic defense of orthodox Christianity. For many years, he taught at Princeton Theological Seminary before leaving in protest to its gradual liberal lean. He and other like-minded men such as Carl McIntire soon founded Westminster Theological Seminary. Before long, they had completely withdrawn from the now liberal main Presbyterian denomination. They founded the Orthodox Presbyterian Church, which today is largely orthodox in doctrine and has several hundred churches.

In 1910, 1916, and 1923, the Presbyterian denomination voted that every candidate seeking ordination must agree with the inerrancy of Scriptures, the virgin birth, the deity of Christ, the substitutionary atonement, the bodily resurrection, and the authenticity of Christ's miracles. The more progressive element soon began trying to find a way around such requirements.

In 1924, about thirteen hundred Presbyterian pastors signed "The Auburn Affirmation" which revealed some of the thinking that led to the downfall of the Presbyterian denomination as a whole. It revealed that good men of sound doctrine erred in not fighting with and separating from those who held wrong doctrine: "Furthermore, this opinion of the General Assembly attempts to commit our church to certain theories concerning the inspiration of the Bible, and the Incarnation, the Atonement,

Good men of sound doctrine erred in not fighting with and separating from those who held wrong doctrine.

the Resurrection, and the Continuing Life and Supernatural Power of our Lord Jesus Christ. We all hold most earnestly to these great facts and doctrines; we all believe from our hearts that the writers of the Bible were inspired of God; that Jesus Christ was God manifest in the flesh; that God was in Christ, reconciling the world unto Himself, and through Him we have our redemption; that having died for our sins He rose from the dead and is our ever-living Saviour; that in His earthly ministry He wrought many mighty works, and by His vicarious death and unfailing presence He is able to save to the uttermost. Some of us regard the particular theories contained in the deliverance of the General Assembly of 1923 as satisfactory explanations of these facts and doctrines. But we are united in believing that these are not the only theories allowed by the Scriptures and our standards as explanations of these facts and doctrines of our religion, and that all who hold to these facts and doctrines, whatever theories they may employ to explain them, are worthy of all confidence and fellowship."

The Presbyterian denomination of the 1920s was more concerned with unity than they were with truth. In a pattern that was also being repeated at the same time in the Northern Baptist Convention, the Fundamentalists on one side opposed the Modernists on the other. Between the two of them gathered a band of men – largely orthodox in doctrine – who refused to be militant and separatist. That refusal doomed the orthodox doctrinal foundation for thousands of churches and the price is still being paid today. For seven years, I pastored in an area of Pennsylvania that was largely Presbyterian. I did occasionally meet a born-again Presbyterian, but almost every one I encountered was lost. A century later, we are seeing the fruit of the failure of good men to fight for the truth.

The heritage of that compromising middle group is not found in the failures of the Presbyterians and the American Baptist Convention alone. It is also found in the New Evangelical movement birthed in the 1950s and continued on into our day via the Contemporary Evangelical movement. It is built on accommodation rather than confrontation. It is built on dialogue and relationships. It seeks to hold orthodoxy while rejecting militancy and separatism (personal and ecclesiastical). In this it sows the sad seeds of its own demise in future generations.

The battles among Baptists paralleled the Presbyterian arc in time and manner. With the advent of strife over the issue of slavery and the coming of the Civil War, the Baptist denomination split into two groups – Northern (now American) Baptist Convention and the Southern Baptist Convention.

The Southern Baptist Convention resisted the inroads of the liberals a little longer; though by the 1970s, almost all of its seminaries had succumbed. A long and protracted fight between the liberals and the conservatives in the succeeding two decades saw the Southern Baptist Convention, in the main, return to orthodox doctrine. Speaking broadly, though orthodox, they would not consider themselves as Fundamentalists. While I could not personally be a part of the SBC for many reasons, I readily admit there are many good men in it with whom I share much doctrinal agreement.

The Northern Baptist Convention lost its seminaries (such as the University of Chicago Divinity School) to liberals much earlier than the SBC. Consequently, its battles took place concurrent with the Presbyterians. In the 1920s, Fundamentalists attempted to get the NBC to adopt a written, orthodox doctrinal statement. The liberals resisted and were helped along like the Presbyterians by men of orthodox doctrine who did not want to fight or separate. Men such as W. B. Riley, Oliver Van Osdel, and Robert Ketchum saw their denomination's theological drift and attempted to stop it. While trying to purify the NBC, they also established parallel religious organizations composed solely of Fundamentalists for organizational purposes. When the liberalism could not be checked, these parallel organizations became the genesis of such fundamental fellowships as the Conservative Baptist Association and the General Association of Regular Baptist Churches. Today the GARBC, birthed in Chicago at the Belden Avenue Baptist Church, has fourteen hundred member churches and is orthodox in doctrine. I grew up in a GARBC church. Again, it has many good men and churches; it has continued its ecclesiastically separatist position and voice. However, because of its weaknesses in other areas, I could not be a part of it now.

Other influential men came out of the Southern Baptist Convention in the mid-twentieth century and established large churches and schools. One of these men, J. Frank Norris, led in the founding of the Baptist Bible Fellowship, which currently represents about four thousand churches. It is similar to the GARBC in many respects. Others of these men, such as Lee Roberson (Southwide Baptist Fellowship and Tennessee Temple University), John R. Rice ("Sword of the Lord"), Lester Roloff, and Jack Hyles (Pastors' School and Hyles-Anderson College) built followings amongst the more independent type of men. These men saw the continual pattern of error that crept into man-made ecclesiastical structures beyond the church. They resolved to only associate voluntarily with other men with whom they agreed. I freely confess that is my heritage (my father led my home church out of the GARBC in 1990) and the pattern for my fellowship.

There are roughly ten thousand American independent Baptist churches associated in arrangements like these. They have established their own local church-based colleges, seminaries, publishing houses, missions agencies, and periodicals. They hold no formal association; rather, they fellowship with men and churches of like mind and practice.

In addition to Presbyterian and independent Baptist Fundamentalists, there are also non-denominational Fundamentalists. Methodism as a denomination fell to Liberalism with more of a whimper than the sound and fury of the Presbyterian and Baptist battles. Here and there, especially in the Wesleyan, Holiness, and Asbury movements, you will find some Fundamentalists. Bob Jones University, founded by the Methodist evangelist Bob Jones, has historically been fundamentalist while at the same time non-denominational. They have been rather influential in the Fundamentalist movement worldwide.

Episcopalians, while nominally Protestant, never were very orthodox in doctrine, especially in the United States. Lutherans vary in their orthodoxy, but a substantial wing of their denomination holds to the major doctrines of the faith and are our brethren in Christ. The Charismatic movement began around the same time as Fundamentalism and developed in a completely distinct way. Few, if any, Charismatics would allow themselves to be called or would call themselves Fundamentalists. We share many similar doctrines, but there are some deep differences. They largely go their way, and we go ours. I personally have known and respected some Pentecostal pastors, though I could not fellowship with them in any organized capacity.

Other organizations such as the Independent Fundamental Churches of America are largely fundamentalist. About a thousand churches strong, they consist mostly of Bible-type churches. There are also some fundamentalist movements in other countries of varying strengths. The independent Baptist movement in the Philippines is growing rapidly. I will speak more of this later. Fundamentalism, as represented by Ian Paisley, has a loud but tenuous hold in Ireland. There are also small groups in England, Australia, and India.

As you can see, Fundamentalism is varied and diverse. It also has a history, speaking strictly of the movement itself, flowing back 150 years. Others point to our established orthodoxy and assert that Fundamentalism is simply New Testament Christianity. Both explanations hold true to form. Fundamentalism is orthodox, militant, and separatist. No, it is not

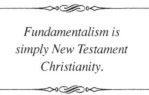

Fundamentalism is simply New Testament Christianity.

always independent Baptist. In a sense, that grieves me; but in a larger sense, I rejoice. These men and churches are my brethren in Christ. They, too, are willing to stand boldly and contend vigorously for the faith. I am pleased to be in their number.

Where are we right? In this: we are Fundamentalists. We are not alone in this, but along with many others, we are right. I am a Fundamentalist. I do not shrink from it; I will not run from it. It means something, and that something is what I believe and practice. I will pigeonhole no man, and I embrace all of God's family. But our crowd is orthodox, militant, and separatist. In this we are right.

We Use the King James Version

The translation was extraordinarily well done because to the
translators what they were translating was not merely a curious
collection of ancient books written by different authors in different stages of culture, but the word of God divinely revealed
through His chosen and expressly inspired scribes. In this conviction they carried out their work with boundless reverence
and care and achieved a beautifully artistic result... they made
a translation so magnificent that to this day the common human
Britisher or citizen of the United States of North America accepts
and worships it as a single book by a single author, the book
being the Book of Books and the author being God.
-George Bernard Shaw

Wait a minute! Put down the pitchfork, and lower the
torches. Perhaps in this generation, I should say step
slowly away from your keyboard. Yes, I am fully aware that not
all independent Baptists use the King James Version. I also realize
some independent Baptists view the fact that most do use the KJV
as a weakness. Well, we shall simply differ there, my friend, and
I seriously doubt it will be the last time you will differ with me in
this book. It probably is not even the first time. In fact, the only
thing about this book of which I am certain is that everybody will
dislike some of it, and some people will dislike most of it.

Let us come back to the subject at hand. In my opinion, it is
almost certain that a healthy majority of independent Baptists use
the King James Version exclusively. Further, it is my opinion that

those who do not exclusively use the KJV will gradually cease being independent Baptists over time. You do not, of course, have to agree with either of those last two sentences. But if I am correct about both of them, then the fact that most do use the KJV is a certifiable strength.

Look at it this way. There is not a single, good argument against the use of the KJV by English-speaking people. Most proponents of modern versions assert that the language of the KJV is archaic and thus unreadable in our generation. If the KJV's language is archaic for this generation, then it has already been archaic for at least several centuries. But through those centuries, several hundred million children – including me and including my own – have mysteriously managed to understand it just fine. What a miracle! Or perhaps the KJV is not nearly as hard to understand as the publishers of modern versions would have us think.

Even if they are correct, that is not a good argument. It is a convenience argument. If convenience is the leg we stand upon, no one will ever diligently work at studying the Bible ever again. One of the most important things any Christian can ever learn is the necessity of working to acquire an understanding of scriptural truth. Would someone please tell me what is so ungodly or unreasonable about asking people to look up an occasional word in a dictionary? To the contrary, such work is precisely what we are called to do in relation to God's Word. *(II Timothy 2.15)* In other words, I contend that having a Bible that does not read like a novel is actually a good thing. It is good for us to view the Scriptures differently than we do any other book. It is good that it reads differently. It is good that we must occasionally, as young people, dig out the meaning of a word or phrase.

Surprisingly (or not), there is a paucity of arguments against using the KJV. They are hard to find. The KJV is so widely revered and has been for so long that there are very few arguments against it at all.

On the other hand, there are a number of good arguments in support of using the KJV. In this chapter, I will briefly present to you five of them. I admit I am not a textual scholar. My aim in this chapter is not to convince any man via a pile of facts that his preferred modern version is wrong. Instead, I simply desire to show you that it is a good thing that a healthy majority of independent Baptists use the King James Version.

The Language

Several years ago, the KJV celebrated its fourth centennial. More accurately, I should say the English-speaking world celebrated it. From far and wide via sources secular and spiritual, the Word of God produced at Hampton Court in the early seventeenth century was lauded. It was heartwarming, indeed, that year to pick up the paper or come across a link to an article (as happened time and time again) that spoke of what a massive accomplishment the KJV was and is. Even Christians who prefer modern versions were encouraged to hear the Bible spoken of so positively and so often that year.

Many things were alluded to in these articles and celebrations. For instance, its enduring influence over centuries was pointed out. How it has shaped the English language and informed our common Western cultural heritage was referenced. But again and again, indeed in every single article I read that year, the classic beauty of the language of the KJV was mentioned. The simple truth is that there has never been a book written in the English language that contains such beautifully moving language as the King James Version. There is dignity here. There is poetry here. There is majesty here. There is awe here.

Alexander McCall Smith, longtime professor of medical law at the University of Edinburgh, said: "Even those who can no longer accept biblical claims – or indeed the relevance of the Bible in the modern world – can appreciate the beauty of the language used, its cadences and its gorgeous, resonant strength. Compared with the language of modern translations, it is vivid, echoing and magisterial. Children exposed to the language of the King James Bible will appreciate the sense of theatre, the sense of awe that suffuses virtually every sentence."

Adam Nicolson, the secular British author who wrote *God's Secretaries: The Making of the King James Bible* referring to the classic patina of its prose said, "The language of the King James Bible is the language of patriarchy, of an instructed order, of richness as a form of beauty, of authority as a form of good; the New English Bible is motivated by the opposite, an anxiety not to bore or intimidate. It is driven, in other words, by the desire to please and, in that way, is a form of language which has died."

On a previous centennial – the 1911 one – Presbyterian theologian Cleland Boyd McAfee (best known as the author of the hymn *Near to the Heart of God*) penned a book on the influence of the King James Version. In it, he credits the KJV as a literary inspiration for a veritable plethora of the greatest English authors. Men and women of the caliber of John Milton, John Bunyan, John Dryden, Joseph Addison, Alexander Pope, Percy Bysshe Shelley, Lord Byron, Samuel Taylor Coleridge, Sir Walter Scott, William Wordsworth, Robert Burns, Charlotte Bronte, Thomas Grey, Jane Austen, Robert Browning, Charles Dickens, George Eliot, Robert Louis Stevenson, Alfred Lord Tennyson, Thomas Babington Macaulay, William Makepeace Thackeray, and John Ruskin on the British side are the roll call of the English literary hall of fame. On the American side, McAfee cites Benjamin Franklin, Edgar Allen Poe, Washington Irving, William Cullen Bryant, Ralph Waldo Emerson, Oliver Wendell Holmes, James Russell Lowell, Henry Wadsworth Longfellow, Henry David Thoreau, and John Greenleaf Whittier. Not all of these were Christians or even good men, but all of them wrote beautifully, constantly referencing the King James Bible.

Sir Thomas Hall Caine, a Victorian era author and playwright, said: "I think I know my Bible as few literary men know it. There is no book in the world like it, and the finest novels ever written fall far short in interest of any one of the stories it tells. Whatever strong situations I have in my books are not of my creation, but are taken from the Bible."

It is my experience that people of all religious stripes and backgrounds sit in silent contemplation at the precious comfort of *Psalm 23*.

The Lord is my shepherd; I shall not want.
He maketh me to lie down in green pastures:
He leadeth me beside the still waters.
He restoreth my soul:
He leadeth me in the paths of righteousness for his name's sake.
Yea, though I walk through the valley of the shadow of death,
I will fear no evil: for thou art with me;
Thy rod and thy staff they comfort me.
Thou preparest a table before me in the presence of mine enemies:
Thou anointest my head with oil;
my cup runneth over.
Surely goodness and mercy shall follow me all the days of my life:
And I will dwell in the house of the Lord for ever.

There is no sweeter description of love in all of human language than the time-honored cadence of *I Corinthians 13*.

Though I speak with the tongues of men and of angels, and have
not charity, I am become as sounding brass, or a tinkling cymbal.
And though I have the gift of prophecy, and understand all mys-
teries, and all knowledge; and though I have all faith, so that I
could remove mountains, and have not charity, I am nothing.
And though I bestow all my goods to feed the poor, and though I
give my body to be burned, and have not charity,
it profiteth me nothing.
Charity suffereth long, and is kind;
charity envieth not;
charity vaunteth not itself, is not puffed up,
Doth not behave itself unseemly,
seeketh not her own,
is not easily provoked,
thinketh no evil;
Rejoiceth not in iniquity, but rejoiceth in the truth;
Beareth all things,
believeth all things,
hopeth all things,
endureth all things.

Charity never faileth:
but whether there be prophecies, they shall fail;
whether there be tongues, they shall cease;
whether there be knowledge, it shall vanish away.
For we know in part, and we prophesy in part.
But when that which is perfect is come, then that which is in part
shall be done away.
When I was a child, I spake as a child, I understood as a child,
I thought as a child: but when I became a man, I put away
childish things.
For now we see through a glass, darkly;
but then face to face:
now I know in part;
but then shall I know even as also I am known.
And now abideth faith, hope, charity, these three;
but the greatest of these is charity.

The Translators

When James I heeded the request for a new English translation at Hampton Court, he called together forty-seven of Britain's most brilliant men. This group, linguists par excellence, included men who, as children, learned Greek and Hebrew concurrently with English. Their long and deep familiarity with the original languages is almost impossible to replicate in our more casual modern day. John Bois, who learned Greek and Hebrew by the age of six, studied sixty grammars on his way to becoming a Greek professor at Cambridge University. Lancelot Andrewes spoke fifteen languages. Miles Smith was labeled by a contemporary as "a very walking library." Andrew Downes was described as the "chief of learned men in England." John Rainolds was likened to a third university, after Oxford and Cambridge. Richard Brett was adept in Latin, Greek, Hebrew, Chaldee, and Arabic. Henry Savile, a world-traveling mathematician and scholar, tutored the queen in Greek. Twenty-seven of the translators had earned doctorates.

Intellectual gifts alone are not sufficient for such a holy work. Men who would be called to choose the very words in which the common people heard from God must needs be deeply spiritual as well. And they were. Among their number were pastors and preachers of rare power. Relating an anecdote about Lawrence Chaderton, one author wrote, "Having addressed his audience for two full hours by the glass, he paused, and said, 'I will no longer trespass on your patience.' And now comes the marvel; for the whole congregation cried out with one consent, 'For God's sake, go on, go on!' He, accordingly, proceeded much longer, to their great satisfaction and delight." George Abbot preached 260 messages expositorily from the book of Jonah. Such preaching compels depth in both pulpit and pew, and is not coincidentally rarely found in our own day.

In addition to intellectual brilliance, sheer preaching ability, and doctrinal orthodoxy, there lived in them a genuine Christianity. Samuel Ward's diary contains frank confessions of his own weaknesses, admitting his struggles with gluttony and inattention. He reproaches himself for not making God his last thought of the day. He asked the Lord to help him desire Sundays more than Mondays and to protect him from delighting in the pleasures of the world. These are not the words of a carnal man full of ambition and pride. Lancelot Andrewes spent five hours in prayer every morning.

The translation with which they gifted the world was the full fruit of a seventeenth century England soaked in the Word of God. Church attendance was compulsory. Ten thousand pulpits thundered out the Word of God for hours on end each week. And this scripturally rich society built families in love with God. In the flyleaf of John Bois's *Book of Common Prayer* is this note in his own hand: "This was my mother's book; my good mother's book. ... She had read the Bible over twelve times, and the Book of Martyrs twice; besides other books, not a few." Not a wonder then that he would spend time every day on his knees with each of his seven children in prayer.

I believe in the sovereignty of God. If He so chose, He could have had His Bible perfectly translated by gorillas pounding away on typewriters. But generally speaking, God uses men who love Him and know Him. Such men, though sinners one and all, laid their many talents at their Master's feet for years. The result – in the providence and grace of God – is simply astounding.

The Approach to the Translating

As can be imagined, with men of such spiritual and academic integrity, great care was taken over each word written. The translators were divided into six groups. Each group was given responsibility for a section of the Bible. Each man in the group, ranging from seven to ten men, personally translated the entirety of the section assigned to his group. Once all the men in the group had each finished their individual work, all of the group's translations were brought together and compared word by word. Over much discussion, a unanimous consensus emerged from the entire group as to one singular translation. This process of painstaking care over each word was duplicated in all six groups. Subsequently, the six finished sections were sent to all of the other groups. Each group then went over each word already attained by the consensus of the other five groups. If any group objected to any word from any other group's section, their translation was returned to that group with the reasons for the objection. Once complete agreement was obtained, a final edit was undertaken by a select committee. In this manner – by repeatedly going over each word of the text individually, jointly, severally by group, and once more for good measure – the King James Version was presented to the English speaking world.

The translation was thus achieved with exacting care. But in addition to this, there was also an accompanying philosophical approach married to the word. Eugene Nida, one of the twentieth century's world-class linguists, was a sometime missionary, pastor, and translator. Though an ordained Baptist, he was ecumenical in approach. He sought to bridge the gap between the Roman Catholic Church and various American Bible societies. It was Nida who first introduced the world to the terms *dynamic equivalence* and *formal equivalence*. For the purposes of this writing, the KJV was translated via formal equivalence while the modern versions Nida worked on were translated via dynamic equivalence.

What is the difference between the two? The purpose of dynamic equivalence is to convey to the reader of the modern version the same sense or understanding that a reader of the original would have experienced "back in the day." From one vantage point, this makes sense; and indeed, the phrase often used to explain dynamic equivalence is *sense-for-sense translating*. Formal equivalence, on the other hand, involves a more literal rendering of the text. In contradistinction, the phrase used to describe it is *word-for-word translating*. It follows the grammatical forms of the original as closely as possible. It is more concerned with translating each word accurately; dynamic equivalence is more concerned with translating each thought accurately.

In my view, when translating the Word of God, the correct approach is a word for word translation. In the Scripture, God places great emphasis on each individual word. For instance, the phrases *word of God* and *words of God* is found fifty-five times in the Bible. *Every word of God is pure:...(Proverbs 30.5) ...man shall not live by bread alone, but by every word of God. (Luke 4.4) ...the word of God is quick, and powerful, and sharper than any twoedged sword,...(Hebrews 4.12) ...the worlds were framed by the word of God... (Hebrews 11.3)* To the contrary, only thrice does Scripture reference the thoughts of God. *(Isaiah 55.8-9, Jeremiah 29.11, Micah 4.12)* Thus it is that orthodox doctrine includes a belief in verbal inspiration – that God wrote each word of the Bible.

I do not mean to imply that God's thoughts are not at all important. They certainly are. After all, that is what I diligently endeavor to communicate when I preach – what did God mean when He said thus-and-such in this passage? But I would not dream of claiming that my sermons are always a completely accurate rendering of what God meant when He said something. *For my thoughts are not your thoughts, Neither are your ways my ways, saith the LORD. For as the heavens are higher than the earth, so are my ways higher than your ways, and my thoughts than your thoughts. (Isaiah 55.8-9)* God does not think like us at all. In a sense, then, it is the height of arrogance and foolishness to think I can convey the sense of the thought of God with complete accuracy. I do not have that capability, and no matter how many accredited degrees a man may have behind his name, neither does he. My sermons are a commentary, a commenting on what I think God said in the Scripture. But the only portion of my messages that is ever and entirely free of error is the portion when I simply read the Word of God.

The safety, the security of inerrancy, is in the individual word. It is not in my concept or sense of the thought. Amongst other works, Nida published a sense lexicon of the New Testament. Most Greek words have

> *The safety, the security of inerrancy, is in the individual word.*

more than one definition. Nida's lexicon attempts to give his best sense of the specific definition for the word in question. I own that lexicon. Occasionally I refer to it. But Nida's lexicon is not authoritative; it is commentary, albeit a learned commentary. The only authoritative source on my desk is the Word of God itself.

Between 1604 and 1611, forty-seven men scattered in six groups between Cambridge, Oxford, and the Jerusalem Chamber at Westminster Abbey labored to translate each word. They did not seek to convey to the English reader their best guess as to the thought behind the sentence. They simply gave the sense of each word as they came to it. As is the case in every translation, there was not always a direct word available. In such cases the integrity of the KJV translators is revealed in the italicized words common only to the King James Version. But to the best of their ability, knowledge, and effort, they simply gave us in our language each word God said. And I will take that approach to the Word of God over the other any day of the week.

A Wide Acceptance

For centuries, the KJV reigned supreme in the English-speaking world. Although new translations were periodically attempted, none gained any substantial hold on the public until Westcott and Hort's Revised Version in 1885. Like a dam bursting, this launched upon the world a veritable flood of revisions, translations, and editions. Apparently, those who found the KJV's verbiage to be archaic found the English language to be changing at warp speed. In the last century, more than one hundred major versions have been gifted to the English-speaking world.

With such a plethora of choices available to the average person combined with the venerable condition of the KJV, one would expect to find it mostly inside museums at this point. If one did so expect, one would be found to be egregiously mistaken. The KJV is the most widely used English version – still.

The KJV is the most widely used English version – still.

In 2011, the KJV's fourth centennial, Philip Goff, Arthur E. Farnsley II, and Peter J. Thuesen launched a systematic examination of the Bible's place in American life. They undertook this on behalf of Indiana's academically respected Purdue University. Their peer-reviewed report, produced in 2014, is by turns encouraging, fascinating, and horrifying. For instance, they found that eight out of ten Americans consider the Bible to be the inspired Word of God. Their purpose was to investigate the personal Bible use of the average person. The detailed report they issued broke the data down by economic class, ethnicity, geographical region, educational attainment, gender, age, etc. Their numbers indicated that fifty percent of the American public read the Bible privately in the past year. Further, nine percent – 29,000,000 people – read it every day.

Along with all of the above and more, they also ascertained which specific version was being read. Five percent read from the Living Bible; six percent read from the New American Standard Version; seven percent read from the New Revised Standard Version; nineteen percent read from the perennially best-selling New International Version. But a staggering fifty-five percent read from the matchless King James Version. That is not just a plurality but an outright majority! It nearly triples the amount of the closest competitor. In other words, last year 88,000,000 Americans personally choose to read from the King James Version. Widespread acceptance indeed.

Surely the average American pastor of any stripe would realize that using the KJV would appeal to the widest number of people. Sadly, this is often not the case.

On a recent trip, I found myself on a Wednesday night in Lancaster, Pennsylvania. Not being aware of any specific church in the area, I reached for my phone and searched "independent baptist churches lancaster pennsylvania." I found several to choose but none with any good websites. Running a little blind, I chose one and showed up for the mid-week service. After interrupting the praise band (which consisted of two people) practicing in the main auditorium, I was directed to a back room where about fifteen people had gathered for Bible study.

The pastor happened to be teaching expositorily that night from *James 1*. He had helpfully printed out a fill-in-the-blank outline. I accepted it and the warm welcome which accompanied it and took at a seat at the long table with the rest of the group. Of course, he did not know I was a pastor, and I saw no reason to broadcast the fact.

I was pleased to see that everyone at the table had brought a Bible. That pleasure rapidly turned to discombobulation as we took turns by course reading verses from *James 1*. Hardly anyone in the room had the same Bible. The resulting Bible study lurched back and forth between Bible styles, this one's phrasing different than the phrasing of that one. But that was only jarring. And probably it was only jarring to me. In and of itself, it did not impact the teaching of the Word of God specifically until the pastor began to drill down in an effort to teach each individual word. He simply could not. It was intellectually, stylistically, academically, and practically impossible for him to place emphasis on any particular word in *James 1*. He simply could not, for we were all looking at different words.

His lesson was fine. He said nothing out of line scripturally. He seemed like a good man, and I will gladly share Heaven with him someday. But inside, my heart was grieved for what the hungry people at the Lancaster church were missing. There was no corporate reading of the Word. There were no precious phrases common to all. There was no in-depth examination of individual words in direct context. Instead, there was a mixture in which each man found it necessary to filter the words of his pastor and the words of his neighbor through the entirely different strainer sitting on the table before him.

I suppose someone reading this may think I am foolish for reacting in such a way. After all, many modern-day Christians routinely experience such Bible studies and think nothing of it. That may well be, but I am heartily glad millions of independent Baptists do not. Nor should they for one moment think such an approach is necessary, let alone wise. The KJV is beautiful, scholarly, and reliable. And it is patently understandable.

The Underlying Greek Text

The New Testament was originally written in Greek. At the dawn of the Reformation, a movement began to compile the available Greek manuscripts into an authoritative Greek text that would be available for translators and scholars. Led by Erasmus, who published the first Greek text in 1517, and later improved upon by Stephans, Beza, and Elzevir, this textual family was the basis for the King James New Testament. With some disparity but much similarity, it is known by names such as the Byzantine Text, the Received Text, the Antiochan Text, or the Majority Text. Its manuscript base ranges from the ninth to the fourteenth centuries.

In the latter half of the nineteenth century, a movement began in England to undertake a dramatic revision of the 250-year-old KJV led by Brooke Foss Westcott and Fenton John Anthony Hort. Westcott and Hort decided not only to retranslate the Bible but also to compile a new, underlying Greek text for the New Testament. This modern Greek text rested largely upon two New Testament-length manuscripts that were not available to earlier compilers. The first was Sinaiticus, discovered by Tischendorf at a monastery in the Sinai Peninsula in 1859, and the second was Vaticanus, first catalogued in the Vatican library in 1475 but not completely transcribed until the nineteenth century. Both of these manuscripts have been reliably dated to the fourth century, and together they largely form the basis for a rather different Greek text now known as the Alexandrian Text or Critical Text.

In the intervening time period since the publication of Westcott and Hort's Revised Version in 1881, almost every English translation since has used the Critical Text as the base of its New Testament. The KJV, of course, used the Received Text.

I freely confess I am not a textual expert, but as I understand it, the main claim for the superiority of the Alexandrian Text over the Received Text is the age of its primary manuscripts – the fourth century as contrasted with the Received Text's ninth through fourteenth centuries. The implication, if not outright assertion, is that the older text basis is more accurate since it brings us nearer to the time of the originals. Operating under the assumption of *lectio brevior,* the idea that scribes over time had a tendency to add information rather than delete it, Westcott and Hort routinely favored the shorter readings and produced a substantially shorter Greek text. (Not coincidentally, the New International Version, for example, contains sixty-four thousand fewer words than the KJV. That is three- fourths the size of the book you are holding in your hands at the moment.)

Just because a manuscript is older, however, does not mean it is better. Sometimes a manuscript is still around simply because it has been used so rarely that it has not worn out. For example, I have four Scofield KJV Bibles in my office. Two of them are entirely separated from the binding and have become the equivalent of loose-leaf Bibles. On the other hand, I have a New Living Translation Bible that is in excellent condition simply because I never use it. I do not believe it is reliable. Yet a thousand years from now, there is a much greater chance that the latter remains while the former will have disappeared. Similarly, older manuscript authorities may very well owe their survival to abandonment by God's people.

It is true that the manuscript basis for the Received Text is younger. It is also indisputably true that it has a much wider base than the manuscripts used for the Critical Text. When a large body of ancient manuscripts are seen to be in agreement, this harmony becomes a great support to the manuscript's claims on legitimacy. Simple math supports this. The nearer a reading is to the original, the more time it has had to produce numerous descendant copies.

Dr. Maurice Robinson, who has taught Greek, New Testament, and textual criticism at Southeastern Baptist Theological Seminary since 1991, is a supporter of the Byzantine Text. He explained it this way: " 'Reasoned transmissionalism!' Had any text type other than the Byzantine more closely represented the autograph form of the text in any New Testament book, that text type should have thoroughly permeated the primary Greek speaking region of the Empire beyond the first few centuries. Any later developing 'new' text type would fail to dominate against a presumed liturgically entrenched and widely disseminated 'original' text form."

Robinson's point is that the Critical Text did no such thing, thus indicating its inherent inaccuracy. There are roughly five thousand Greek manuscripts extant in the world as of this writing, and ninety-nine percent of them agree with the Received Text against approximately one percent that agree with the Critical Text. Such numbers indicate that no matter the age of individual manuscripts, the Received Text body itself is older and thus closer to the originals. The larger the family, the older the original source must be.

Not only are the Received Text manuscripts much more numerous than the Critical Text, they are also much more unified. The Critical Text is based mostly on two manuscripts; yet those manuscripts – Vaticanus and Sinaiticus – disagree with each other over three thousand times in the Gospels alone. On the other hand, the much bigger Received Text base agrees with itself to a much greater extent. Dr. Wilbur Pickering defends the Majority Text in his 1981 book *The Identity of the New Testament Text* in this way: "A better though more cumbersome way to describe the situation would be something like this: 100% of the manuscripts agree as to say 80% of the text; over 99% of the manuscripts agree to another 10% of the text; over 90% of the manuscripts agree as to another 3% of the text. Only 3% or less of the text to less than 90% of the manuscripts agree."

The supporter of the Critical Text who rejects the Received Text must account for its widespread existence. He does so by maintaining it has its roots in fabrication. But if he complains of fabrication, how can he possibly believe this fabrication was done with almost universal unity? The stubborn fact of the matter is the

Received Text is both much more prevalent and much more unified than the Critical Text.

In addition to these facts, there is the weight of the early translations which is significant. By virtue of the conditions required for an accurate translation, an ancient version will always have a higher reliability factor than any single codex or manuscript. In other words, since translations require painstaking compilation and comparison of manuscripts by informed men, then an ancient translation that agrees with the Received Text reveals that the cream of the crop of the Early Church held a Received Text position. Additionally, ancient translations have the ability to show that the Received Text predates or is at least contemporary with the Critical Text, thus robbing the latter of its greatest claim to support. A partial listing of ancient translations that support Received Text readings include the Aramaic Peshitta (145), the Latin Itala (200), the Gothic (330), and the Armenian (436).

Lastly, there is the support of the church fathers, the influential church leaders in the early centuries after Christ. They were fond of writing long letters to one another and to other churches. In these letters (many of which survive today), we find numerous Scripture quotations packaged around whatever particular theological question they were discussing. These surviving letters are full of New Testament references, providing a valuable witness to the prevailing text of their day.

Keep in mind that Westcott and Hort put great stock in the age of the Critical Text manuscript base. They asserted that the Received Text base did not exist prior to A.D. 350. Quoting Hort, "The text found in the mass of existing manuscripts does not date further back than the middle of the 4th century. Before that text was made up other forms of text were in vogue."

Briefly then here is the fatherly testimony: Tertuallian, Iranaeus, Hippolytus, Origen, and Clement alone cite Scripture over thirty thousand times. The great majority of these citations agree with the Received Text, and all five of these men died before Vaticanus and Sinaiticus were copied out. Dean Burgon, the nineteenth century's avowed foe of Westcott and Hort, wrote several books defending the Received Text. His editor, Edward Miller, explains it this way:

"As far as the Fathers who died before 400 A.D. are concerned, the question may now be put and answered. Do they witness to the Traditional Text as existing from the first, or do they not? The results of the evidence, both as regards the quantity and the quality of testimony, enable us to reply, not only that the Traditional Text was in existence, but that it was predominant, during the period under review."

As with the ancient translations, such testimony is more reliable than any solitary codex. Burgon himself established this. "It has been pointed out elsewhere that, in and by itself, the testimony of any first rate Father, where it can be had, must be held to outweigh the solitary testimony of any single codex which can be named... For instance, the origin and history of Codexes A, B, Aleph, C is wholly unknown: their dates and the places of their several production are matters of conjecture only. But when we are listening to the articulate utterance of any of the ancient Fathers, we not only know with more or less precision the actual date of the testimony before us, but we even known the very diocese of Christendom in which we are standing. To such a deponent we can assign a definite amount of credibility, whereas in the estimate of the former class of evidence we have only inference to guide us. Individually, therefore, a Father's evidence where it can be obtained, *caeterius paribus*, is considerably greater than of any single codex." The Early Church fathers thus establish that the Greek text of the KJV was flourishing as early as the fourth century making it at least as old as Vaticanus and Sinaiticus.

On the Critical Text side of the scale, there is age. But on the Received Text side of the scale, there is an explanation for that age, a prevailing number, unity, and age itself via the testimony of the ancient translations and the Fathers. I will happily take the Received Text and thus the KJV, thank you very much.

Where are we right? In this: along with nearly ninety million Americans, we use the King James Version.

We Hold Standards

Take the high road.
-Clarence Sexton

I had the privilege of growing up in a Christian home. My father, who was raised strict Catholic, was converted at twenty-five. The change in him was immediate and deep. An independent Baptist pastor led him to Christ on a Friday night. He attended a church prayer breakfast the next morning. Within a week, he was attending every available service. Within a year, he was enrolled in a local church Bible institute. Within four years, he had moved his growing family to a different state to attend Bible college. Within seven years, he was pastoring his own independent Baptist church.

I reference this in order to show you that everything in his life changed and changed quickly, dramatically, and deeply. When my father trusted Christ, he did not play around. He hit the ground running and continued running hard after the Lord in the decades that followed. Among other things, his concept of family and of parenting changed deeply as well. Both my mother and he led our family full throttle into the conventional wisdom of the conservative 1960s independent Baptist movement.

For example, my parents did not (and still do not) own a television. We were enrolled in a Christian day school from kindergarten through twelfth grade. The music in our house was classical or hymns. The hair on the men was short, and the skirts on the women were long. No matter how broke we were, we always wore dress clothes to church. We did not attend theaters, dances, or pool halls.

When the village we lived in allowed community bingo around the Fourth of July festival, Dad went to the mayor and protested.

As a result of this approach to parenting, one of the earliest things I remember realizing was that our family was different. We were different from the children in the neighborhood around us. We were different from most of the children in our Christian school. We were different even from many of the children in our church. What we did was different. What we wore was different. Where we went was different. What we enjoyed and did not enjoy was different.

> *The best word I can think of to describe how we were raised as children is sheltered.*

The best word I can think of to describe how we were raised as children is sheltered.

This is not a book on the family. I make no pretense to expertise in that area, and even if I do write something about that, it will not be for many years yet. But I will say – and happily so – that the way I was raised was very good for me. It was good for this basic reason: it protected me. It protected my flesh from openly developing spiritually damaging appetites. It protected my impressionable mind from foul language, sexual banter, and some aspects of negative peer pressure.

At its root, standards (defined as an acceptable code of conduct) are about protection. There are three great enemies of the Christian man: the world, the flesh, and the devil. Standards protect us from most aspects of the first and some aspects of the latter two. They are guidelines that inform what we allow and do not allow, protecting us from temptation.

Protection from temptation is a scriptural concept. It is a worthwhile goal. ...*lead us not into temptation...* (*Matthew 6.13*) James 1 dwells on this extensively. My Dad calls this passage the anatomy of temptation. It reveals how the devil works. *But every man is tempted, when he is drawn away of his own lust, and enticed. Then when lust hath conceived, it bringeth forth sin: and sin, when it is finished, bringeth forth death.* I vividly remember my father illustrating this in a message with a dodgeball marked "death." He put me into a corner marked "sin," and I found I had no way to escape "death." Gradually, he allowed me wider leeway around the auditorium in progressive steps marked as "lust," "enticed," and "drawn away." The ultimate protection was when I avoided even being drawn away. At that point there was no possibility of choosing actions that would inevitably or even potentially result in death.

Solomon speaks similarly in *Proverbs 4. Enter not into the path of the wicked, and go not in the way of evil men. Avoid it, pass not by it, turn from it, and pass away.* A path is a route that has a destination. If I do not want to end up at a certain destination, I need to avoid the path that leads to that destination. *Proverbs* speaks often of paths and where they lead us–*paths of life, right paths, path of the wicked, path of the just, path of life,* etc. For example, sexual sin surely leads to death. *For her house inclineth unto death, and her paths unto the dead. None that go unto her return again, neither take they hold of the paths of life. (Proverbs 2.18-19)*

A wise man then thinks about where his current path is going to lead him. *Ponder the path of thy feet,... (Proverbs 4.26)* An even wiser man thinks about where his future path is headed. He thinks it through before he ever gets on the wrong path. He consciously seeks to avoid not just the wrong destination but even setting foot on the path that leads to the wrong destination.

My parents designed my childhood spiritually with a large emphasis on protection. They attempted to shelter me from being both enticed by sin and drawn into sin. They attempted to protect me from the entrance to the wrong path rather than trying to pull me off of the wrong path once I had meandered down it for a while. Certainly, no protection is foolproof; and there dwelt within my sinful heart a natural inclination to foolishness. A parental philosophy of sheltering cannot protect any child from his own wicked heart. But the standards they imposed on me and my siblings did offer us a good measure of that protection.

I am no longer a child, but I have found that the applied principle of standards is still a wise one. The world is still out to get me. *(John 15.19)* My heart is still deceitful and

> *The applied principle of standards is still a wise one. The world is still out to get me.*

desperately wicked. *(Jeremiah 17.9)* The devil is still stalking his prey. *(I Peter 5.8)* Yes, I have more experience now than I did as a young person. Yes, I have more backbone now. Yes, I have more maturity now. But I still need protection from temptation.

Please do not misunderstand me. I do not believe the application of standards produces holiness. In fact, I will speak to this error in a later chapter of this book and mayhap in a book entirely of its own. But I am weary with hearing it said that applying standards produces wickedness. I am weary with the philosophy that says externally mandated rules result in hypocrisy. On the contrary, standards are not the problem. I make no claim that they are the entirety of the solution, but they definitely are not the problem. Indeed, in my view derived as I believe from God's Word, standards are a blessing.

The independent Baptist movement handed my parents a set of guidelines. It handed them a principled approach to parenting that involved standards of behavior designed to protect their children. Those standards did protect me. In turn, I largely embraced them for myself and my own children.

In the past fifty years, millions of independent Baptist children have grown up with similar standards. That is not a bad thing. It is not a handicap. It is not an anchor around the neck of the growth of our movement. It is not a hindrance to holiness. It is not a spur to hypocrisy. It is applied wisdom. It is principle turned into practice. It is a blessing and a benefit.

Where are we right? In this: we hold standards.

We Are Evangelistic

I still, from my armchair, preach in great revival campaigns. I still envision hundreds walking the aisles to accept Christ. I still feel hot tears for the lost. I still see God working miracles. Oh, how I long to see great revivals, to hear about revival crowds once again! ...I want no Christmas without a burden for lost souls, a message for sinners, a heart to bring in the lost sheep so dear to the Shepherd, the sinning souls for whom Christ died. May food be tasteless, and music a discord, and Christmas a farce if I forget the dying millions to whom I am debtor; if this fire in my bones does not still flame! Not till I die or not till Jesus comes, will I ever be eased of this burden, these tears, this toil to save souls.
-John R. Rice

One of the marks of a sincere Christian is a concern for the eternal destiny of the lost world around him. This concern, not wanting any man to experience the eternal horrors of hell, arises from natural human sympathy and is combined with an appreciation for the emphasis that is placed upon it in the Word of God.

Such an emphasis is found in the Old Testament. Solomon tells us we are wise to win souls. *(Proverbs 11.30)* Ezekiel presses our responsibility heavily upon us. *(Ezekiel 3.18)* Daniel motivates us with rewards. *(Daniel 12.3)*

The importance of witnessing is found in exponentially increasing quantities in the New Testament. The mission statement of the church is the Great Commission. *(Matthew 28.19-20, Mark 16.15)* John quotes Jesus to the effect that we are supposed to go and bring forth fruit. *(John 15.16)* Jesus said that if we follow Him as we are commanded, we will find ourselves fishing for men. *(Matthew 4.19, Mark 1.17)* James said that we should endeavor to save souls. *(James 5.20)* Jude motivates us to do so with fear and compassion. *(Jude 23)* Jesus said people are ready to be saved; they just need to be told. *(John 4.35)*

There are numerous examples in Scripture of God's people having a passion for souls. Paul was so burdened for the lost he was willing to endure hell if it meant their salvation. *(Romans 9.3, 10.1)* By all means, he wanted to save some. *(I Corinthians 9.22)* The early church endured persecution, but it only spurred them on to a greater witness. *(Acts 8.4)* Jesus felt a compelling need to endure Samaria so that He might witness to the woman at the well. *(John 4.4)* As He died, He still sought to win men to God. *(Luke 23.43)*

Christianity includes within its boundaries many graces, but surely witnessing ought to be prioritized. I am not seeking to minimize prayer, Bible study, love for our neighbor, building a good marriage, raising godly children, pursuing wisdom, living in the joy of Christ, being holy, praising God, having faith, or any other important aspect of our religion. But what is the point of all of these if we let them die with us? We must pass it on.

A soul-winning Christian is not necessarily a mature Christian, but a mature Christian is a soul-winning Christian.

As a Christian grows in grace, he inevitably comes face to face with his own responsibility in this area. If he chooses to yield, he has the potential for future growth. If he chooses to excuse himself with any one of a thousand possibilities happily handed to him by the devil, he will plateau. Eventually, he will backslide. A soul-winning Christian is not necessarily a mature Christian, but a mature Christian is a soul-winning Christian.

Just as with other aspects of Christianity, this one is not limited to a personal responsibility alone. Just as churches have a corporate duty to be holy and to exercise faith, so they have a corporate obligation to witness for Christ. A non-soul-winning church is rather an oxymoron in terms; the very purpose of the church is rooted in world evangelism. Jesus instructed us to ...*Occupy till I come. (Luke 19.13)* The original language behind the word *occupy* means to carry on a business. What business is that? In context, the Father's business is the Son's purpose. *For the Son of Man is come to seek and to save that which was lost. (Luke 19.10)* Make no mistake; the church is a business. It is not in business to make money. It is in business to reach souls with Gospel.

Every single theological definition of the church I have ever encountered says something to this effect: "the church is a group of believers called out and assembled together for the purpose of carrying out the Great Commission." The church I pastor printed a phone book in 1925. They had the wisdom to place this statement in the frontispiece: "The purpose of this church shall be to promote the interests of the Kingdom of God, evangelize the unsaved, and edify those of the faith. To this end the church shall maintain regular meetings and seek to create and cultivate an interest in and devotion to missions at home and abroad." The church must be after people with the Gospel, or it is recklessly negligent of the primary point of its own existence.

This is not easy to do. There is little the devil fights harder than a soul-winning, missions-minded church. He attacks it on all fronts constantly. A church that is gathered together enjoying each other's company and heedless of the lost world outside its walls is no threat to his kingdom. But a church that is pursuing sinners with the Gospel draws his attention like a lodestone.

Growing up in a pastor's home and now pastoring for nineteen years, it has been my experience that there is no single thing more difficult to do than to get God's people to develop a sustained burden for witnessing. It is easier to get a man to tithe. It is easier to get a woman to yield her wardrobe to Christ. It is easier to heal the dead, cast out the sick, and raise the devil than it is to develop a soul-winning church.

It can, however, be done. Church history is filled to the brim with records of men, ministries, and movements who have given themselves to pursuing sinners for the Saviour. This is by no means historically limited to independent Baptists, but it does visibly and deeply mark our story.

The first nationwide Baptist organization was built around missions. The Northern and Southern Baptist Conventions which resulted from that original organization produced mission boards. The fundamentalist battles that split the Northern Baptist Convention in the 1920s produced (even in its infant Baptist Bible Union days) missions agencies. The General Association of Regular Baptist Churches, the Fundamental Baptist Fellowship, the Conservative Baptist Fellowship, and the Conservative Baptist Association all produced mission boards. On the southern side, the weakness of the Southern Baptist Convention produced the World Baptist Fellowship, the Baptist Bible Fellowship, and the Southwide Baptist Fellowship. All of these, particularly the BBF, fervently embraced missions.

A partial list of current American independent Baptist missions agencies includes the International Board of Jewish Missions, Baptist International Missions, Incorporated, the Global Faith Mission Agency, Macedonia Baptist World Missions, International Gospel Missions, Baptist International Outreach, Baptist Evangelistic Missionary Association, Word for the World Baptist Missions, Vision Baptist Missions, Fundamental Baptist Missions International, Independent Baptist World Missions, Truth for Today Baptist Missions, Final Frontiers Foundation, the Gospel Preacher Association, Baptist Bible Fellowship International, the World Baptist Fellowship Mission Agency, Jewish End-Time Ministries, Beacon International Baptist Mission, Mount Abarim Baptist Mission International, Points North Baptist Mission, Heartland Baptist Missions, Reach International Ministries, Baptist Mid-Missions, Central Missionary Clearinghouse, the Association of Baptists For World Evangelism, Continental Baptist Missions, Baptist Mission to Forgotten Peoples, Independent Baptist World-Wide Mission, World-Wide New Testament Baptist Missions, Fundamental Baptist Home Missions, Incorporated, Independent Baptist Fellowship International, and Open Door Baptist Missions.

Many of these were founded out of the initial enthusiasm incumbent in the associations emerging from the Fundamentalist-Modernist controversy. Others were the dream of one particular man who was burdened for a certain people group or geographical region. Most of the newer ones are ministries of specific local churches. This is due at least in part to an increased understanding of the importance of the doctrines of autonomy and perpetuity I discussed earlier. But however they came into existence, the point is they exist. And they cumulatively include on their rolls conservatively more than 5,000 independent Baptist missionaries.

The independent Baptist emphasis on evangelism is not only global; it is also local. Independent Baptist churches pioneered the bus ministry. All across the United States hundreds of thousands of children will ride a bus to an independent Baptist church this Sunday. Under the aegis of pastors with national influence, the bus ministry caught on in thousands of churches in the latter half of the twentieth century.

This corporate evangelism emphasis is not only seen in specific ministries but in legacies as well. The independent Baptist movement has preached more, written more, and pushed more for personal soul winning than any other denominational group in twentieth century America. Other groups have had influential men stand up such as D. James Kennedy and Ray Comfort; for this I am grateful. But one cannot study soul winning in the last century without coming across John R. Rice, Lee Roberson, Curtis Hutson, and Jack Hyles again and again and again.

Please do not misunderstand me. I do not believe for one moment that only independent Baptists care about lost people. Wide swaths of the Charismatic movement and the Contemporary Evangelical movement dedicate themselves to church planting, mass evangelism, media evangelism, and niche evangelism. To the extent that they genuinely preach Christ, I rejoice in it all. *(Philippians 1.18)* But no Presbyterian, Lutheran, Methodist, Southern Baptist, or contemporary non-denominational church member has ever handed me a tract. None of them have ever knocked on my door. I have never run into their people publically confronting people with the Gospel or rounding up children to ride a bus to church on Sunday. Independent Baptist churches by the thousands do so every week of the year. It is deeply implanted into our DNA. It is who we are.

While watching fireworks in Youngstown, Ohio one July night, a man handed me a tract. He was an independent Baptist. Answering my front door in Chicago one Saturday afternoon, I found two Hispanic soul winners smiling at me. They were from a local Spanish-speaking independent Baptist church. I have spotted tracts in doctor's offices, hospital waiting rooms, phone booths, restaurant tables, car windshields, and truck stop rest rooms. Five out of six were placed there by independent Baptists.

Many years ago, a family visited our church on a Sunday night. Sitting in the foyer afterward, the husband gently grilled me about our church. Amongst other questions he asked, "What does your church do for evangelism?" I explained to him that we met weekly each Saturday morning, divided up in teams of two, and went house to house on the streets directly adjacent to our church building. I told him we passed out tracts, invited people to church, and attempted to win them to Christ if they were willing to listen. I informed him that we offered individual training for those doing this work, that we followed up on contacts, and that we incorporated a mentoring type of discipleship program afterward.

He sat there quietly for a long minute. Then he looked at me and said, "We are searching for a church. We have visited about a dozen. Yours is the only church that has answered that question so simply. All the rest talked about their basketball tournaments or their community leaf raking program. Your church is the only church that just tries to talk to people about Jesus." That man and his family still attend our church.

That does not mean that every other church in my city is not evangelistic. It does not mean that we are the only ones who love God. It does mean that in that man's experience, the only kind of church that placed a great emphasis on individually witnessing to the lost was an independent Baptist church. His limited experience coincides with my own deeper knowledge base.

Within one mile of my church building, there are nearly 200,000 people. In twelve years, I have once come across a charismatic church sharing the Gospel with the lost in my neighborhood. I have repeatedly come across Mormons and Jehovah's Witnesses sharing their false doctrine. And more times than I can count, I have seen independent Baptists going house to house passing out tracts and telling people about Jesus. I suspect my neighborhood is like yours.

God knows my heart. I am not boasting on our behalf or seeking to belittle others. Beloved, I am rejoicing as I write this chapter. God has graciously drawn our churches to Himself in this area. We were birthed for evangelism. Our history is filled with evangelism. Just now we are circling the block and the globe carrying the good news of Gospel to every creature. It is a wonderfully precious fact. Where are we right? In this: We are evangelistic.

We Are Prudent

Think not that Prudence dwells in dark abodes,
She scans the future with the eye of gods.
-William Wordsworth, *At Bologna, In Remembrance
of the Late Insurrections*

W ise men are cautious men. I do not mean to say that wise
men sit still while their world crumbles around them. I
do mean to say that wise men diligently examine as many possible
ramifications of a decision as are feasible before making that decision. *A wise man feareth, and departeth from evil: but the fool
rageth, and is confident. (Proverbs 14.16)* Pride is the outstanding
characteristic of the fool. Conversely, humility is essential to
wisdom. Wise men embrace humility, and it is seen in that they
chase instruction. *...the wise seeketh knowledge. (Proverbs 18.15)*
Wise men are not overconfident in their own ability. They do not
trust their own perception. Thus, they move ahead cautiously. They
wait. They watch. They think. They weigh. They examine. They
pursue counsel. Then they move forward.

> *Wise men constantly ask,
> "Where will this road
> lead us?"*

The scriptural word for this
wise caution is *prudence. The
simple believeth every word: but
the prudent man looketh well to
his going. (Proverbs 14.15) A prudent man foreseeth the evil, and
hideth himself:... (Proverbs 22.3)*
Prudence looks down the road as far as it possibly can in order to

discern what is coming. Wise men constantly ask, "Where will this road lead us?" As much as possible, they attempt to answer that question not based on the now but on the future.

The first time I bought a car I was a simple young man. I looked to see if it had any rust at the present moment. I looked to see if it started easily at the present moment. I looked to see if the tire wear was even at the present moment. None of those were wrong necessarily, but what I did not do was look to see what that car would be like five years down the road. I did zero research on the historical patterns of that car's reliability. Thus, I had no idea that the car under discussion had a predilection to wheel bearing issues and CV joint problems. I did not realize that car had a tradition of transmission trouble. It was only six years old when I bought it, but the three more years I managed to eke out of it cost me thousands of dollars as I tried to address the ensuing complications. A prudent young man would have avoided that 1985 Ford Tempo. Unfortunately, I was not a prudent young man; I was a simple young man.

Independent Baptists, on the whole however, are prudent people. We are cautious about what is new.

Many years ago when I first came to Chicago, the pastor of the biggest Baptist church on this side of town invited me to lunch. (I will be forever grateful to him for introducing me to Greek food.) In the course of our conversation, he likened independent Baptists to the caboose on a train. From his point of view, we eventually end up where the rest of American Christianity is, but we just get there later.

He had a point. Generally speaking, we resist things that are new and embrace things that are old. Most men of educated opinion agree with this critique. There is, however, a difference in perspective. Many men I know think this is a weakness. I think it is a strength.

Often the difference in perspective breaks along age lines. Older men are often conservative. Younger men are often innovative. Older men are often questioning, hesitant, and slow to move. Younger men are often frustrated by this. "Young man in a hurry" is not a colloquialism for nothing. The younger men I know in the independent Baptist movement are much more prone to embrace change than the older men.

It is my view that while the young men are certainly not entirely wrong, the balance of wisdom lies with the old men. *With the ancient is wisdom; and in length of days understanding. (Job 12.12)* To their credit, the young men in our movement know this. This knowledge on their part governs their pursuit of change. In this fashion, the caution of the wise old men permeates our movement to a great degree as it should. The problem lies in that the young men often view the older men as obstacles that must be overcome in this area rather than as resources to be mined. It is a difference of perspective.

It is biblical to be cautious of that which is new. The oft-cited *meddle not with them that are given to change* is certainly appropriate. But the case for prudence does not rest on *Proverbs 24.21* alone. It rests much more broadly on the whole concept of wisdom. It rests on the entire tenor of the book of *Proverbs.*

Truth by definition cannot be new. It is a fixed point. *For ever, O Lord, thy word is settled in heaven. (Psalm 119.89)* This is why we must be cautious when the doctrine we hold and the practice we execute is somehow different from our fathers. We must make sure it is rooted in the Scriptures.

For the most part, the problem in our day does not lie with doctrine, though I believe that day is coming. The churches that have embraced innovative change as a core philosophy will eventually improve themselves to theological death. There is little settled about them. Everything is in flux. Change is the air in which they breathe and operate. Sooner or later, their own internal philosophy will bridge the wall they have built around doctrine. Driven by pragmatism, peer pressure, or persecution, their doctrine will inevitably succumb.

We are only now, however, beginning to discern the dim outlines of this coming doctrinal shift. On the other hand, the speed with which American Christianity has dramatically refashioned the entire concept of church is downright startling.

This is not intended to be an issue-driven book, but let me illustrate my point using music. Several years ago, I decided to do an intensive study on contemporary Christian music and its use in the church. It was relatively easy to find books written against CCM.

It was much harder to find books written for CCM. The music section of my bookshelf contains twenty-five books about music; only one of them is pro-CCM. This was not because I was not interested in hearing both sides in the debate. It is rather because one side of the debate has not thought it through very much. That sounds harsh, but I was forced to that conclusion. Nobody writes books supporting CCM because those who use it do not think such books need to be written. They do not attempt to discuss the ramifications of this great change simply because those ramifications have not even occurred to them. Innovatively driven ministries, methods, and philosophies are not built to think through the long-term consequences of their choice. They do not look down the road because it is not in their DNA.

However, it is in our DNA. The religious groups that are resisting CCM are either doing so for largely traditional reasons – they are liturgical in nature – or because they believe CCM is wrong or leads in the wrong direction. Independent Baptists are not liturgical. Our reasoning is not that CCM will damage our ritual but rather that it sends a church down the wrong road. We have looked down that road and seen where it goes. We do not like where it goes. So we avoid getting on that road. We are prudent.

We are rarely on the cutting edge. We do not, as a rule, inaugurate changes in doctrine or method. Consequently, we are never associated with the "in crowd." I cannot remember any case of an independent Baptist being nationally recognized by the wider religious world as "cool." Those to whom such things are important – and there have been some – simply do not stay independent Baptist. They cannot, for to pursue what is new is anathema to our approach.

In the short term, this often seems to harm us. Every week of my life someone walks into my church building as a brand new visitor and chooses never to return. Many times this is due to our music. This is not because our music is unenthusiastic or poorly done. It is because our music is not hip. It is not like the music at all the other churches with which they are cross shopping us. Just recently I sat in the living room of a thirty-something couple and listened as the wife explained the problem with our church. "I love your preaching, Pastor Brennan, but I love the music at this other church. If I could just combine their music with your preaching, it would be the perfect church." Apparently, my preaching alone could not keep that couple; for they are currently attending a contemporary church.

On the other hand, this helps us in the long run. Take, for example, the concept of commitment. The average contemporary evangelical church in America tries to function with a scarcity of commitment. It sells itself as fun, non-confrontational, practical, and hip. Its underlying philosophical approach breeds followers with a lack of commitment. They only follow as long as it stays fun, as long as no one confronts them, as long as they feel like the teaching is applicable to their stage of life, and as long as it bears some semblance to cool.

By contrast, independent Baptists may lose some people initially, but those that we keep are kept long term. We make the front door small and the back door even smaller. The typical independent Baptist church draws from a wide radius. Our people are willing to travel a distance and do so several times a week.

Not only is this deep difference in commitment true now, but it will be increasingly true in the decades to come. Persecution is coming to America. It is not a question of *if* but rather a question of *when*. Christianity was born and came of age under the persecution of the Roman Empire. We blossomed and bore much fruit in an extremely harsh environment. When such an environment comes again, what will be the result? Committed Christians who are already used to paying a price for their Christianity will take it in much better stride than those who are not. Churches built on *Thus saith the Lord* will be much less prone to bend under the pressure than churches built on sermons about last summer's Hollywood movies.

Prudence looks down the road to see what is coming and adjusts itself accordingly. Prudence proceeds with caution. Prudence is … *swift to hear, slow to speak, slow to wrath: (James 1.19)* Prudence takes its considerable time to understand what is coming. *(Proverbs 14.8)* Prudence takes the long view and thus protects us. *(Proverbs*

20.17) Wisdom dwells with prudence. *(Proverbs 8.12)* We are wise to embrace prudence and hold her close.

Where are we right? In this: we are prudent.

We Believe in Education on Fire

O, that my tongue were in the thunder's mouth!
Then with a passion would I shake the world.
-William Shakespeare, *King John*

I n the independent Baptist movement, it is Lee Roberson that is largely credited with emphasizing that everything rises and falls on leadership. I do not intend for this book to be solely for or about pastors. At the same time, I cannot avoid touching on both the good and bad aspects of leadership. Our movement is schizophrenic. If Lee Roberson is correct, this must be laid directly at the feet of that leadership.

Let us back that up for a moment. In order to understand our movement's strengths and weaknesses, we must understand the equivalent characteristics in our leaders. But in order to understand our leadership, we need to begin before they are leaders. Where do our leaders come from? How are they chosen? How are they developed?

In this book, I will attempt to answer those questions from several angles. Allow me to begin with what I believe is a strength. We believe in education on fire. We believe that young men training for the ministry should – to borrow a turn of phrase – be on fire for God. It was said of the Apostle John that *He was a burning and a shining light:... (John 5.35)*

What does it mean to "be on fire for the Lord"? Surely, some of that is passion. I do not believe emotions should lead us around by the nose, but I have no patience for a religion without them.

102

When Jeremiah wanted to quit the ministry, he found it impossible because ...*his word was in mine heart as a burning fire shut up in my bones, and I was weary with forbearing, and I could not stay. (Jeremiah 20.9)* The two men unknowingly walking with our risen Lord on the road to Emmaus asserted afterwards that they should have realized just Who He was. ...*Did not our heart burn within us, while he talked with us by the way, and while he opened to us the scriptures? (Luke 24.32)* The independent Baptist movement seeks to keep its young ministers passionately in love with the Lord *(Luke 10.27)*, with the Word of God *(Psalm 119.97)*, and with the souls of men. *(Matthew 9.36)*

David Martyn Lloyd-Jones said it this way in his third volume on *Ephesians*: "We should never study the Bible or anything concerning biblical truth without realizing that we are in His presence, and that it is truth about Him. And it should always be done in an atmosphere of worship. Biblical truth is not one subject among others; it not something that belongs in a syllabus. It is living truth about a living Person. That is why a theological college should be different from every other kind of college." There must first and foremost in our Bible colleges be a passion for God and for the souls of men.

> *A theological college should be different from every other kind of college.*
> -David Martyn Lloyd-Jones

Surely the twin of passion is enthusiasm. Young men are by nature enthusiastic. Most of the time, they simply need pointed in the right direction, and they will charge hell with a squirt gun. We cultivate this wonderfully well in our young ministers or "preacher boys" as we term them. Our college chapel services are purposely designed to be fiery and enthusiastic; our weekend ministries are exuberant. Indeed, the young men in these systems of ministry training are often practically fanatical in their pursuit of souls.

This pursuit of souls and embrace of fiery preaching is at the very core of what I am attempting to convey is our strength. The whole idea of John shining and burning was in reference to these things. In the greatest sermon ever preached, Jesus used the illustration of a shining, burning light as a beacon calling men to God.

(Matthew 5.16) As children in Sunday school, we sang "This little light of mine, I'm gonna let it shine." We are to *..shine as lights in the world; (Philippians 2.15).* The people of this world are blinded. They desperately need someone who will shine the light of the glorious Gospel of Christ into their lives and who will burn themselves up in the process, if necessary. *(II Corinthians 4.4)* To be on fire for the Lord is to pursue Him and to pursue souls with a fanatical enthusiasm. It is to know no limits. It is to throw yourself body and soul into reaching men and women and boys and girls with the Gospel. It is to love Him with all your heart, soul, and mind. It is to passionately plead with others to do the same. It is to be all in, to hold nothing back, and to surrender every part of yourself to ministry.

There are several keys to building an environment in which preacher boys receive an education on fire. The first is to set that education directly in the middle of a thriving, local church. It does not have to be a big church. In fact, big churches have just as many liabilities as they do assets. But it does need to be a church wholly alive and passionately pursuing sinners with the Gospel. This is the environment in which a preacher boy should learn.

Doing so marries his ministerial training to the local church. It magnifies the local church in his mind and in his philosophical approach. It also surrounds him with regular people. It gives him an active pastor as a model. It gives him an intimate acquaintance with what a healthy body of Christ should be.

In conjunction with this is the vital necessity of the preacher boy immersing himself in ministry. This centers him. It is a weekly reminder that the very point of his ministry is reaching, teaching, and building people.

Many years ago, I walked into the Girard Free Library in Girard, Ohio. Strolling past the circulation counter, I took a left hand turn into the stacks. In so doing, I walked directly past a librarian's desk. Amongst the piles of books and papers was a sign that stopped me dead in my tracks. It simply said, "Please interrupt me." The librarian loved books, but her job was to help people. If she was not careful, she would get so involved in her books that she would forget her task. So she solicited interruptions.

A preacher boy who sits in class twenty hours a week desperately needs the interruption of active ministry. His first passion must be God, but his second passion must be people. Ministry is people. It is loving them, winning them, serving them, and building them for the glory of God. His schooling must include large chunks of time, effort, money, sweat, and tears devoted to ministering to real people. In a very real sense this is exactly our method. And it is genius.

I am familiar with the arguments against such an approach. It runs the risk of turning the preacher boy into the equivalent of slave labor in another man's ministry. Sometimes it is pursued in an unbalanced manner. Tunnel vision produces a guy who never wants to leave his training ministry. Unscrupulous leaders take advantage of his enthusiastic naiveté. All of these potential dangers, however, do not overrule the potential dangers of ministry training in a classical seminary setting alone.

My last two years of high school I spent my summers traveling through the American South with veteran evangelist Joe Boyd. He was in his mid-seventies at the time with a lifetime of accumulated wisdom and experience available to me. Riding along in the bus with him one day, we were talking about this very matter. I was asking his opinion of how I should pursue my future ministry training. Joe Boyd was no intellectual slouch. He held a Bachelor's degree in accounting from Texas A&M University and a Master's degree in theology from Southwestern Baptist Theological Seminary. When he read his New Testament, he usually read the Greek version. His library contained thousands and thousands of volumes. In response to my query, Dr. Boyd made a statement I will never forget. He looked at me and said, "Son, don't get scholarship with a cold heart."

Don't get scholarship with a cold heart.
-Joe Boyd

By far this is the great danger in a ministerial education. It is the inculcation of a dead scholarship, a factually overstuffed mind paired with a spiritually lifeless heart. Seminaries staffed by barren academics produce men deep in arcane knowledge yet absent of a passionate desire to reach people with the Gospel. I have met them here and there. My predilections run to books and study, and I could easily have been numbered among them. God in His mercy spared me that. For ministry training, he placed me squarely in the center of a church that passionately pursued sinners. And the potential dangers I faced there were far less than those I would have faced in an ivory-towered seminary somewhere.

Intellectual pride is a subtly damning temptation. It builds a man secure in his own ability and knowledge. Such a man stands in the pulpit every week and leads God's people away from the heartbeat of God – the salvation of sinners. He may wax eloquent. He may impress the simple and even sway the sophisticated. He may publish papers and author books. Learned men may direct commendations his way. But an intellectually oriented ministry usually fails to minister to the real world needs of God's people. What is worse, it almost always produces a church educated far beyond its spiritual readiness to perform.

Church history is filled with examples of denominations that exalted intellectual credentials above scholarship on fire for God. They litter the English and American past like the debris of a lost civilization. If you stay with me through the end of this book, you will discover that I am no fan of ignorance; but the truth is, I cannot think of a denomination destroyed by too much passion. I can, however, think of several destroyed by too much erudition.

The Scripture says of Christ, ...*The zeal of thine house hath eaten me up. (John 2.17)*

Where are we right? In this: we believe in education on fire.

We Have Prophets

Historians are prophets with their face turned backward.
-Johann Friedrich Von Schiller

I do not want you to misunderstand this chapter title before we even get started; please bear with me. The position of prophet is one of great significance. In the Old Testament, the prophets were God's mouthpiece speaking His words to His people. Their role was different than the priest; he was charged with ministering for the people in the service of the Lord. Their role was different than the king; he was charged with executing God's instructions on a national scale. The prophet's role was primarily one of revelation. He set before the people exactly what it was that God was telling the people to do.

Prophets are not limited to the Old Testament alone. The New Testament has much to say about prophets and prophecy. As with the Old Testament, sometimes their job was to reveal the future. More often, it was simply to establish the specific words of God during an era in which the canon of Scripture had not yet been completed.

I am a Baptist. As such, I believe in the sufficiency of Scripture alone. Although I believe God spoke in the past through revelations and visions, I do not believe that is the case any longer. I reject the concept of extra-biblical revelation. I am thus termed a *cessationist* in contrast to our charismatic friends who are termed *continuationist*. I believe in the Holy Spirit, and I believe that He is active on Earth today. I do not believe His ministry to us now includes new revelation from God.

The clearest extended discussion of this in Scripture is found in *I Corinthians 12-14*. The Corinthian church struggled with an awful misunderstanding and misapplication of the gift of the tongues. Their practice was confusing and dangerous. Paul carefully explained their mistakes and urged them toward a correct practice.

As long as the position of prophet existed, men took advantage of it. They claimed to be speaking for God when He had in fact given them no such message. *(Jeremiah 23.21)* It took approximately sixty years from the time Christ ascended for the New Testament to be finished. During that time period, God gave the gift of tongues so churches could verify that someone who claimed to be speaking prophetically actually was. Their inspired revelation could not be accepted at face value. It had to be confirmed. *(Hebrews 2.3-4)* God used the sign gifts – tongues, visions, miracles, etc. – in order to confirm to the early church that what the church was hearing was directly from God. *(Mark 16.20, I Corinthians 1.4-7)*

The authoritative structure for determining this validity was the "in part" system. The sign gifts were distributed amongst the individuals in the church as checks and balances; one would speak in tongues, one would interpret, one would discern whether the spirit was genuine, etc. *(I Corinthians 12.7-11)* Together, all of these gifts applied jointly brought an edifying message to the church.

In *I Corinthians 12-13*, there is a small Greek phrase used five times, transliterated as *ek merous*, which means "by part or in portions." *Now ye are the body of Christ, and members in particular. And God hath set some in the church, first apostles, secondarily prophets, thirdly teachers, after that miracles, then gifts of healings, helps, governments, diversities of tongues. (I Corinthians 12.27-28)* In other words, the Corinthian church had been allotted or apportioned the parts necessary for her edification.

I Corinthians 12 was written to demonstrate how each member (by way of their allotted part) contributed to this edification. In *I Corinthians 13*, Paul begins to differentiate between those gifts that will endure throughout the entire church age and those that will not. *Charity never faileth: but whether there be prophecies, they shall fail; whether there be tongues, they shall cease; whether there be knowledge, it shall vanish away. (I Corinthians 13.8)* In what way does prophecy fail? It does not fail by being ineffective or failing to come to pass; rather it fails by becoming inoperative. Prophecy, at some point, would cease to exist as a gift. Prophets would cease to exist as an office.

When does Paul say this will take place? Well, at the very moment Paul was writing, the "in part" system was still in operation. That is how they knew that God was speaking. *For we know in part, and we prophesy in part. But when that which is perfect is come, then that which is in part shall be done away. (I Corinthians 13.9-10)* The "in part" system would be finished when *that which is perfect* arrived. We often speak of the following two verses as Heaven, but the context is talking about sign gifts, church edification, and the part that members have in establishing the revelation of God to His church. They are not about Heaven. *When I was a child, I spake as a child, I understood as a child, I thought as a child: but when I became a man, I put away childish things. (I Corinthians 13.11)* The church in its infancy had to rely on a system of receiving knowledge that would no longer be used when the church reached maturity. *For now we see through a glass, darkly; but then face to face: now I know in part; but then shall I know even as also I am known. (I Corinthians 13.12)*

In those days, the church had a potentially flawed understanding of God's will based on the "in part" system of sign gifts. Later, when *that which is perfect* came and the church reached maturity, the knowledge of God's will would be crystal clear to one and all within the church. Is this talking about Heaven? No. It is talking about God's Word.

Scripture elsewhere clearly likens itself to a mirrored piece of glass which allows us to see our true condition as reflected in God's revelation. *(James 1.23-25, II Corinthians 3.16-18)* Only the Bible – the complete canon of Scripture, *a glass* –gives us an unveiled, transforming look at both our depraved selves and the glory and will of God. The Scripture alone is all that we need; God Himself makes that crystal clear at the very end of the Bible. *(Revelation 22.18-19)*

It follows then that when I assert that independent Baptists have prophets, I most certainly do not mean the formal position. We have the perfectly complete and entire Word of God. There are no more prophets. God is not continuing to reveal His Word to men. He stopped at *Revelation 22*.

What do I mean then? Why do I say that the independent Baptist movement has prophets? I say this because we do. *Prophecy* and *prophesy* are not just used in the New Testament in the formal sense. They are also used in a preaching sense. In other words, to prophesy was not just to tell the future or reveal the inspired words of God. Sometimes it meant simply to preach. *(I Thessalonians 5.20, Romans 12.6)* In this sense, to prophesy is simply to preach about Jesus Christ. *...for the testimony of Jesus is the spirit of prophecy. (Revelation 19.10)*

At the same time that there is a distinction between the formal role of prophet and that of preacher (my preaching is not authoritative unless I am directly reading the Word of God), there is also a connection. New Testament preachers carry the heritage of the prophets. We stand in their modern-day place telling the people what God said. Our job is not priestly; it is prophetic. It is to urge upon the people a strict obedience to the already revealed will of God as found in the pages of Scripture.

In this sense, we are to carry the spirit of the old time prophets with us. We are to be similar to them in ministry. We are to be marked by the same characteristics with which they were marked. And I think to a very real extent, we do and are. In this chapter, I offer you three characteristics that exemplified the prophets. I think these characteristics are found in large proportions among us.

Preaching

The prophets have largely come to us in written form. In their own day, however, they were known primarily as preachers, not as writers. Elijah preached the devil out of Ahab and the prophets of Baal. Elisha followed fast on his heels. Jeremiah wept while he preached, yet he preached on. Ezekiel preached against the wickedness of the nations around Israel. Hosea preached the great love and longsuffering of God. Joel preached the day of the Lord. Amos preached that people ought to prepare to meet God. Jonah's preaching brought a foreign city to its knees in sackcloth and repentance. Micah preached the Lord's controversy with His people. Habakkuk preached faith in God. Haggai preached the people toward a renewed commitment. Zechariah preached about the Messiah. Malachi preached reform to Israel's leadership. But one and all, they preached. Even in the New Testament, the prophetic ministry was marked as a preaching ministry. *In those days came John the Baptist, preaching in the wilderness of Judaea,... (Matthew 3.1)*

In my opinion, the greatest preacher in the Bible outside of Jesus is Isaiah. His pulpiteering was matchless, and his book contains perhaps the single best definition of preaching in the Scripture. *Cry aloud, spare not, lift up thy voice like a trumpet, and shew my people their transgression, and the house of Jacob their sins. (Isaiah 58.1)*

Preaching confronts passionately. We are to *cry aloud*. There is here a sense of urgency; the idea is that this message is vital.

Preaching confronts wholeheartedly. We are to *spare not*. Do not ask the God-called preacher to tread lightly. Do not ask him to tiptoe through the tulips. Do not give him a list of things about which he should not preach. Do not ask him to be mindful of the visitors or the senior citizens or the new converts or the little children. He must preach freely.

Preaching confronts clearly. We are told to *lift up thy voice like a trumpet*. The herald cannot hide any portion of the King's message. The people must hear it plainly. They must understand exactly what is required of them.

Preaching confronts revealingly. We are to *shew*. We are to convince men of what is wrong and what is right. We are to be logically and emotionally persuasive.

Preaching confronts specifically. What are we to shew? We are to shew *their transgression*. We are not to waffle on endlessly about things other people are doing wrong. We are to plainly, forcefully, and powerfully confront the sin of our own hearers.

Preaching was a priority in biblical times. When God saw the wickedness of the world in Genesis, who did He send? He sent *Noah... a preacher of righteousness. (II Peter 2.5)* When God wanted to reach the sex-soaked, sports-mad, money-chasing city of Corinth, what did He do? He sent a preacher. *For Christ sent me not to baptize, but to preach the gospel: not with wisdom of words, lest the cross of Christ should be made of none effect. For the preaching of the cross is to them that perish foolishness; but unto us which are saved it is the power of God. (I Corinthians 1.17-18)* Jesus was a mighty preacher. *(Matthew 4.17, 4.23, 9.35, 11.1, 12.41)* He commissioned His apostles as preachers. *(Matthew 10.7, 10.27)* The early church was marked by an emphasis on preaching. *And daily in the temple, and in every house, they ceased not to teach and preach Jesus Christ. (Acts 5.42)* Stephen was martyred while preaching. When persecution sent them running, *...they that were scattered abroad went every where preaching the word. (Acts 8.4)* On the side of the road, Philip *...opened his mouth, and began at the same scripture, and preached unto him Jesus. (Acts 8.35)* When he was done with the Ethiopian eunuch, he *preached in all the cities, till he came to Caesarea. (Acts 8.40)* Paul got saved *And straightway preached Christ in the synagogues,... (Acts 9.20)* He preached so long he put men to sleep and raised them from the dead. *(Acts 20.9)*

As of this writing, I have been a preacher for twenty-eight years. I have the wonderful privilege and high responsibility of occupying a pulpit several times a week. If my church does not sing well, I am disappointed. If my church does not give well, the cause of Christ is hindered. If my church does not pray well, our ministry is anemic. But if my church does not listen to preaching well, we are sailing at breakneck speed toward the reefs of tragedy.

There is no orthodox religious movement in America today with a greater emphasis on preaching than the independent Baptists. Our services include music, fellowship, giving, and prayer; but they prioritize preaching. Our people have grown to delight in preaching. A service is a good one or a bad one based on the preaching. They bring their Bibles with them to church and they expect to use them. Our movement's emphasis on preaching has created thousands of churches and millions of people with a hunger and thirst for righteousness. No other kind of church in America conducts as many preaching services on a yearly basis in America as we do. No other group of pastors preaches as often in a week. No other church builds people with such a hunger for and delight in preaching.

There is no orthodox religious movement in America today with a greater emphasis on preaching than the independent Baptists.

Discernment

Discernment is the ability to notice things to which others are completely oblivious. The first use of the word in the Bible is in the context of Isaac's failure to recognize Jacob under his Esau disguise. *(Genesis 27.23)* Implicit in the idea of discernment is the capacity for distinguishing between good and bad. *(II Samuel 14.17, 19.35)* Discernment sees beneath the exterior. It is not deceived by a seeming smoothness but unerringly narrows in on the rocks just beneath the surface.

Discernment is closely allied in *Proverbs* with *understanding*. The three great words of *Proverbs* are *knowledge, wisdom,* and *understanding.* Knowledge is the what. Wisdom is the how. Understanding is the why. Paul prayed that the Colossians *...might be filled with the knowledge of his will in all wisdom and spiritual understanding. (Colossians 1.9)* The knowledge of the will of God is to know what it is God wants you to do. Wisdom is to know how to do what it is God wants you to do. Understanding is to know why God wants you to do it and why you should do it how you should do it. Set in this framework, discernment implies that you can see what others cannot – the real *why* behind what everyone else sees, knows, or does.

Solomon's great request upon assuming the throne lays this out clearly. *Give therefore thy servant an understanding heart to judge thy people, that I may discern between good and bad:...(I Kings 3.9)* Discernment is ever the work of mature, experienced Christians. *But strong meat belongeth to them that are of full age, even those who by reason of use have their senses exercised to discern both good and evil. (Hebrews 5.14)* In contradistinction, simple (a Bible word for those who are not rebellious but rather ignorant) people have little discernment. They look down the road, but they do not know how to see around the bend. Their vulnerability is compounded by their naïve gullibility in making decisions. The simple young person chooses friends based on shared interests. Their wiser, more mature parent looks beneath the surface. What is that individual's character? Do they exercise self-discipline? Do they work hard? Is there in them a respect for authority? Are they a person of integrity?

Discernment married with understanding is borne out in decision making. Because it sees clearly what others cannot, it has the capability of making better choices. *...the children of Issachar, which were men that had understanding of the times, to know what Israel ought to do... (I Chronicles 12.32)* They knew what choices Israel ought to make because they discerned the future consequences of those choices.

It takes no great skill to fall in love. Conversely, it takes the diligent and painstaking work of discernment to discover ahead of time what kind of groom or bride that individual will become. Goethe's apt description applies here: "It is easier to perceive error than to find truth, for the former lies on the surface and is easily seen, while the latter lies in the depth, where few are willing to search for it." But such effort is most assuredly worthwhile. Choices informed by discernment work out for the long term at a much higher percentage rate than choices made without it.

The prophets were men of discernment. Their sermons are chock-full of allusions to upcoming disasters that somehow the rest of God's people did not notice at all. I realize their writings are inspired, but I do not think – and you may certainly disagree – that some of them knew they were being inspired as it happened.

In other words, sometimes their minds worked normally. Their thoughts flowed naturally. The depth of wisdom inherent in their observations was the result of a profound acquaintance with understanding and discernment.

Moses is a jaw-dropping example of this. Certain passages in some of his sermons in *Deuteronomy* read like an after history of the nation of Israel. For instance, in *Deuteronomy 28* Moses contrasts the blessing and cursing of God. Blessing, loosely described, is the favor of God. It is His beneficent attention. Cursing is the opposite. It is the disfavor of God. To be cursed is to draw God's malicious notice. In much of *Deuteronomy,* Moses sets this distinction before God's people and tells them that their future – blessing or cursing – will be the distinct result of their choices now. *Behold, I set before you this day a blessing and a curse; (Deuteronomy 11.26)* In *Deuteronomy 28,* Moses expands on what these mean in varied and specific detail. That curse included famine, pestilence, drought, defeat, theft, rape, and ultimately captivity at the hands of a foreign power. *The Lord shall bring thee, and thy king which thou shalt set over thee, unto a nation which neither thou nor thy fathers have known; and there shalt thou serve other gods, wood and stone. And thou shalt become an astonishment, a proverb, and a byword, among all nations whither the Lord shall lead thee... Thou shalt beget sons and daughters, but thou shalt not enjoy them; for they shall go into captivity. (Deuteronomy 28.36-37, 41)* Thus it is that Moses passionately urges them to choose carefully what kind of a life they will live. *I call heaven and earth to record this day against you, that I have set before you life and death, blessing and cursing: therefore choose life, that both thou and thy seed may live:... (Deuteronomy 30.19)*

Moses had discernment. He looked down the road and around the bend and saw the horrors that awaited Israel if she chose to disobey God. If ever a man was right in what he saw, it was Moses. In a sense, the entire second half of the Old Testament is the story of Israel's captivities. Why did those captivities come? They came because a disobedient people failed to heed the discernment of their prophet. They could not see what Moses saw, and so they assumed he was wrong. He was not; they were. And their nation paid a hefty price for it.

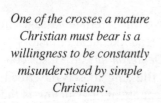

One of the crosses a mature Christian must bear is a willingness to be constantly misunderstood by simple Christians.

One of the crosses a mature Christian must bear is a willingness to be constantly misunderstood by simple Christians. Where the simple Christian sees nothing amiss, the mature Christian sees great danger. When he warns of that danger, he is often ridiculed and ignored. He is shouted down, laughed at, and ignored just as Noah was when he predicted the entire Earth would flood.

The story of God's men is the story of rejection. It is par for the course. This is because God's men are supposed to be excellent at discernment. If they fail to teach their people the importance of heeding that discernment, the result is often disastrous.

One of the great strengths of the independent Baptist world is that we have a keenly honed ability to look down the road and around the bend. If we allow a Sunday school teacher to reference another Bible version, where will that take us? If we incorporate this kind of music, where will that take us? If we bend on this standard, where will that take us? If we read these authors, where will they take us? If we cancel a service for the Super Bowl, where will that take us?

In this we are set in complete contrast to so many of the contemporary evangelical pastors of the day. They rarely ask the question, "Where will this take us?" Instead, they just want to know what will happen right now if I do or allow or promote or incorporate or emphasize such and such a thing. The contemporary approach, by definition, is immediate. It is caught up in the now.

I find this alternately infuriating and heartbreaking. It produces big crowds and seeming momentum now while simultaneously doing great damage to the cause of Christ down the road. Our nation's government is damning our grandchildren to economic purgatory by borrowing money like it is going out of style. Our politicians are committing national suicide while buying votes with future generation's money. In a very real sense, there is little practical difference on the spiritual side with many contemporary religious movements. They are embracing all manner of things so that their crowds may swell, their books may sell, and their paid appearances may multiply. But they are using zero discernment. It is fairly easy to spot an independent Baptist. He is the lonely guy being ridiculed by all the rest. He is the man who sees the inevitable conclusion of bad decision making and is crucified when he speaks up. He is the guy whose sermons are full of warning that the bridge is out up ahead.

While this is an often lonely and thankless task, it is an undeniable strength. It has protected thousands of churches from the spiritually decaying culture around us. Other movements have surpassed us by leaps and bounds, but I am utterly convinced that there is deep staying power for the cause of Christ in the independent Baptist movement. That staying power is the result of good choices informed by mature discernment.

Steadfast

I confess I wanted to title this portion "Stubbornness." I like that word. It implies a fierce determination not to be moved. It would be hard, however, to support this section with Scripture since every case in which the Bible uses the word "stubborn" carries a negative context.

Steadfast, on the other hand, is a perfectly good word. The dictionary defines it as firm in purpose and unwavering. In the Old Testament, the original language carries connotations like fortify, stiffen, obstinate, and permanent. In the New Testament, we see similarities such as firm, solid, and establish.

Ruth was steadfast in her determination to follow her mother-in-law. Jesus was steadfast in his decision to head to Jerusalem. *...therefore have I set my face like a flint,... (Isaiah 50.7)* The early church *...continued stedfastly in the apostles' doctrine and fellowship, and in breaking of bread, and in prayers. (Acts 2.42)* Stephen *...looked stedfastly into heaven,...(Acts 7.55)* while being martyred.

As with the other characteristics, this one rises in stark relief in the lives of the prophets. From all sides, they were pushed, pulled, prodded, and driven; yet they continued undeterred. For example, Jeremiah sent a letter from God to King Jehoiakim. The rebellious king burned Jeremiah's letter. *Then Jeremiah took another roll, and gave it to Baruch the scribe, the son of Neriah; who wrote therein from the mouth of Jeremiah all the words of the book which Jehoiakim king of Judah had burned in the fire: and there were added besides unto them many like words. (Jeremiah 36.32)* You just have to love that last phrase. Jeremiah preached an unpopular message of repentance and then an even more unpopular message of surrender to Babylon. He was ignored, mocked, and jailed. In the solitary confinement of a mud pit, he refused to trim his message.

During the days of the divided monarchy, Ahab sought to enlist Jehoshaphat in his ongoing war with Syria. Ahab cared naught for God's opinion, but Jehoshaphat asked Ahab to obtain prophetic permission. *I Kings 21* tells us Ahab gathered the four hundred toadies that called themselves prophets and promptly obtained the permission for which he had well paid them. Jehoshaphat was no dummy. He knew a set up when he saw one and pressed Ahab for an enquiry with a genuine prophet. Ahab grudgingly admitted he knew of one ...*but I hate him; for he doth not prophesy good concerning me, but always evil:*... When Micaiah was finally called he was given a dressing down before he ever walked out the door to see the two kings. *And the messenger that went to call Micaiah spake unto him, saying, Behold, the words of the prophets declare good to the king with one assent; let thy word therefore, I pray thee, be like one of theirs, and speak thou good.* There could be no doubt of Ahab's expectation for the direction of Micaiah's prophecy.

Micaiah, however, did not care what the messenger or the king

———∾◦⟨ℰ⟩◦∾———

If independent Baptists have a strength in the world, surely it is this: we are obstinately steadfast.

———∾◦⟨ℰ⟩◦∾———

thought he ought to say. ...*As the LORD liveth, even what my God saith, that will I speak.* When Micaiah's prophecy predicted doom for the enterprise and death for one of the kings, he was slapped for his trouble, put in prison, and fed ...

with bread of affliction and with water of affliction... Ahab promised to release Micaiah upon his victorious return. Micaiah rejoined, *...If thou certainly return in peace, then hath not the LORD spoken by me...* Sure enough, the battle went badly; Israel lost; Ahab's blood was licked by the dogs as the sun set.

Micaiah, against all the pressure his world could bring for him to bear, stood like a rock. He was steadfast.

If independent Baptists have a strength in the world, surely it is this: we are obstinately steadfast. There is something rooted deep within us that pushes back against all of the pressure of the world. The salmon are the independent Baptists of the sea. They, like us, are always swimming upstream.

I pastor in Chicago. The governor, the mayor, and the county board president lead the gay pride parade a million people strong down Halsted Street five miles from my church building. The street corners in that neighborhood are adorned with permanent rainbow sculptures anchored to the city sidewalk. The political and popular pressure against our kind of religion is large and growing. The gangs grant us no respect. They tag our building, shoot out our headlights, icepick our tires, and key our vans. The decent people in this city want nothing to do with us. When they do choose to answer our knock on their door, it is not unusual at all to be greeted with a snarl and a slam. Even the religious people in this city look at us like we are two-headed creatures from outer space. "You still use what Bible?" "You still have an organ?" "You still have a Sunday night service?" "What, no screen in your auditorium?" "You preach how loud?" "How long?" "How often?" "Seriously, you require a dress standard from your teachers?" "What planet are you from?"

I suspect your church is like mine. No, not necessarily in specifics but if it is independent Baptist, it is similar in spirit. To quote a pastor friend I had lunch with recently, we have a S-P-I-N-E. We have a backbone. No, we are not the only ones with a backbone. Indeed, I suspect we will be pleasantly surprised when push comes to shove just how much backbone there still is in American Christianity. But if any group is stubbornly steadfast it is us. Thanks be to God. That is a wonderful thing.

The prophet Daniel saw things others of his generation missed entirely. Daniel stood steadfastly against pressure his entire life. He stood as a young man alone and unpopular in a strange land. He stood as a middle-aged man toiling away as a bureaucrat in the government of a heathen king. He stood as an old man facing down yet another world power. He stood against his peers. He stood against his leadership. He stood against his government. He stood even in the face of a pride of snarling lions. He just stood.

The oldest member of my church is remarkably, at eighty-four, an active soul winner. He attends every service. He teaches Sunday school. He visits and prays with me during the week. He is a great blessing to me and to our church. For over fifty years he served as a pastor in the Christian and Missionary Alliance. Some time ago, his church asked him to retire, and the government took away his driver's license. He was forced to find a new church close to his house. He walked into ours on a Wednesday night and found a home. It is a privilege to serve the Lord with Miguel Bless.

He has never been a Baptist. I have never been Christian and Missionary Alliance. But he is a fervent Fundamentalist, and we share a great many beliefs in common. We also share an admiration for the leading light of the Alliance, A. W. Tozer. It does not hurt our admiration of him that Tozer pastored the bulk of his years in the same city in which Miguel and I both serve the Lord.

In his book *Of God and Men*, Tozer says it this way:

"Today we need prophetic preachers; not preachers of prophecy merely, but preachers with a gift of prophecy. The word of wisdom is missing. We need the gift of discernment again in our pulpits. It is not ability to predict that we need, but the anointed eye, the power of spiritual penetration and interpretation, the ability to appraise the religious scene as viewed from God's position, and to tell us what is actually going on.

...Where is the man who can see through the ticker tape and confetti to discover which way the parade is headed, why it started in the first place and, particularly, who is riding up front in the seat of honor?

Not the fact that the churches are unusually active these days, not what religious people are doing, should engage our attention, but why these things are so. The big question is "Why?" And no one seems to have an answer for it. Not only is there no answer, but scarcely is there anyone to ask the question. It just never occurs to us that such a question remains to be asked. Christian people continue to gossip religious shoptalk with scarcely as

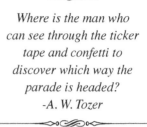

Where is the man who can see through the ticker tape and confetti to discover which way the parade is headed?

-A. W. Tozer

much as a puzzled look. The soundness of current Christianity is assumed by the religious masses as was the soundness of Judaism when Christ appeared. People know they are seeing certain activity, but just what it means they do not know, nor have they the faintest idea of where God is or what relation He has toward the whole thing.

What is needed desperately today is prophetic insight. Scholars can interpret the past; it takes prophets to interpret the present. Learning will enable a man to pass judgment on our yesterdays, but it requires a gift of clear seeing to pass sentence on our own day. One hundred years from now historians will know what was taking place religiously in this year of our Lord; but that will be too late for us. We should know right now.

If Christianity is to receive a rejuvenation, it must be by other means than any now being used. If the church in the second half of this century is to recover from the injuries she suffered in the first half, there must appear a new type of preacher. The proper, ruler-of-the-synagogue type will never do. Neither will the priestly type of man who carries out his duties, takes his pay and asks no questions, nor the smooth-talking pastoral type who knows how to make the Christian religion acceptable to everyone. All these have been tried and found wanting.

Another kind of religious leader must arise among us. He must be of the old prophet type, a man who has seen visions of God and has heard a voice from the Throne. When he comes (and I pray God there will be not one but many) he will stand in flat contradiction to everything our smirking, smooth civilization holds dear. He will contradict, denounce and protest in the name of God and will earn the hatred and opposition of a large segment of Christendom.

Such a man is likely to be lean, rugged, blunt-spoken and a little bit angry with the world. He will love Christ and the souls of men to the point of willingness to die for the glory of the one and the salvation of the other. But he will fear nothing that breathes with mortal breath."

The independent Baptist movement is blessed. We have prophets. May God grant it always be so.

We Produce Commitment

When you have bacon and eggs for breakfast, the chicken makes
a contribution, the pig makes a commitment.
-Fred Shero

O n average, independent Baptist churches have a higher
percentage of committed members than other types of
churches. For example, we generally draw from a wider radius than
most churches. Our people are willing to spend more time com-
muting to our services. We are the only remaining orthodox group
in America – aside from some charismatics and Southern Baptists
– that still maintain Sunday night services on a wide scale. We put
more soul winners and bus workers on the streets each week than
any other group. Generally speaking, our percentage of tithers is
higher than the average American church.

Of course, I am not saying that other kinds of churches have
no committed members. I am saying that our churches breed commitment by default and it shows.

Amongst thoughtful men (those who are not simply doing
what they do because they have always done it that way), there
are two prevailing church philosophies in America today. (By
philosophy, I mean the underlying rationale that drives how you
approach leading a church.) One is seen in the tag line "Come as
you are." It seeks to make people comfortable. It actively works
at being as non-threatening as possible. It intentionally pursues a
casual atmosphere. Its campuses resemble malls on the big side
and restaurants on the small side. It tries not to look like church,

act like church, or sound like church lest it offend the very people it is seeking to reach.

I would liken the second approach to a cafeteria line. A person holds his tray out, and they fork over what he is going to get regardless of whether he wants it or not. It is what it is. It is not going to gloss over off-putting aspects of itself in order to be more appealing.

Both of these philosophical approaches are sincere. The first sincerely wants to reach more people for Christ. The second sincerely wants to please God.

Please do not misunderstand me. I do not mean to imply that the first approach has no interest in pleasing God nor that the second approach has no interest in reaching people. I am rather attempting to explain what drives them.

Additionally, there are some churches that seek to synthesize both philosophical approaches. Their attempt reminds me of the man who tried to walk the fence. Sooner or later, he had to come down on one side or the other.

The first approach points like an Irish setter to *I Corinthians 9.19-22. For though I be free from all men, yet have I made myself servant unto all, that I might gain the more. And unto the Jews I became as a Jew, that I might gain the Jews; to them that are under the law, as under the law, that I might gain them that are under the law; To them that are without law, as being without law, (being not without law to God, but under the law to Christ,) that I might gain them that are without law. To the weak became I as weak, that I might gain the weak: I am made all things to all men, that I might by all means save some.*

The second approach references the tenor of Jesus Christ's ministry. While His life was marked deeply by compassion, there was in Him no soft pedaling of anything. He made no attempt to make people comfortable. He presented the truth and demanded that men immediately conform themselves to it.

The single biggest proof of this is His world's reaction to His coming. They mocked and assaulted Him. Numerically, His ministry was a bell curve, but He produced many more lasting enemies than He produced lasting converts. The local religious leaders disliked Him. The national religious leaders attacked Him. His three-and-a-half years of ministry produced an exponentially increasing resistance to His message. There were repeated attempts on His life. By the end, there was an organized conspiracy in the Sanhedrin designed to assassinate Him.

The primary aim of this chapter is not to disprove or attack the first philosophy. But I do think it is quite a stretch to cultivate such a philosophy from that passage. Paul worked hard at reaching people, and he sought to do so from a platform to which they could relate. His conversations in Athens show this. But what he did not do was build his entire ministry around making people feel comfortable. He did not purposely soft pedal anything in order not to offend. He was firm in and free with his convictions. A woman said to Billy Sunday one time, "You are rubbing the fur the wrong way." He replied, "Then turn the cat around." Paul would have liked that.

One of the godfathers of this philosophy is Willow Creek Church in Barrington, Illinois. I have been to their campus for a service. You will not find a cross anywhere. This is purposeful rather than accidental, for the sight of a cross might offend an unsaved visitor. Such would have been anathema to Paul. He embraced ...*the offence of the cross*... *(Galatians 5.11)* Yes, he wrote *I Corinthians 9.19-22* and practiced it, but it does not mean all that it has been held to mean in our generation.

With that being said, it then does not follow that the only other alternative is aiming to purposely offend. The second philosophical approach is often painted as heedless by those who disagree and are indifferent to the pain they inflict with their preaching and their stand. Jesus Christ's earthly career stands in stark contrast to that. His life must ever inform our own. It is very possible to be compassionate and welcoming while also being an unbending, rock-ribbed Fundamentalist at the same time.

Independent Baptists use the second philosophical approach. Our preaching is oft marked by the prophetic phrase *thus saith the Lord*. We offer no apology for our belief systems or for our attempts to propagate them. We call men to leave where they are and to change. If unrepentant sinners return to our services week after week, we begin to worry. The tone of our churches calls men not to be comfortable with the world but to abandon it. We are much more Winston Churchill than Neville Chamberlain.

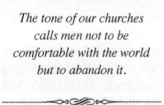

The tone of our churches calls men not to be comfortable with the world but to abandon it.

We can debate the validity of the differing approaches, but we cannot debate what they produce. The first approach generates crowds. The second approach builds disciples. When the music of the first one stops, everybody gets off the merry-go-round. The second one well grasps *Luke 14.27And whosoever doth not bear his cross, and come after me, cannot be my disciple.*

Let us take for an example something I referenced earlier – the Sunday night service. In the United States, it is fast becoming an endangered species. This is true in spite of the fact that *Hebrews 10.25* instructs us not to cancel services but to add them as we get closer to the time of the Second Coming. You can try to debate that if you like, but there can be no debate that it takes a greater level of commitment to have one. The members of your church have to go home and then come all the way back again. In addition, these services are often longer than the morning service. Likewise, the pastor must also take upon himself the extra work of preparing an entirely different sermon each week.

I have spoken with numerous pastors whose churches do not have a Sunday night service. These men come from a wide variety of religious traditions. Many of them have tried repeatedly to start or build a Sunday evening service. Without exception, they all point to a lack of commitment as a primary cause.

Why then do independent Baptists still have them in thousands and thousands of churches? Indeed, it is the exception rather than the rule to find them absent. Simply this: our entire approach generates commitment.

I do not mean this as cynically as it sounds, but people gravitate toward the level their leadership allows them to be. What makes exceptional CEOs and exceptional generals is that they refuse to accept substandard work. They demand better, and though at first that demand is met with resistance, it results in a culture of excellence over time.

In a sense, the independent Baptist world is similar. American culture is running from commitment as fast as it can. Marriage rates are down, and cohabitation rates are up. Bankruptcy lawyers are doing a booming business. Church hopping and job hopping are a veritable pandemic. But it is not in the DNA of the independent Baptist movement to appease, excuse, or ape the culture. It is in us to call men to a higher standard. And when men are called to a higher standard, they respond.

Jesus most eloquently called men to a higher standard in the greatest sermon ever preached. *Ye have heard that it hath been said* was then followed by the contrast *but I say unto you.* For two thousand years, men have responded to His call.

The problem with American Christianity is not that we are asking too much. It is that we are asking too little. And the groups like ours that are holding the standard high will continue to find that men rally to it.

Where are we right? In this: our movement builds deeply committed Christians.

Book Two–What is Wrong

Write hard and clear about what hurts.
-Ernest Hemingway

A Word of Explanation

I now send forth this volume with an earnest prayer, that the Holy Ghost may bless it, and that God may be pleased to use it for His own glory and the benefit of many souls. My chief desire in all my writings, is to exalt the Lord Jesus Christ and make Him beautiful and glorious in the eyes of people; and to promote the increase of repentance, faith, and holiness upon earth. If this shall be the result of this volume, the labor that it has cost me will be more than repaid.
-J. C. Ryle, *Expository Thoughts on the Gospels: St. Luke*

One of the best of the modern historians is Rick Atkinson. His three-volume set on the history of the American army in World War II is excellent. In the second book, *The Day of Battle,* he speaks in haunting detail of the worst friendly fire disaster of the war.

Following the fledgling American army's defeat of the Axis powers in North Africa in 1943, there arose a vigorous discussion about what the Allied armies should do next. Stalin, as always, wanted an immediate cross-channel invasion of France. Churchill favored a blow to what he termed "the soft underbelly" of Europe, Greece and the Balkans. Roosevelt favored a buildup of forces in Britain as preparation for an early 1944 invasion of the continent.

The policy that resulted was largely a compromise between all three preferences. In order to appease Stalin, the British and American divisions would be kept in combat against the Axis somewhere. Churchill, in turn, was placated with a limited invasion of southern Europe. Roosevelt, too, got his way as the main effort continued to be the all-out preparation for what is now known as D-Day (June 6, 1944).

Thus it was that an invasion of Italy was launched via Sicily in the summer of 1943. Code named "Operation Husky," a massive armada with hundreds of ships battled rough weather in order to land seven divisions across a one hundred mile stretch of Sicilian coastline on July 10. Initial resistance was scattered and light, especially from the Italian army. Within mere hours, however, two experienced German divisions hurled themselves point blank toward the beaches in an effort to drive the Allied armies back into the sea.

The brunt of this counter attack was born by the Big Red One, the U.S. 1st Infantry Division. Major General Terry Allen commanding from the aptly named HQ Danger Forward pleaded with Patton and Eisenhower for reinforcements. Facing the panzers of the redoubtable Hermann Göring Division, Allen's infantry proved unable to the task. By the next day, the ill-equipped, exhausted, sea-sick troops found themselves going the wrong direction – back to the beach. Their retreat would not be stopped until cruisers and destroyers 1,200 yards off the beach engaged panzer tanks individually with their five-inch naval guns.

Just this side of desperation, Patton ordered and Eisenhower authorized an ill-advised reinforcement attempt by a full regiment of the 82nd Airborne Division based in Tunisia. All American ships at sea and front-line Sicilian troops were issued coded instructions informing them that a nighttime parachute drop was planned at approximately midnight. These instructions, issued early that morning, were not decoded and transmitted until late evening. In the chaos of front-line battle, many units failed to receive the news. Before the first paratroop plane arrived overhead, those front-line troops and ships had already fought off twenty-three Luftwaffe sorties aimed at American shipping. In the dark, jumpy and uninformed Allied ships and shore-based AA units hurled distinctive, red American tracer bullets and proximity-fused flak skyward while the parachutes of the 82nd Airborne Division began floating down out of the night sky. C-47s and C-53s were blown from the sky. Paratroopers describe cargo holds in the planes being awash in the blood of their fellows that did survive. Entire sticks of paratroopers prematurely jumped into the sea in an effort to avoid the flak only to find themselves machine-gunned by surrounding American destroyers. Others thudded into the Sicilian sand with a sound described as the thwack of smashing pumpkins. Eight pilots outright refused to green light any jumps, describing them as tantamount to murder; they simply turned back toward Africa. Of the 4,800 men in the 505th regiment of the 82nd Airborne in planes that night, 1,400 still could not be accounted for days later. Sixty of their 144 planes were shot down or damaged.

As God sees my heart, I have no desire to be the guy on the beach launching tracer fire toward those in the sky on my own side. I would not for the world discourage a brother in Christ or seek to make his task more difficult. I am an independent Baptist for many of what I think to be very good reasons. Those who claim the same banner under Christ as I do are not my foe. This book is not designed to attack or injure them. Governor Mike Huckabee once described the American military as being designed to kill people and break things. I do not want my book to kill people and break things, especially on my own team.

With that being said, it behooves me to say that I am not naïve. Ralph Waldo Emerson once said, "To be great is to be misunderstood." I am inclined to believe that being misunderstood is the only sign of greatness I will ever exhibit. Just because I have no intention of injuring independent Baptist men and ministries does not mean they will not feel hurt by what comes next in this book. If that is the case with you or if some principle you hold dear is fired upon in this next section, I simply ask you to keep this word of explanation in mind. I do not hate you. I am not against you. I do not want to discourage you. If you love and serve God, I love you. I am for you.

If I do shoot at something you believe precious, please understand I am not shooting at you. I am shooting at scripturally errant philosophies and practices of ministry that are wreaking havoc through a movement that I love. To borrow another illustration, the doctor who operates on your cancerous tumor is not your enemy. The cancer is your enemy. The doctor is your friend even if he causes you great pain in the short term.

We Are Proud

Pride must die in you or nothing of heaven can live in you.
-Andrew Murray, *Humility*

Peter tells us *the time has come that judgment must begin at the house of God. (I Peter 4.17)* God is nothing if not a consistent God of integrity. The theme of *I Peter* is suffering. That was brought out to me at some length as I preached twenty-five sermons from that precious book recently. At least eight of them were about suffering. The very heart of this message and this book is the context surrounding the above quote. In this context Peter gives various reasons why it benefits us to suffer, not for wrongdoing, but for *righteousness sake. (I Peter 3.14)* Such suffering reveals our underlying character and integrity. Perhaps I should say how we respond to suffering reveals these things. The point in this section of *I Peter 4* is that it is better for us to suffer for right than it is for us to suffer for wrong because God will ensure that all men are examined searchingly by Him.

Remember, God is nothing if not a consistent God of integrity. Where does such a God begin His searching examinations? He begins, in His integrity, with His own. *For the time has come that judgment must begin at the house of God: and if it first begin at us, what shall the end be of them that obey not the gospel of God? (I Peter 4.17)* In other words, He is this hard on us, His own, justifiably; but think how hard He is going to be on those who have rejected Him!

Yet amongst this larger point relating to suffering is the lesser-while-still-applicable point that God's integrity demands of Him that He hold His own accountable first.

In this, Peter is echoing *Ezekiel*, who, in chapter 8, upon digging in the walls, found wickedness and abominable idol worship being conducted secretly in the very Temple itself. *And he brought me into the inner court of the LORD'S house, and, behold, at the door of the temple of the LORD, between the porch and the altar, were about five and twenty men, with their backs toward the temple of the LORD, and their faces toward the east; and they worshipped the sun toward the east. Then he said unto me, Hast thou seen this, O son of man? Is it a light thing to the house of Judah that they commit the abominations which they commit here? for they have filled the land with violence, and have returned to provoke me to anger: and, lo, they put the branch to their nose. Therefore will I also deal in fury: mine eye shall not spare, neither will I have pity: and though they cry in mine ears with a loud voice, yet will I not hear them. (Ezekiel 8.16-18)*

If God would not let the heathen get away with idol worship, He certainly would not let His own get away with it, either. Remember, He is a God of consistent integrity. *He cried also in mine ears with a loud voice, saying, Cause them that have charge over the city to draw near, even every man with his destroying weapon in his hand. And, behold, six men came from the way of the higher gate, which lieth toward the north, and every man a slaughter weapon in his hand; and one man among them was clothed with linen, with a writer's inkhorn by his side: and they went in, and stood beside the brasen altar. And the glory of the God of Israel was gone up from the cherub, whereupon he was, to the threshold of the house. And he called to the man clothed with linen, which had the writer's inkhorn by his side; And the LORD said unto him, Go through the midst of the city, through the midst of Jerusalem, and set a mark upon the foreheads of the men that sigh and that cry for all the abominations that be done in the midst thereof. And to the others he said in mine hearing, Go ye after him through the city, and smite: let not your eye spare, neither have ye pity: Slay utterly old and young, both maids, and little children, and women: but*

*come not near any man upon whom is the mark; and **begin at my
sanctuary**. Then they began at the ancient men which were before
the house. (Ezekiel 9.1-6)*

The principle we see then in both the Old and New Testaments
is that God begins His searching examinations of humanity with
His own people first. The house of God where Peter in the New
Testament said judgment was to begin is clearly revealed in *I
Timothy 3.15* to be the church: *But if I tarry long, that thou mayest
know how how thou oughtest to behave thyself in the house of God,
which is the church of the living God, the pillar and ground of
the truth.*

As a pastor of such a church, I have rightly preached sermons
through these years that roundly condemned all sorts of wickedness
such as abortion, homosexuality, the New Age movement, materialism, hedonism, environmentalism, gambling, drinking, drugs,
crime, and political corruption. Such sermons, while helpful to
numbers of our people, were primarily aimed at the spirit of the
age. As a pastor, I have also rightly pointed out to my people the
varied and grievous dangers of errant branches of Christianity such
as the Charismatic movement, Contemporary Evangelicalism, and
the trendy denominationalism of our day. Yet if I am willing to
point my finger in righteous indignation at the sin going on in other
people's camps, I must, as God's messenger, be just as willing
to point my finger in righteous indignation at the sin going on in
our own camp; and this is precisely what I aim to do in this book.
In so doing, I am going to be brutally honest. I am going to say
exactly what I think. The time for contemplative silence is past.
Some things simply need to be said. It is high time for some can-
cers in our independent Baptist movement to be exposed for the
tumors they are.

If all you had read in this book was the first section, you
would think we are in pretty good shape. After all, we are right
about being Baptists, about being independent, and about being
Fundamentalists. We use the King James Version. We hold standards, chase sinners with the Gospel, exercise prudence, produce
preacher boys with fire, have prophets, and build commitment.

Again and again as I wrote those chapters, I found myself shrinking in my mind at the way they would be perceived. I do not apologize for Book One. I embrace them. I am glad for them. But I do not, for one moment, believe they give us anything to boast about.

To one extent or another, every doctrine and practice that we hold dear can be found in other religious groups. We are not the only Baptists. Some sound Fundamentalists can be found amongst the Bible church movement, the Orthodox Presbyterian Church, and the Lutheran Church Missouri Synod. Our Mennonite brethren use the King James Version and often have higher standards of personal separation than we do. The Contemporary Evangelical crowd contains within it a genuine passion for souls. The Charismatic movement also believes in education on fire. Most, if not all, of these philosophies I have labeled as strengths of the independent Baptist movement can also be found amongst others of God's people.

There is a great danger in thinking your group is the only right group. The Jews fell prey to that by the millions. The great error of Old Testament Israel was idolatry, but the great error of New Testament Israel was an empty and proud profession. The Jews of Jesus' day were quite convinced that they were completely correct, and everyone else was entirely wrong. Again and again, Jesus sought to open their minds and hearts to His desire to reach the Gentiles. He ministered to Gentiles. He did miracles for Gentiles. He ate with Gentiles. He preached about Gentiles. He quoted the prophets favorably about the Gentiles. *And other sheep I have, which are not of this fold: them also I must bring, and they shall hear my voice; and there shall be one fold, and one shepherd. (John 10.16)* Yet no matter how much he sought to rein in the ethnic prejudice of His people, it still knew no bounds. Even His own disciples took years to grasp such truths. And that ethnic and religious pride not only hamstrung the Jewish people, it also almost mortally wounded the early church.

Besides the fact that there are other religious groups with strengths that match our own, the strengths that we hold to so strongly are held solely by the grace of God. In other words, even in the areas in which we are correct, we can find no place of merit. Paul said, *for I know*

137

that in me (that is, in my flesh,) dwelleth no good thing. (Romans 7.18) When I stand before Him at His coming, I will not offer Him

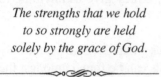

The strengths that we hold to so strongly are held solely by the grace of God.

my standards or my soul winning or my orthodoxy. I will not wave my King James Bible in His face and assert my right to go to the head of the line at reward time. No, I will cast myself at His feet and marvel that He would even allow me into His presence. *But we are all as an unclean thing, and all our righteousnesses are as filthy rags;.... (Isaiah 64.6)*

I am the Lord: that is my name: and my glory will I not give to another,... (Isaiah 42.8) And daily in the temple, and in every house, they ceased not to teach and preach Jesus Christ. (Acts 5.42) ...For thine is the kingdom, and the power, and the glory... (Matthew 6.13) I believe firmly in a pastor-led independent Baptist church, but the day my church becomes about me is the day we have crossed the line into error. In 1895, Rudyard Kipling spoke in his famous poem "If" about the temptation that comes the way of all men who can move crowds of people with their words: "If you can talk with crowds and keep your virtue." Pride is an immense problem for preachers, and I have seen pastors again and again fall prey to the temptation to make themselves the focus of their church.

In 1990 and 1991, I spent my summers traveling with evangelist Joe Boyd. We were in one particular church in Texas (a large and growing church) led by an up and coming pastor. As I climbed onto one of his church buses on our first day, lo and behold, there was a large picture of the pastor at the very front of the bus. Sure enough, that same picture was in the same prominent place inside the front of each bus. I could not help but be reminded of the Communist leaders of Soviet Russia and the cult of personality they cultivated by placing large pictures of themselves everywhere. Sadly, I have run into that same personality cult mindset more times than I can count in independent Baptist preachers in the years since.

It is not difficult to see how such a preacher-focused church can be developed. For some preachers, thousands of people hang on their every word. They are never challenged or told they are wrong.

They are accompanied by a posse everywhere they go. Often when they preach, they are preceded by a glowing introduction and followed with a standing ovation. Following their sermons, numbers of people line up to have their Bibles autographed. People come to their office for counsel and tell them, "No matter what, I will do whatever you tell me." Their sermons are filled with their own personal illustrations in which they are the hero.

In this scenario, sooner or later you begin to believe your own publicity. Your ministry becomes about you, done by you, and molded by you. Your opinion of your own opinion rises higher than is appropriate. You begin to think yourself indispensable. You begin to wrap your entire ministry even tighter to yourself. You see the crowds and think they came to hear you. You see the adoring gazes of those who sit at your feet and think you really do know something. You listen to the rhapsodic introductions and think they are actually true. You bristle when corrected, criticized, or questioned. You lash out when someone crosses you since after all, you are clearly always right. Your vision for your ministry becomes more and more grand, and you see yourself striding across the pages of church history. You see yourself having rescued a degenerate Christianity, brought revival, or built something of which other people will stand in awe. You teach your staff to keep you first and foremost in the minds and hearts of the people with whom they directly work. You cultivate personal loyalty to yourself, personal gratitude to yourself, personal praise about yourself, and then you sell these things to yourself as essential for church unity and progress. You think you know better about every single aspect of your ministry than any other person in your ministry does about any aspect. You see this man worship developing in your people, and you do not see it as dangerous but as good and healthy for your ministry. You mouth occasional platitudes of humility, but in your heart you really think it all revolves around you. You are the straw that stirs the drink. Without you, your ministry would not have come nearly as far. Without you, it would all fall apart.

How do I know all of this? I know because even with the average size ministry that I have, all of these temptations have attacked me. As the pastor of my church, I have the biggest influence, the biggest part in each public service, the most attention, the most praise and thanks, and the most respect. Consequently, I have found how easy it is for pride to creep into my own heart. I preach a powerful sermon, and people are plainly moved. I receive some kind word, gift, or thank-you note. I am recognized in a public meeting somewhere, and the foot of pride gains entrance in my heart.

I have tried to fight it externally. For instance, my name is not on our church sign or our church stationary. I have asked our people not to applaud platform performances. I strive to preach often about the primacy of glorifying God. I regularly remind my people of my own humanity. I have sought to cultivate the kind of church that is willing to offer with a sweet spirit a word of friendly and kind criticism to me. Frankly, sometimes I win that fight in my own heart, and sometimes I lose it.

> *Our work is about Him. When I forget this, God begins to resist what I do even if what I do is His work.*

Our work is about Him. When I forget this, God begins to resist what I do even if what I do is His work. …*God resisteth the proud, but giveth grace unto the humble. (James 4.6, I Peter 5.5)* When I reach this point eventually and inevitably, my ministry comes crashing down with a bang or sliding down with a whimper. The cities of America are filled with the ghosts of great churches – churches now mired in scandal and curled up in pain and whose pastors forgot the simple truth that *He must increase, but I must decrease. (John 3.30)*

Nor is the fault in this area limited to pastors. Members by the hundreds of thousands have willingly sipped the deceitful Kool-Aid of egotism. My church is the greatest church. People across the nation look to us for leadership. We have influence. We are innovative, traditional, talented, qualified, trained, and spiritual. Our assistants and college professors travel and speak around the country. We are the cream of the crop, the cat's meow, the bee's knees, and the bomb diggity. Our church is all that and a bag of chips. We are as cool as the other side of the pillow.

Few church members are as crass as to actually enunciate some of the statements in the above paragraph, but many are not above thinking them. When you lay claim to greatness – for any reason and in any way – you are treading on perilously thin ice under a blazing noonday sun. Spiritual greatness (albeit with the obligatory "praise God" thrown in here and there) is the very worst form of pride. It goes against the very tenor of Who God is and who He instructs us as His people to be.

I do not know a more insidious sin than pride. Like a noxious weed that refuses to be uprooted, it returns no matter how it is attacked. Pride is woven into the fabric of our being. In point of fact, pride was the original sin, *(Isaiah 14.14)* Pride creeps into the most spiritual of hearts and crops up in the most humble of men. Such is awfully true enough. The last thing we need to do is build systems of ecclesiastical and institutional structure which feed that very pride. Pride is so pervasive in the human spirit that if it is not constantly assailed (God forbid that it be encouraged), it will bring ourselves, our families, our churches, and our movement to certain destruction.

Beloved, check your heart this very moment. Mayhap it lurks there even now, coiled and deadly, with fangs bared to strike. God knows I see it constantly in my own heart. But beyond your heart, examine the structure of your ministry's system. Does it nourish pride or besiege it? Is there present a disdainful condescension toward other men and other ministries? Is there a visible swagger? Is there a self-confidence bordering on cockiness? Are others around you comfortable with adulation?

Examine the structure of your ministry's system. Does it nourish pride or besiege it?

Many years ago, I sat in a church service amongst thousands of other Christians. The big name preacher got up and announced his subject as humility. Curiously enough, I heard him preach often; yet that is the only time I recall him preaching on humility. Without batting an eyelash, he proceeded to describe it as a private understanding between you and God that God does the work.

Private? Private??? Did he seriously just stand there and preach that humility is something that must be displayed or realized only in private before God? Yes, he did. Not coincidentally, the plaudits and praise he heaped to himself in his life have been found woefully lacking in death.

Paul was not very private when he mused to the entire church age that he was the chief of sinners and less than the least of all saints. David was not very private when he soliloquized before billions of God's people that he was a worm and no man. Job's public reaction to his own sin even as a mature Christian was to abhor himself and repent in dust and ashes.

Men such as these had seen where pride led. Paul watched Judas Iscariot implode straight into hell. David saw Saul sin away a kingdom for himself and his posterity. I, too, have seen where pride leads. It leads to empty church buildings, closed Christian schools, shattered reputations, fatherless children, imprisoned pastors, burned-out missionaries who abandon the field and an independent Baptist movement on the brink of irrelevancy. In short, it leads to destruction.

The story is told of a fly that sat atop a stagecoach driving at top speed through the dusty Western plains. Looking behind him, the fly saw the enormous dust plume trailing the coach and said to himself, "O, what a dust I raise." Many a Sunday school teacher, deacon, soul winner, professor, assistant, and pastor in an independent Baptist church has looked at the work God alone is so graciously doing in their midst and said to himself, "O, what a dust I raise."

Where are we wrong? So grievously in this: we are proud.

We Have Been Transformed by Pragmatism

Crudely, Pragmatism is a form of relativism which holds that any belief that is useful is therefore necessarily true. Conversely, any truth that is inconvenient or non-useful is necessarily untrue.
-Jonah Goldberg, *Liberal Fascism*

If I were forced to choose just one philosophy I could excise from the independent Baptist movement, it would be pragmatism.

What is pragmatism, and why am I so violently against it? Paul, who is often cited in defense of pragmatism, in fact, established the opposite as the norm when he said, *And my speech and my preaching was not with enticing words of man's wisdom, but in demonstration of the Spirit and of power: That your faith should not stand in the wisdom of men, but in the power of God. (I Corinthians 2.4-5)* Man's wisdom is a scriptural phrase that simply means pragmatism. There is a way to get things done that just makes sense to people, a conventional wisdom, if you will. It springs from the starting point of the desired result and works backward in order to ascertain which methods will best obtain that result. It is exemplified in the phrase "the end justifies the means."

Pragmatism is at a veritable epidemic level in modern American culture. The success of a college sports program is measured in wins. Starting with that as the desired end point, pragmatism offers up deceit and recruiting violations. It insists on a lack of integrity and morality. It pampers over-indulged athletes. It finds suspicious doctors to inject steroids. And then it delivers wins by the boat load. Pragmatism offers weary parents easy medicine in lieu of hard discipline, a capitulated abandonment of rules in place of stubborn enforcement, and quick money given to children instead of hours of time in order to achieve peace in the home. Pragmatism offers politicians compromise rather than principle and sound bites rather than serious study and discussion. Pragmatism sends them chasing after klieg lights. It beckons with the siren song of borrowing instead of rigorous fiscal discipline. In so doing, pragmatism fails entirely to deliver statesmen. But that was not its goal. Instead, it delivers election returns. Pragmatism drives the media, advertising, and show business industries. It is the mother's milk of the business world. It sells itself as offering the fastest, surest way to the best result, and our culture has swallowed it hook, line, and sinker.

To varying degrees, all of the above scenarios are bad. Other than parenting, however, they pale in comparison to the awful results that come when pragmatism finds its way into the New Testament church. A church is supposed to be built to please the Lord, to reach the lost, and to edify His people. That is the end game in mind. But when the end game instead becomes attracting the most people into a room, the process changes completely. Pragmatism maximizes the emotion of music and de-emphasizes the confrontation of preaching. Pragmatism seeks to make the lost comfortable by making the church environment as much like the world as possible. Pragmatism embraces marketing and the constant shifts of emphasis and action in order to appeal. Pragmatism sells, promotes, and manipulates. When church growth and ministerial success are your aims, pragmatism inevitably becomes your guiding philosophy.

> *When church growth and ministerial success are your aims, pragmatism inevitably becomes your guiding philosophy.*

Why is this so awful? Why is it bad to aim for church growth? It is erroneous because it builds a church that chases the world in its effort to reach the world. It builds a church that is hollow, inauthentic, uncommitted, confused, and ignorant. Compromise becomes not an occasional thing but a core value. Worldliness is now a virtue instead of a vice. While the resulting conglomeration may resemble a church, in reality, it is nothing like what God intends a church to be. It has abandoned all of that as inconvenient and hampering in its effort to attract the largest crowd possible.

Not only do the results indicate that pragmatism is an awful approach (ironic, right?), but scriptural teaching is clear and plain on the matter. Results are not our concern. It is not our place to worry or care for what happens afterwards. For instance, Shadrach, Meshach, and Abednego, when called to bow before the golden image of Nebuchadnezzar, said, *...we are not careful to answer thee in this matter. If it be so, our God whom we serve is able to deliver us from the burning fiery furnace, and he will deliver us out of thine hand, O king. But if not, be it known unto thee, O king, that we will not serve thy gods, nor worship the golden image which thou hast set up. (Daniel 3.16-18)* The result did not matter, only the obedience.

The Bible is the revelation of God. It shows us Who God is and what He expects of us. The best single word I can think of to sum up what God expects from us is not *results*; it is *obedience*. God tells us to pray; we say, "But when will we get an answer?" God calls us to witness; we say, "But when will we get a response?" God urges us to read the Bible; we say, "But I am not getting anything out of it." In each of these cases and in a myriad of others, we are placing the focus entirely on the wrong side of the equation. Our job is the obedience; His job is the outcome.

> *The best single word I can think of to sum up what God expects from us is not* results; *it is* obedience.

Pragmatism screams, "That does not make any sense! You cannot do that! It is not going to work!" Noah builds an ark anyway. Jeremiah preaches on anyway. Moses returns to Egypt anyway. Peter steps out of the boat anyway. Jesus goes to the cross anyway. The false philosophy of pragmatism drove Abraham and Isaac to separately represent their wives as their sisters. The false philosophy of pragmatism nearly kept Naaman a leper. In case after case in the Bible, we see simple obedience emphasized and the repercussions left to Providence.

I am not preaching fatalism. I am not advocating a calvinistic *que sera sera*. I am saying that an unhealthy preoccupation with whether something will work or not is absolutely killing American Christianity. It is driving us away from obedience and into the false arms of the glory of our own wisdom. And along the way, it is sidetracking churches, waylaying pastors, and ambushing greatly sincere and sincerely wrong men and women.

In response to my rejection of pragmatism, I am offered objections by others. The first invariably revolves around Paul's ...*I am made all things to all men, that I might by all means win some. (I Corinthians 9.22)* Yet surely this is balanced by Paul's emphatic rejection of man's wisdom in the same epistle. Furthermore, it must also be balanced with all of the enumerated Scriptures and examples that point in the direction of an obedience-oriented Christianity in place of a results-oriented Christianity. Did Paul work hard at reaching people? No doubt. But he did not prioritize innovation and relevance. He did not prioritize attracting people to his newly formed churches. He prioritized an obedience that was so non-pragmatic that the inevitable result was persecution and flight.

Others have said to me, "You don't like pragmatism, eh? So you want to do what doesn't work then?" The snide intention is to display the silliness of insisting that the outcome is not important. Yet I never said the outcome is not important. What I do maintain is that the outcome is not my responsibility. The result is not my place to produce. It is not about clinging bitterly to what no longer works and howling as the darkness closes in on my crumbling kingdom. It is about giving myself to obey God and resting on simple faith in Him to produce whatever He chooses from that obedience.

I full well realize that there are certainly times and places in which it is appropriate to ask the question, "What will work best here?" If I am tasked with getting a stump out of the ground, it is valid to figure out whether an ax, a shovel, or a stump grinder is better. For that matter, maybe I can just set it on fire. Perhaps I will just look at all of these options and conclude that I ought to simply leave the stump right where it is. But such an outcome-oriented approach must be set aside when it comes to the spiritual. The entire tenor of the Bible is against it. With great grief, I say that the entire tenor of American Christianity is increasingly for it. The ensuing collision is one in which the Bible will come out with flying colors, but American Christianity will be strewn in pieces all across the highway.

The great problem here, from my vantage point, is not just that pragmatism has invaded American Christianity. After all, this is not a book aimed at American Christianity. It is that the independent Baptist movement has imbued the contagion that infects everyone else. Or perhaps I should say that we have finally begun to suffer the results of the disease after testing positive for the bacteria for decades.

Pragmatism, while endemic in the wider Christian community, has had a firm hold in the independent Baptist movement at least since the 1970s. We have chosen our leaders on the basis of the size of their churches and then trotted ourselves to their annual conventions in order to learn their secrets. Those conventions, by and large, were not about the importance of holiness, grace, faith, wisdom, and prayer; but rather they were "how-to manuals" on building ministries. They did not emphasize obedience so much as inculcate in us a passionate pursuit of growth via whatever new idea we could glean.

That hurt us, but it did not hurt us in visible ways immediately. Like a bomb with a delayed fuse, that pragmatism lay ticking quietly just waiting to go off. After all, our preaching was still central and fiery. Our music was still God-honoring. We went soul winning and ran buses and started Christian schools with good motivations. But when the 1970s became the 1990s, gradually it dawned on us that we were not the largest anymore. And as the 1990s transitioned to the twenty-first century, the middle-aged men stepping into leadership began to cast their inspiration-seeking eyes on the Bill Hybels and Rick Warrens of the world. After all, what they were doing was obviously working. Let us send our staff over there to glean some good ideas from them.

The pragmatism that became embedded in the independent Baptist movement forty years ago is literally shredding us now. The old men were pragmatic but fierce. The middle-aged men were more pragmatic and shaky. The young men are so fiercely pragmatic that they are abandoning even being independent Baptist by droves or are seeking to drag our movement "into the 21st century." After all, the old independent Baptist way does not work anymore, and what works is king.

For instance, let me briefly mention the team missions concept. Its basic idea is that we send a team of missionaries to the foreign field instead of just one couple. A large church chooses from amongst their staff five or six couples and sends them over as a group. The reason for such an approach is that a group tends to become less discouraged than one family. Thus, quitting is minimized. More importantly, the group produces bigger results faster than the old-fashioned way.

The problem with the team missions concept is not the result. I cannot argue with that. In point of fact, it was built with the result in mind, and it is producing that result. The problem is not even with the idea of sending a team of people instead of the traditional couple, for we find examples of that in *Acts*. The problem lies in the fact that as it is currently structured it violates the vital principle of the autonomy of the local church. A man who goes alone to India and establishes a church there establishes an autonomous, local church. A team going to India but is controlled from the States establishes a branch of the Baptist megachurch back in America. The church in India has no say in its own staff. Constant reference must be made to the headquarters in America in order to see what can be allowed next. This is entirely true as well of the increasing numbers of independent Baptists that are transitioning into a multi-site operation. Beloved, that is denominationalism of the worst kind. It is unworthy of being called an independent Baptist work in any respect.

Over lunch one day with a dear friend of mine, this subject came up. He is on staff at a large church that has much invested in this type of missions project. When I brought up the fact that its structure is entirely non-Baptistic and wrong, he looked at me in exasperation and said, "But it works." I know. I completely agree. In the short term, it is producing something grand. Over time, it is asphyxiating the core of who we have been fashioned to be according to the Word of God.

Books are another sad illustration of our decline into pragmatism. Pastors of yore used to be referred to as divines, meaning a theologian or a scholar of religion. The Puritans, for examples, had divines. Their books – both the ones they read and the ones they wrote – reflected it. That orthodox, passionate, yet scholarly heritage could still be found in our fundamentalist founding fathers. R. A. Torrey's early twentieth century *The Fundamentals* are filled with articles and essays of depth, written by learned men. If we fast forward in time fifty years, we come to the beginning of the boom of the independent Baptist movement, and if we examine that boom from the standpoint of books instead of the standpoint of church size, the measurement is quite different. Books on theology and the great scriptural themes are replaced by books about how to boost church attendance, run a music program, parent a family, and structure a ministry.

The result of a further fifty years of this type of writing and reading is the idea that books are all about how to accomplish something. The truth is our bookshelves ought to be weighted more to the side of how to understand some spiritual truth, exercise some spiritual grace, or grasp the inherent riches of some biblical book rather than how to organize a Sunday school.

Nor is a wrongly weighted bookshelf – when it exists – the only bad result. Increasingly, younger independent Baptist pastors find themselves confronted with a maddening lack of depth in the books available to them in our circles. In frustration, they have begun to read the thematic, theological, and expositional books of the Contemporary Evangelical crowd. Is it any wonder our concept of grace is weakening? Is it any wonder we lose men to Calvinism? Other issue-oriented examples could be given ad nauseam. One of the causes is the almost complete paucity of independent Baptist books with depth. We have been so busy writing "how-to volumes" instead that we have lost the capacity and even the desire to write books that will be worth reading a hundred years from now.

I sat down once with the pastor of one of the larger independent Baptist churches in America. I explained to him that I had the opportunity to write books, and I wanted to write books of substance. I asked him for his advice on what I should write about. He looked at me slightly nonplussed and said, "Well, write something 'how-to.' Those are always needed." With great effort I restrained myself from strangling him. Our bookshelves groan under the weight of books rapidly outdated and of little use to the deeper needs of men. But that is all we know anymore because that is all we are anymore – pragmatic men driven to passionately pursue a result. We have become dependent on the next big idea.

We have become dependent on the next big idea.

One of the concepts for which independent Baptists have long been criticized is our willingness to use promotions of one sort or another to boost church attendance. For instance, I swallowed a goldfish for the first time as a sixteen-year-old bus captain. On that particular Sunday, I saw a substantial increase in attendance. After all, what child does not, at some point, want to have a goldfish—not to swallow – but to take home? (Whether his parents wanted him to have one or not is an entirely different matter.)

Over time, promotions were used not just to boost attendance but to motivate those doing the work of bringing in the unchurched as well. When it was announced that thirty brand new visitors on the Big Day would get you a go-kart of your own, the mad rush was on! Sure enough, visitors came by the dozens, and the go-kart was duly handed over. But in so doing, what did we teach the young person who won the go-kart? Have we taught him to serve as to the Lord or to seek to impress men? Have we taught him to the primacy of winning and an ungodly glory in competition? Have we taught him to be spiritually minded or carnally minded?

"But it worked! Thirty people heard the Gospel, and some of them got saved. That wouldn't have happened if you had not motivated him with a go-kart." Aye, in the short term, it worked. But in the long term, we failed to teach him the life-transforming lessons of spiritual maturity. In the long term, we failed to teach him to embrace God as his motivation; we failed to teach the grace poured into our lives via the Holy Spirit as his help. In the long term, we missed out on a lifetime of him accessing that grace in which he unknowingly stands to reach many more people than he did on that Big Day. We have short-circuited a lifetime of Spirit-enabling productivity in order to obtain a visibly good result on the Big Day. Please do not misunderstand me. I am not against all promotion. I am not saying that attendance campaigns are evil. I am not celebrating an anemic us-four-and-no-more Christianity. I do not believe it is wrong to examine how a church might improve and grow. God forbid! I am, though, saying that we are foolish to drink from the muddy waters of the contemporary stream of American Christianity simply because their crowds are bigger than ours. I am saying that the constant prioritization of what works will result in the eventual abandonment of much of the strengths I spoke of in Book One. I am saying that pragmatism has grabbed ahold of our throat so tightly that even through our death rattle we will wheeze, "But it works," as our movement slides into spiritual unconsciousness.

We are foolish to drink from the muddy waters of the contemporary stream of American Christianity simply because their crowds are bigger than ours.

Where are we wrong? In this – we have been transformed by pragmatism. In the short term, it is looking very good. In the long term? Well, let us not think about that. What was last week's attendance again?

We Elevate Young Men

Mistakes are the usual bridge between inexperience and wisdom.
            -Phyllis Theroux

Young men are energetic, enthusiastic, and fiery. Young men have a lust to build something. Young men have the curious combination of courage and ignorance necessary to push past obstacles. Young men do not take "no" for an answer. Chances are if you find a man charging hell with a squirt gun, it will be a young man. Young men are flexible, innovative, demanding, and questioning. Young men have historically made the greatest mathematicians, physicists, and inventors.

Young men have not, however, historically made great pastors or spiritual leaders. We notice that we are cautioned about just such a matter by the Apostle Paul. *Not a novice, lest being lifted up with pride he fall into the condemnation of the devil. (I Timothy 3.6)* Indeed, the tone of the Word of God is one in which the aged man is promoted, and the young man is held back. Elihu wisely let Job's older friends exhaust themselves before he offered any opinion. *I said, Days should speak, and multitude of years should teach wisdom. (Job 32.7)* This is precisely because the wisdom and experience of age are explicitly linked in Scripture. *With the ancient is wisdom; and in length of days understanding. (Job 12.12)* Jehovah instructed the Jews to pay homage to their aged. *Thou shalt rise up before the hoary head, and honour the face of the old man, and fear thy God... (Leviticus 19.32)* Conversely, He never instructed them to honor the young. David is described as dying ...*in a good old age, full of days, riches, and honour:... (I Chronicles 29.28)* A good young age? No such phrase is found in the Word of God. The aged are labeled as having understanding. *(Job 12.20)* The aged women in contrast with the young women are explicitly called to be teachers. *(Titus 2.3)*

There are, of course, exceptions to the rules implicit in the above paragraph. Jesus was only thirty years old when He began His public ministry. God used men such as Gideon, Daniel, Joseph, and David in their youth. Indeed, age in and of itself is no automatic guarantee of wisdom. *(Ecclesiastes 4.13)* One can be a fool at any age. But by and large, those exceptions prove the rule. A querulous old man is common; a foolish one is not so common. I know none of the latter in the ministry. Yes, Charles Spurgeon began his pastorate at the Metropolitan Tabernacle at nineteen, but there are not many Spurgeons in church history.

One of the negative consequences of entwining pragmatism through the core identity of the independent Baptist movement has been the elevation of young men. This weakness is not found among us alone. In point of fact, it is actually worse in the contemporary evangelical wing of American Christianity, but it is found widely in us.

I know what some of you are thinking at the moment. "What in the world is he talking about? No group on the planet has spent more time honoring and listening to old men." In many ways that is true. Attending conferences while growing up, it was common to hear an old man headline the evening services. But there are three key areas in which this wisdom has left us. Allow me to lay them briefly before you.

Conferences

The first area in which we have elevated young men is quite often in the very conferences where the old men preach. Such conferences usually contain afternoon sessions in which various "how to" aspects of ministry are presented. Who teaches these sessions? Young men do. They are chosen largely on the basis of the size of their churches. Such men are assumed to have good ideas because their churches are growing. The old men get a respectful hearing in the evening services, but it is the young men who heap to themselves influence during those afternoon sessions.

I am conscious as I write this that it may come across as sour grapes. God is my witness that such is not my motivation. Instead, I am simply casting my mind back across a great many young men who stood to teach me something. Their names scroll before me in my mind's eye notorious for how they flamed out of the ministry, brought shame to God's name, and ushered their ministries to the very brink of extinction. On the other side of the equation, I see my father – pastor for thirty-nine years, husband for fifty-three years, father of six, and grandfather of eleven – who has never graced a platform of this type in his life.

What is the reason for such a dichotomy? Simply this: my father never pastored anything larger than an average-sized church and never promoted himself in any way. His operating watchwords in the ministry have been faithfulness, fidelity, consistency, and caution. Who wants to learn from someone like that? After all, what kind of a crowd would he draw? If we put him up as a teacher, he would not draw flies. No, let us trot across the hall to hear this new thirty-something wonder who has taken his church from fifty to five hundred in three years. That is where the answers to my ministry's problems must lie. Do not bother with the fact that this man's marriage, parenting, preaching, pastoring, praying, faith, holiness, wisdom, leadership, consistency, study, integrity, and teaching have not been proven for any real length of time.

Colleges

Much worse than this, however, has been the now ingrained habit among independent Baptist Bible colleges of hiring young professors. Pastors of the large churches that sponsor such Bible colleges often become overly protective as they age – afraid of questions, fearful of contrary opinions, and downright scared of disloyalty. Consequently, their hiring choices become driven out of fear rather than out of a genuine desire to edify the preacher boys under their care. Who do they thus hire? The answer is as patently obvious as it has become absurd. Immediately following commencement, they hire their own graduates.

Someone has well said, "Young preachers are like wasps. They are never bigger than when they are first hatched." I cast my mind back to my own Bible college experience in some horror in this respect. The men who taught me how to pastor had never pastored. Most of them had never even left the system in which we all were cultivated. It is no coincidence that ignorance, pride, insecurity, authoritarianism, and pragmatism ruled the day. It took me years to overcome the corresponding weakness in my own ministry. Not coincidentally, as the young professors' influence receded, my own father's influence increased.

Young preachers are like wasps. They are never bigger than when they are first hatched.

The truth is I should have known this all along. Jesus was not proud. Jesus was not dictatorial. Jesus was not manipulative and ambitious. He never shouted down questions. Yes, He did occasionally exercise anger in His ministry, but it was rare rather than common. Such were the faults of the young men placed over me in my training.

The tragedy of such an inbred system is two-fold. First, it fails to realize its own weaknesses because it only hires from within. There are no fresh eyes and no new broom to sweep clean. Second, it perpetuates and magnifies its weaknesses in the men it produces. Take pride for example. I have known some proud old men in ministry but not many. God has a way of purging us of it (or at least from the outward exhibition of it) as the years become decades. But young men are notorious for such pride. It is the very reason Paul warned that inexperienced men should not be put into places of leadership. *(I Timothy 3.6)* Proud young men influencing even younger men inevitably produce flashy, loud ministries that eventually crater into destruction. Pause and think for a while, and I am sure that you can come up with quite a list of such men.

I realize older, more experienced men in ministry often have contrary opinions to the established wisdom of the school. The truth is, that within limits, that is a strength and not a weakness.

Older, experienced men are less mouthy and thus, less interesting. Again, I would argue that this is not a weakness but a strength. We could do with a little less flash and a little more actual content in the independent Baptist college environment. Experienced men are often not teachable nor as moldable in the purposes of the institution. Yet what they bring to the table in that timeworn cliché is so much greater than what the young men bring. They bring balance, wisdom, experience, knowledge, understanding, discernment, prudence, and patience. Such men have a track record in family and ministry that indicate a character worthy of a great trust. Such men have not been handed anything. They have fought and clawed and scratched for years to get their platform; we would be wise to usher the young men down and the older men up.

Online

One of the curious and wonderful things about being independent Baptist is the diversity of views we hold. I think if you get four independent Baptists together, you will get six opinions on any one subject. If you wrote this book, for instance, you might very well label something a strength that I have labeled a weakness and vice versa.

Such is the case with the third area in which our movement has elevated young men, namely, the internet. It is no secret that in our generation young people are more active and attuned to the online world than senior citizens are. Certainly, there are exceptions to both of these broad brushes, but generally speaking, the graph runs from high to low in relation to internet activity and age.

The practical result of this in the context in which I am speaking is that the younger men in our movement own the internet. They are the ones that are active on social media. They are the ones with up-to-date websites. They are the ones blogging. They are the ones using new media to expand the message. And they are the ones diving headlong into conversations and discussions. Even a casual perusal through my contacts reveals a more than four-to-one split, with the far greater numbers of active internet users on the side of the younger men.

In the first two areas I cited above, the younger men have been granted a platform for which they have been proven feebly prepared. In this last area, however, the younger men have not been granted anything. They own it by default. They simply engage in much larger numbers and in far greater detail.

There are some contributing factors to this that I understand, and perhaps some I do not. It is hard to teach an old dog new tricks. The more experienced men in our movement did not grow up in the freewheeling online world of discussion, argument, and give-and-take that now exists. They are often uncomfortable not just with the technology but with the climate of controversy that the online environment fosters. Others perhaps feel it is unseemly or a waste of time. Some shrink from confrontation. Still others think it is inappropriate to disagree publicly or to enter in to what amounts to an argument. Some feel this so strongly that they believe either participation, conversations, or both should be stopped period or vigorously preached against.

Let me reach again to my father for a concrete illustration. I know that he and my mother often read the dialogue that takes place on my Facebook page, yet they absolutely never comment. This is not because they do not have an opinion, for they often share that opinion with me days later in a random phone call. They just cannot bring themselves to put that opinion into digital words on a screen. What is the result of such an unwillingness? Frankly, their wisdom goes no further than my ear in the phone call. The mature generation does not share their experienced and knowledgeable perspective with the wider independent Baptist community. They do not write. They do not engage. They do not discuss. They do not conversate. They do not share. They do not proffer. They do not blog. They do not tweet. They do not update. Some of them read in silence, and others ignore it altogether. And in consequence, only the younger men are heard.

We are all familiar with the tale of foolish Rehoboam. *...he forsook the counsel which the old men gave him, and took counsel with the young men that were brought up with him, that stood before him. (II Chronicles 10.8)* Rehoboam was absolutely wrong-headed in his approach, but at least he had the opportunity to make a choice. The old men were ignored, but at least they spoke up. So often I find myself staring at a screen during the middle of an important discussion of one kind or another, wishing that the seventy-year-old Brother So-and-So would tell us what he thinks. But he rarely does.

I would have no man violate his conscience. I am sensitive to the fact that in my current middle age, I do not personally know what it is like to be an older person. But there is a movement taking place amongst the younger generation of independent Baptists, and often that movement has no influence from the wiser generation ahead of us. As kindly and lovingly as I know how, I plead with that wiser generation to speak up. You do not have to spend six hours a day online. You do not have to join every social media start-up. You do not have to insult people. You do not have to know everything. But a voice unspoken is always a voice unheard. God gave you a voice to use. The internet is simply another way of speaking with that voice. Speak up, beloved.

There is a hastiness in younger men that often results in unwise courses of action. There is a boldness in younger men that sometimes brings about experimental change resulting in disastrous consequences. There is a pride in younger men that is not yet tempered by a lifetime of watching the devil flay the spiritual skin from the unwary. If these weaknesses are not countered, we will inevitably find ourselves innovating our way right out of the old time religion and into something unrecognizable in future generations.

I do not believe that all change is bad. I do not think our concept of God and church and spirituality and ministry must be forever kept in stasis. There is nothing inherently spiritual about stagnation. But American Christianity is changing at warp speed. That change has worked its way even into the conservative bastions of the independent Baptist movement. And we need the perspective of the older men on the issues of the day. Speak up, beloved.

Recently my wife and I were lying in bed together at the end of the night. As is our custom, we were sharing some thoughts about the day as husbands and wives are wont to do. I curled up next to her, kissed her hair, and said, "You don't look a day older than when we got married." She batted her eyelashes at me. I should have known to leave well enough alone and quit while I was ahead. But I had to go one step farther. Unfortunately, in an attempt to continue the compliment I said, "No, you don't look a day older but you do look wiser." The batted eyelashes disappeared and through a glare she said to me, "Everybody knows that those are the same thing."

Well, not everybody. Apparently independent Baptists do not. Where are we wrong? In this: we elevate young men.

The Emperor Has No Clothes

Your minister may be a man of God indeed, and worthy of all
honor for his preaching and practice; but do not make a pope
of him. Do not place his word side by side with the Word of
God. Do not spoil him by flattery. Do not let him suppose
he can make no mistakes. Do not lean your whole weight on
his opinion, or you may find to your cost that he can err. It is
written of Joash, King of Judah, that he *did that which was right
in the sight of the Lord all the days of Jehoiada the priest. (2
Chronicles 24:2)* Jehoiada died, and then died the religion of
Joash. Just so your minister may die, and then your religion may
die too; – may change, and your religion may change; – may go
away, and your religion may go. Oh, be not satisfied with a religion built upon man! Be not content with saying, "I have hope,
because my own minister has told me such and such things."
Seek to be able to say, "I have hope, because I find it thus and
thus written in the Word of God." If your peace is to be solid,
you must go yourself to the fountain of all truth. If your com-
forts are to be lasting, you must visit the well of life yourself,
and draw fresh water for your own soul. Ministers may depart
from the faith. The visible Church may be broken up. But he
who has the Word of God written in his heart, has a foundation
beneath his feet which will never fail him. Honor your minister
as a faithful ambassador of Christ. Esteem him very highly in
love for his work's sake. But never forget that infallibility is not
to be found in godly ministers, but in the Bible.

-J. C. Ryle, *Warnings to the Churches*

I sat staring at the blinking cursor on my screen. I had nothing. I needed to respond to a hurting man, and I had nothing to offer. I had known him for twenty years, on and off. Years ago, he had taken my place as the bus captain of a route I loved. He had married a beautiful girl who had been one of my bus workers. For a number of years now, they had joyfully served on the staff of a large independent Baptist church. And they were now telling me their emperor had no clothes.

The emperor in question had a nationwide ministry. The emperor in question was innovative, generous, personable, passionate, talented, and experienced. He was also cursing a blue streak at his staff in private meetings and coming on to my friend's wife in long, extended, graphic counseling sessions. Even his public actions were increasingly erratic. Arrogance had become the most visible mark of his ministry.

I sat staring at the blinking cursor on my computer screen. I had suspected something was wrong. Now I had confirmation from two eye witnesses that something was terribly wrong. But what do I tell a man who has finally been forced to admit that his pastor is a fraud?

Four years later, I sat down to lunch with another hurting man. He, too, was on staff at that same large church. He, too, had been known and loved by me for twenty years. He, too, had been forced to come to terms with the fact his emperor had no clothes. Not coincidentally, it was the same emperor. In the second man's case, he was forced to admit it when pictures of his pastor in a compromising situation turned up on a cell phone.

An awkward silence enveloped the table where we sat at lunch. His mind was hunched over in pain. My mind ran backward to that blinking cursor on my screen four years before. I had to ask. "Did you ever hear him curse in a staff meeting?"

Like air leaking from a punctured tire, he let out a long drawn out "Yes."

"And you didn't say anything?"

An uncomfortable moment passed.

"No."

I said, "And others heard him do this?"

"Yes."

"And nobody said anything?"

More pain crossed his features.

"No."

I simply had to ask the follow-up question; it begged to be asked.

"Why not?"

Silence. Around us, all the buzz and hum of a normal lunch restaurant rush passed unheeded. At our table, there was only stillness.

Finally, almost angrily, he sought to explain himself, perhaps as much to himself as to me. "I believe in loyalty. I believe in following the man of God without question. I believe that if he is wrong, it is God's job to correct him not mine."

Now angry myself, I hurled back into his teeth, "And that is how you ended up with those pictures on that phone, isn't it?"

I looked across the table at the pinched features of a man I loved, a man who had ministered to me in time of need, a man now in need himself. I had no wish to hurt him further. But some things simply must be said.

The followship philosophy that I had so agonizingly pulled out of him was the very reason we were sitting at that table. To him, his pastor might just as well have been God. You do not tell God He is wrong even when He is wrong. You just sit there, swallow your tongue, nod your head, and say, "Yes sir, that's an excellent idea. Yes sir, I agree with you. Yes sir, you are right. Yes sir, I will find a way to do that."

The position of pastor in the New Testament church is in no way the equivalent of the position of king in the Old Testament. Pastors are not to be kings but servants.

At this point, a certain segment of the independent Baptist world runs to the Old Testament, picks up the story of David and his interactions with Saul, and seeks to club me over the head with it like they do their church people. But that is a non-existent club. Saul was a king of Israel. Israel and the church are two entirely different institutions. *(I*

Corinthians 10.32) The position of pastor in the New Testament church is in no way the equivalent of the position of king in the Old Testament. Pastors are not to be kings but servants. *(I Peter 5.3)* Further, David's position was one of not physically harming the king. David never said it was wrong to speak up when the king was mistaken; he said it was not his place to physically take the king's life.

As much as loyalty is mentioned in some men's preaching, one would think that the Bible would be full of references to it. Curiously enough, the word *loyalty* is not even found in the Word of God. I freely admit the words *faithful* and *steadfast* are found, but they are found in reference to our attitude toward God. The entire tenor of the Word of God is that our faithfulness and loyalty are to be pledged to Him and Him alone. Yet I have heard pastors – highly respected leaders of independent Baptist colleges and mega-churches – vociferously demand in preaching that the men in the congregation stand up in order to pledge their public support of the man of God. Furthermore, I have then heard them berate those who were slowest in rising as disloyal cretins. Such antics have no place in the pulpit of a minister of the Gospel. Such philosophies have no place in the religion of the meek and lowly Nazarene.

Please do not misunderstand me. I am not advocating anarchy. The great mistake of Israel in the age of the judges was found in the sad indictment ...*every man did that which was right in his own eyes. (Judges 21.25)* The New Testament repeatedly calls God's people to follow God's humanly ordained leadership in the local church. ...*Be ye followers of me. (I Corinthians 4.16) ...Be followers together of me,... (Philippians 3.17)*

The New Testament does mandate followship in a local church context, but that followship is not a blanket followship. With meticulous care, the Apostles marked that followship as a limited followship. ...*Ye became followers of us, and of the Lord,... (I Thessalonians 1.6)* If a man is not following the Lord, I cannot, dare not follow him. *Be ye followers of me, even as I also am of Christ. (I Corinthians 11.1)*

I must constantly be on guard that I do not follow some man off into the weeds in my attempt to follow God. I am to watch both his doctrine and his life. I am bound to follow him but only so long as these things line up with the Word of God. *For yourselves know how ye ought to follow us: for we behaved not ourselves disorderly among you. (II Thessalonians 3.7)* The qualification necessary for a leader to call for followship is a Christ-like life. Many preachers love to quote the first part of *Hebrews 13.7, Remember them which have the rule over you, who have spoken unto you the word of God:...* yet oddly leave off the last half of the verse, *whose faith follow, considering the end of their conversation.*

The qualification necessary for a leader to call for followship is a Christ-like life.

I am not supposed to gossip. I am not supposed to slander. I am not supposed to rock the boat, kick in the traces, stir the pot, or do any number of similarly clichéd activities. I am supposed to put my shoulder to the wheel and push as hard as I can in harness together with my church and my pastor as we serve the Lord alongside one another – as long as my pastor is right.

The sad truth is that many an independent Baptist preacher loves that last paragraph – well, at least up to the dash anyway. Oh, they may pay lip service to the dash. They may throw in the obligatory, "I'm not perfect" in a sermon about humility. But the simple fact of the matter is that they have structured their ministries as if they are correct all the time.

Let me give you an example. I love to visit other independent Baptist churches as I travel. I enjoy meeting new preachers. I get some good ideas. It is good for me to sit down and get preached to like any other Christian. Occasionally, however, what I expected to be a distinct pleasure turned into a woeful disaster.

Such was the case with the pastor and church I am thinking of at the moment. Prior to my visit and according to my knowledge, it was an average-sized church in an average-sized town with some above-average ministries. Its website revealed it had an active bus ministry, an internet radio station and media ministry, a daycare, a Christian day school, and a small Bible college all meeting in newly constructed facilities. By anyone's estimation, that is quite an extensive ministry list for an average-sized church in an average-sized town.

I attended all three services on Sunday, and I found something extraordinary. Not counting visitors, the number of adult men in Sunday school was two; in the morning service, there were five; in the evening service there were three. Well, I take that back. The church has four full-time paid staff men, and I did not count them. In actuality, the church, on average, had more paid staff men than it had regular layman for each service.

Financially, this functions because the church makes substantial income from side businesses. Organizationally, it defines the phrase "top heavy." Realistically, it is entirely unsustainable over the long term. The church with a growing national reputation and an impressive number of ministries is actually an empty shell.

Wait just a minute, though. I have not yet even gotten to my point. After the morning service, I joined the pastor for a bite to eat. Over lunch, he began to share with me his vision for future ministries. He laid them out in great philosophical detail. He had to start a Bible college because no one else does Bible college right. He wants to start a mission board for the same reason. He plans to start an evangelists' training school for the same reason. Here is a man who wants to train men in how to start churches, pastor churches, and be evangelists and missionaries. He alone has the real answer to how to do these things. And he has three adult men in his Sunday evening service.

There is a word for such a man as this – delusional. He does not think he is proud, yet he is. He disclaims arrogance, yet insists he alone has the answer for not only the areas of ministry in which he is failing but also the ones which he has never tried. Twice in the course of our afternoon conversation I gently tried to bring up an alternate possibility to a position he was maintaining. He shot them both down quick as a wink. Several times I saw him admonish others around him unpleasantly about some aspect of their conduct or behavior. Why? He is right about everything.

I do not mean to imply he is an awful man; he is far from it. He is a passionate soul winner. He has a great determination. He loves his wife deeply. He has dedicated himself to seeing that his family turns out for the Lord. But he is a legend only in his own mind.

The unvarnished truth is he is an emperor with no clothes. But no one in his church will tell him. His wife will not tell him. His staff will not tell him. His deacons will not tell him. His children will not tell him. No one will tell him. And so he will go on dreaming up grander and grander ministries and building an exponentially leveraged superstructure until the whole thing comes crashing down. This will all happen because no one in his kingdom has the courage to say the emperor has no clothes.

Solomon said it well: *Better is a poor and a wise child than an old and foolish king, who will no more be admonished. (Ecclesiastes 4.13)* Such an emperor who refuses to be admonished is nothing more than a fool.

Why do I care? Why should you care? We should care because kingdoms with naked emperors wreak havoc in the name of Christ. Some wreak havoc when they implode morally as in the first example in this chapter. The young couples in such a system routinely throw the baby out with the bathwater as they abandon the independent Baptist movement for the contemporary evangelical one. The teenagers in such an environment are often deeply scarred. For the rest of their life, they will view all preachers and churches with suspicion. Indeed, in future years they will blame their backslidden condition on some hypocritical preacher in their past who hurt them.

> *Kingdoms with naked emperors wreak havoc in the name of Christ.*

Others, as in my second example, wreak havoc by transferring to impressionable preachers-in-training an arrogant, know-it-all, don't-you-dare-question-me, my-way-or-the-highway attitude. Such men – if they are not rescued by the grace of God from this philosophically disastrous approach – build churches conformed aggressively into their own image. They often seem to succeed for a while. After all, there is a certain percentage of the population that wants someone else to think for them and someone else to tell them what to do. But by and by the structure becomes an empty shell. The young people that it produces will sooner or later begin to ask questions. Their questions being viewed with suspicion as attacks, they eventually walk away. If the ministry can attract any men and women who think for themselves, it cannot keep them. If it does happen to catch a person with a backbone, it soon finds that person leaves. The end result is nothing built that glorifies God, edifies the saints, and advances the cause of Christ. It is rather a false front that glorifies the preacher, conforms the saints to his image, and advances the causes he deems justified.

Beloved, we are in the last days. The world system is visibly shifting to embrace the godless anti-Christ. Should the Lord tarry His coming, the family of God will have much to endure. The end of the Church Age will be marked by the same spilled blood that identified it at the beginning. We will not breed a Christianity that will stand in such a time by conforming them to a man's image. They will not grow a backbone because of our frequent admonitions not to quit, but rather they will grow a backbone by the grace of Almighty God. And if they cannot even stand up to their own church leaders when those leaders are wrong, how will they ever stand up when their nation's leaders are wrong?

In entirely too many circles, we have taught our people not to question the pastor. He is the man of God standing in God's place. He mounts the pulpit, and we tremble. He casts his fierce glance our way, and we drop our eyes in submission. He disposes, and we do not propose at all. He moves, and the entire congregation seconds that move.

Where are we wrong? In this: the emperor has no clothes, and yet we remain silent.

We Demand Veto Power

We think ourselves possessed, or at least we boast that we are so,
of liberty of conscience on all subjects and of the right of free
inquiry and private judgment in all cases, and yet how
far are we from these exalted privileges in fact.
-John Adams, Letter to Thomas Jefferson, January 23, 1825

In the American system of government as it was originally
designed, the power to legislate was granted to Congress. To
legislate is to decide on a course of action and to mandate that
action. In the spirit of checks and balances, the framers of the
Constitution wisely included a limit on Congress' authority to legislate. They granted the President the power to veto any bill he saw
fit; at the same time, it gave Congress the ability to override that
veto with a two-thirds majority vote in favor.

When we descend from the national level to the personal one,
we see that legislation is nothing more or less than the decision of
the individual to undertake a particular course of action. The ability
to make such decisions in freedom is a particular right granted to
us by Almighty God. Adam and Eve were given reign to choose for
themselves what they did and did not want to eat in the Garden of
Eden. *(Genesis 2.16)* When Moses raised money for the building of
the Tabernacle, he asked contributions from …*everyone whom his
spirit made willing,… (Exodus 35.21)* John recorded the importance
of free will in the very last chapter of the Bible. …*And whosoever
will, let him take of the water of life freely. (Revelation 22.17)* This
concept is thus found literally from beginning to end in the Bible.

In the first chapter of this book, I briefly outlined the Baptist distinctives. You may remember I paid scant attention to individual soul liberty as I intended to return to it later in the book. I simply summarized it with E. Y. Mullins explanation: "The great principle underlying religious liberty is this: God alone is the Lord of my conscience."

Such a concept of soul liberty was a revolutionary idea in its time. Historically, during Europe's Dark Ages, one did not have the freedom to choose his own religion. It was chosen for him before he was born on the basis of his ethnicity, parentage, or the particular principality in which he lived. If his prince was Catholic, so was he; if his prince was Protestant, so was he, etc.

Baptists have ever been the world's greatest champions of liberty. This is precisely due to our firm conviction that no one can or should force you to believe or practice anything. You alone are responsible to God for what you believe and practice; therefore, you must be free to choose how to live in the context of worship.

This concept springs from Paul's discussion of personal responsibility in *Romans 14. But why dost thou judge thy brother? or why dost thou set at nought thy brother? for we shall all stand before the judgment seat of Christ. For it is written, As I live, saith the Lord, every knee shall bow to me, and every tongue shall confess to God. So then every one of us shall give account of himself to God.* You cannot give an account to God for me. I must do it for myself. It then follows that I should be free to live just as I believe God wants me to live since I am the one who has to answer to Him for my life.

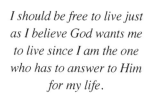

I should be free to live just as I believe God wants me to live since I am the one who has to answer to Him for my life.

God in His sovereignty chose to enlighten every human being individually in relation to Himself. *That was the true Light, which lighteth every man that cometh into the world. (John 1.9)* A just God would not call on each individual man to answer for himself without at least giving each of us some light. Thus, God is fair to demand of each of us that individual account since He has given to each of us light about Himself and a free will to choose whether to obey Him or not. Since these are true and we are individually held responsible by God, then we must have the individual freedom of conscience in order to choose to do so.

J. D. Freeman, the pastor of the Bloor Street Baptist Church in Toronto said it this way in 1905: "Our demand has been not simply for religious toleration, but religious liberty; not sufferance merely, but freedom; and that not for ourselves alone, but for all men. We did not stumble upon this doctrine. It inheres in the very essence of our belief. Christ is Lord of all... The conscience is the servant only of God, and is not subject to the will of man. This truth has indestructible life. Crucify it and the third day it will rise again. Bury it in a sepulcher and the stone will be rolled away, while the keepers become as dead men... Steadfastly refusing to bend our necks under the yoke of bondage, we have scrupulously withheld our hands from imposing that yoke upon others... Of martyr blood our hands are clean. We have never invoked the sword of temporal power to aid the sword of the Spirit. We have never passed an ordinance inflicting a civic disability on any man because of his religious views, be he Protestant or Papist, Jew, or Turk, or infidel. In this regard there is no blot on our escutcheon."

We often think of this right as being guaranteed to Americans in the Bill of Rights of our Constitution. And it is. "Congress shall make no law respecting an establishment of religion, or prohibiting the free exercise thereof." At its root, however, this is not a right founded upon the American Constitution; it is a right plainly established by God from the dawn of Creation.

The English Baptist John Bunyan wrote the book more people have bought and read than any other book in human history, *Pilgrim's Progress*. He wrote that book while incarcerated in the Bedford County Gaol (British for *jail*) in 1660. Why was he in jail? He refused to accede to the state's demand that he be licensed by them to preach the Gospel. The duly recorded conversation at his succeeding trial between the Baptist John Bunyan and Judge Wingate is eye-opening on this matter of individual soul liberty.

Judge Wingate: Mr. Bunyan, you stand before this Court accused of persistent and willful transgression of the Conventicle Act, which prohibits all British subjects from absenting themselves from worship in the Church of England, and from conducting worship services apart from our Church. You come, presumably, with no legal training, and yet without counsel. I must warn you, sir, of the gravity of the charge, the harshness of the penalty, in the event of your conviction, and the foolhardiness of acting as your own counsel in so serious a matter. Are you cognizant of these facts, and do you understand the charge?

Bunyan: I am, and I do, M'lord.

Judge Wingate: In truth, I hope you do. Now, I hold in my hand the depositions of the witnesses against you. In each case, they have testified that, to their knowledge, you have never, in your adult life, attended services in the church of this parish. Each further testifies that he has observed you, on numerous occasions, conducting religious exercises in and near Bedford. These depositions have been read to you, have they not?

Bunyan: They have, M'lord.

Judge Wingate: In that case, then, this Court would be profoundly interested in your response to them.

Bunyan: Thank you, M'lord. And may I say that I am grateful for the opportunity to respond. Firstly, the depositions speak the truth. I have never attended services in the Church of England, nor do I intend ever to do. Secondly, it is no secret that I preach the Word of God whenever, wherever, and to whomsoever He pleases to grant me opportunity to do so.

Having said that, M'lord, there is a weightier issue that I am constrained to address. I have no choice but to acknowledge my awareness of the law which I am accused of transgressing. Likewise, I have no choice but to confess my guilt in my transgression of it. As true as these things are, I must affirm that I neither regret breaking the law, nor repent of having broken it. Further, I must warn you that I have no intention in future of conforming to it. It is, on its face, an unjust law, a law against which honorable men cannot shrink from protesting. In truth, M'lord, it violates an infinitely higher law, the right of every man to seek God in his own way, unhindered by any temporal power. That, M'lord, is my response.

Judge Wingate: This Court would remind you, sir, that we are not here to debate the merits of the law. We are here to determine if you are, in fact, guilty of violating it.

Bunyan: Perhaps, M'lord, that is why you are here, but it is most certainly not why I am here. I am here because you compel me to be here. All I ask is to be left alone to preach and to teach as God directs me. As, however, I must be here, I cannot fail to use these circumstances to speak against what I know to be an unjust and odious edict.

Judge Wingate: Let me understand you. You are arguing that every man has a right, given him by Almighty God, to seek the Deity in his own way, even if he chooses, without benefit of the English Church?

Bunyan: That is precisely what I am arguing, M'lord. Or without benefit of any church.

Judge Wingate: Do you know what you are saying? What of Papists and Quakers? What of pagan Mohammedans? Have these the right to seek God in their own misguided way?

Bunyan: Even these, M'lord.

Judge Wingate: May I ask if you are particularly sympathetic to the views of these or other such deviant religious societies?

Bunyan: I am not, M'lord.

Judge Wingate: Yet, you affirm a God-given right to hold any alien religious doctrine that appeals to the warped minds of men?

Bunyan: I do, M' lord.

Judge Wingate: I find your views impossible of belief. And what of those who, if left to their own devices, would have no interest in things heavenly? Have they the right to be allowed to continue unmolested in their error?

Bunyan: It is my fervent belief that they do, M' lord.

Judge Wingate: And on what basis, might I ask, can you make such a rash affirmation?

Bunyan: On the basis, M'lord, that a man's religious views or lack of them are matters between his conscience and his God, and are not the business of the Crown, the Parliament, or even, with all due respect, My lord, of this Court. However much I may be in disagreement with another man's sincerely held religious beliefs, neither I nor any other may disallow his right to hold these beliefs. No man's right in these affairs are secure if every other man's rights are not equally secure.

The heart of every true child of God thrills to read such boldness and courage. It is a clear and cogent explanation of the doctrine of individual soul liberty by a man who spent the next twelve years of his life behind bars proving he actually believed it.

Therein lies the rub. Many a Baptist pays lip service to the doctrine of soul liberty while at the same time violating it in body and in spirit. How so? We violate it by demanding or acceding to the awful doctrine and practice inherent in the phrase "veto power."

The power to legislate on a national level is the power to decide on a course of action and mandate obedience. On an individual level, the power to legislate is a man's own free will. He alone has the right to decide what God wants him to do and be, for he alone will answer to God for it. The ungodly concept of veto power puts a club into the hands of the pastor. It allows him to stand over the prone body of his Christian brother and take away his ability to individually legislate his own course of action. It says, in essence, "Give me your will. Let me decide what you should and should not do for God."

Bear in mind, there is no scriptural backing for such an approach by the New Testament pastor. Yes, I am familiar with *Hebrews 13.7* and its teaching that the pastor has authority in the church. Such a teaching is also implied in the New Testament word *bishop* which literally means boss or overseer. I am a pastor. I do not apologize for being authoritative at church. I decide or delegate the deciding of any number of things in the assembly of God's people. But what I do not do or perhaps I should say have, is the right to lord it over the conscience of my people. I can and should set parameters for how people serve the Lord in our church; what I cannot do is take away from them their God-given right to determine for themselves what God wants them to do.

I cannot count the number of times I have heard a Baptist pastor ask his people to give him veto power over their decisions. And I understand the motivation from which it springs – a sincere desire to protect the uninformed and carnal Christian from a dangerous decision. But while I may offer my informed and spiritual opinion upon his proffered course of action, I cannot make that decision for him. I cannot take that decision out of his hands. He alone will answer for it; he alone must make it.

> *God does not tell the preacher in some magical way what His will is for your life.*

I am not God. Yes, in a sense, I represent Him. I speak on His behalf before His people. But I have no special insight into the will of God for another man that he himself does not have. He and I have equal right to access the throne of God. Such a doctrine is clearly understood as another Baptist distinctive, the priesthood of the believer. Yet another Baptist distinctive says that the Bible alone is our sole authority for faith and practice. God does not tell the preacher in some magical way what His will is for your life. No, God hands both of you the Bible and says, "Here is My will for your life. Study it out, and follow it."

The pastor has no right to take the place of God in the life of a believer. He receives no private divination of God's will. Perhaps he may have more experience as a mature believer in discerning right and wrong. *(Hebrews 5.14)* But experience and position do not equal inspired knowledge and veto authority. He has no right to pull a man into his office and – outside of plain Scripture – claim the authority to declare something or other to be either in or out of the will of God for another person. The will of God is not at the determination of the pastor. God never gave him that authority.

The concept of veto power defies the very Baptist distinctives we claim to hold dear. If it be found, let it be found amongst the charismatics. If it be found, let it be found in the overbearing control of each man's life as represented in any number of cults and false religions. But let it not be found amongst Baptists.

Let us love one another. Let us pray for one another. Let us minister to one another. Let us support one another. Let us counsel with one another. But let us not demand the right to make another mature human being's decisions. Let us not sign away the rights to our own conscience. For we alone will answer to God for how we have lived and served Him in that Great Day.

Each man in our midst was made in the image of God. Each man has direct access to that God. Each man has the same Bible, the revelation of God and of God's will for us. Each man has an inherent right to the liberty of his own conscience. It is past time for us to turn from mere lip service to these precious truths; instead, let us live them.

Where are we wrong? In this: we demand veto power.

We Cover Up Sin

Fearful leaders side-step issues instead of dealing with them,
cover up mistakes instead of owning up to mistakes; they skulk
back into the shadows and hope that the crisis – whatever it is
– will somehow blow over instead of facing their fears. Worse,
they resort to lies and deception to cover up the truth.

-Lee Ellis, *Leading With Honor:*
Leadership Lessons From the Hanoi Hilton

I tremble with this one, for in saying what I am about to say, I
am placing a gun to my own head. Yet it cries to be said, and
above all it is right.

The Pastoral Epistles were written specifically to pastors in
order to tell them how to lead their local churches. It was also
written to churches in order to tell them how to choose their pastor,
relate to their pastor, treat their pastor, etc. I have often heard
preachers use texts from the Pastoral Epistles to explain to their
people what a preacher's responsibilities are and are not and what
the people's responsibilities are and are not. It is true that perhaps
these sermons were sometimes used to beat people over the head,
but then again, maybe I am being uncharitable in saying so. After
all, I myself have preached from these books as well. But there is
one passage in *I Timothy 5* that very suspiciously in my forty-two
years in church I have only heard referenced once (and that one
time the pastor twisted it to make it say the exact opposite of its
intended meaning.) In other words, the silence from the independent
Baptist movement in preaching this text – let alone applying

176

this text – is absolutely deafening. *Them that sin rebuke before all, that others also may fear. (I Timothy 5.20)*

The context reveals that Paul was referencing preachers who are accused of what we would term "great moral failures." *Against an elder receive not an accusation, but before two or three witnesses. (I Timothy 5.19)* Now this verse I have certainly heard railed on a time or two in my life. It soundly establishes the acting principle that a church should not consider seriously disciplining its pastor unless there is a pile of evidence as to what has been done. This rightly protects the pastor from the talebearing gossips spoken of so often in *Proverbs*. This is a scenario experienced by every genuine man of God at some point in his ministry. However, once a church has painstakingly sifted the evidence and come to the undeniable verdict that their pastor has committed some great moral lapse, why is it, I ask you, that no one goes on the next verse? *Them that sin rebuke before all, that others also may fear. (I Timothy 5.20)* We fire him and justifiably so if he commits adultery, molests a child, or embezzles the offerings. But what we do not do is publicly and formally announce what he has done to the wider Christian community – and scripture is clear this is a thing we are supposed to do.

In my experience, there are several excuses offered up at this point in the narrative. Supposedly, they are so compelling as to enable public silence. For instance, we are instructed not be negative. My response is, "Says who?" There is no scriptural instruction in this context to keep silent simply because the publicity is negative. Actually, the opposite is true. Scripture is absolutely filled to the brim with examples of negative messages given publicly. What is so ironic about this is that we are quick to be negative about every other Christian group under the sun until it is our ox that is being gored.

Another statement that often comes up at this point is "We aren't supposed to judge." Yes, we are. *Judge not according to appearance, but judge righteous judgment. (John 7.24)* Judgment must be cautiously done. Yet once we have carefully judged the preacher to be in great moral sin, then said judgment needs announced.

Some will, at this point, throw out *...love covereth all sins.* I agree that *Proverbs 10.12* is found in the Bible, but a clear and contextually appropriate section of that same Bible explains that this does not apply to pastors, at least not in the sense of keeping quiet about their sin. Pastors have a greater influence, a greater visibility, and a greater opportunity to damage the cause of Christ. *...unto whomsoever much is given, of him shall much be required: and to whom men have committed much, of him they will ask the more. (Luke 12.48)* I do not want to write this sentence, but if I desire the privilege of anonymity in my sin, then I had better resign the pastorate. We are public men ministering in a public way. If we are found out, we are to be publicly exposed.

If I desire the privilege of anonymity in my sin, then I had better resign the pastorate.

It boggles my mind that in our hyperconnected, social media-soaked world, so many independent Baptist leaders still think sin can be covered up. Their attempts to do so look increasingly feeble and pathetic to anyone with the ability to type a phrase or sentence into an online search engine. The word *desperate* comes to mind. And desperate men frantically trying to keep some moral implosion secret draw the attention of the online community like my alley garbage cans draw rats. To the hypocrisy of moral implosion is added the deceit of cover-up. We then wonder why the younger, tech-savvy generation refuses to listen to our pontifications.

Undeniably, the independent Baptist movement has an absolutely disastrous record in this respect. My first experience with this came as a teenager. The pastor of a local church with which I was rather familiar launched himself into evangelism. I heard a whisper here and there, but it was not until much later that I put two and two together and learned the truth. He had been confronted by some concerned staff members, and basically ran away into the night. Yet no one ever thought it a helpful idea, I suppose, to inform a very impressionable teenager in an appropriate yet open way of just what exactly he had done wrong. Two years later while I was considering Bible colleges, a public attack was launched against the founder of the college I was considering. I read the original article, and for the first time became aware of the depravity of his son. Shortly afterward, we received and I read this founder's answering defense. In that defense, he asserted that he had no prior knowledge of his son's immorality before recommending him to the pastorate. As much as it pains me to say it, that was an utter lie. I have personally spoken with half a dozen individuals who have confirmed to me that they confronted him with his son's sins prior to this and that he refused to heed them. It is this very culture of silence that *I Timothy 5.20* was designed to prevent.

Sadly, this type of sweep-it-under-the-rug-and-hope-no-one-notices activity is not confined to that particular ministry. It is written deep into the independent Baptist genome. After being a leader in our movement for decades, one pastor was arrested after being accused of molesting twenty-one individuals when they were children. He would die shortly before his trial began the following year. However, in addition to the awful tragedy that this series of sins produced in the lives of these children, when the leadership of his church originally discovered these facts a decade prior, they simply announced his resignation with the affirming words that it did not concern anything "sexual or immoral." The pastor in question then proceeded to raise money from independent Baptist churches all across the country – including mine in Chicago – and headed overseas as a missionary. A wolf was released into another sheepfold with nary a warning to those sheep. To this day, his home church and pastor in America has not, to my knowledge, apologized for their cover-up.

As a good independent Baptist, I have read every issue of the leading periodicals of our movement for decades. As this story unwound across the pages of the internet, I eagerly awaited one particular editor's take. Curiously, month after month went by with nary a word. Finally summoning up my small courage, I wrote him and told him that inasmuch as his periodical had played a tremendous part in lifting up this wolf's ministry publicly, it owed the country a public announcement of the man's sin. I still read that periodical every issue; I am still waiting for that announcement.

A few years ago another pastor whose picture graced an independent Baptist publication on occasion and spoke in their national conferences committed suicide after being discovered in an adulterous relationship. For some reason, this periodical could spare lots of ink and column inches to promote him but nary a drop of ink to reprove his actions before the very public to which they had lifted him up. Yet who can blame the editor? He was simply continuing a long tradition of these curious silences. The largest independent Baptist national conferences ever held in the 1970s were led by a veritable "Who's Who" of independent Baptist pastors. Numbers of these men were later found out in confirmed egregious sin. But the periodical never uttered a peep.

This tragic approach of cover-up is not limited to that generation of independent Baptist leaders. Not long ago a pastor hanged himself in jail after being arrested for the sexual assault of a woman he had picked up in a bar while supposedly attending a revival in another state. I had heard him preach just prior to this at a national independent Baptist conference, and his sermons had been published on occasion. Knowing the editor in question to be a man of integrity, I awaited a statement in his paper. When it came, tucked away in the back, the short paragraph made no mention of his sin or even of the cause of his death. It simply asked people to pray for the family. I stood there holding that periodical, knowing that once again a national independent Baptist publication was willing to publicize a man's ministry but unwilling to publicize that man's sin.

I can hear them now. "We must keep it quiet for the cause of Christ." Will someone please show me that in the Bible? After all, as Baptists our sole authority is the Scriptures. Surely in the case of such momentous life and death decisions, we can point to a clear Scripture verse telling us to hush things up so that the cause of Christ is not brought to reproach. What we find is just as surely the opposite. We are explicitly called to make it public.

Jesus Christ requires of us holiness. Corporate religious institutions and churches can only come to holiness as sin is exposed and repented of.

A dear friend of mine in the ministry conducted a holiness conference at his church every year. Partnering with him in that was an evangelist long known and loved in his church. Right around the time of the holiness conference, this evangelist was found to be discussing in graphic terms sexual activities online with someone he thought to be an underage girl. He was arrested, convicted, and sent to jail. After this hit the news, I called my friend (the pastor of this church) in order to offer him comfort and encouragement. Curiously, he did not seem to need it. He said to me, "Tom, we have been praying for God to show us our sin and for revival to come. Why would we be upset when He answered our prayer?"

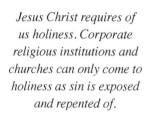

Jesus Christ requires of us holiness. Corporate religious institutions and churches can only come to holiness as sin is exposed and repented of.

His attitude was both refreshing and enlightening. The cause of Christ does not need our cover-up. The cause of Christ calls for an open denunciation of sin, for only in that way lies the pathway of holiness.

Where are we wrong? Deeply, in this: driven by fear and riven by pragmatism we cover up sin. And then scratch our heads in puzzlement when genuine holiness is found all too often to be a foreigner in our movement.

We Love Bad Preaching

It is better to preach five words of God's Word
than five million words of man's wisdom.
-C. H. Spurgeon

I ndependent Baptists love to preach and to listen to preaching. You will recall I devoted some space to it in Book One. I do not know an orthodox Christian movement in the world today that embraces preaching with more delight or that has more fervent preaching. In a typical year, the average independent Baptist will hear two to three times more sermons than his Christian friends of other denominations. We hear preaching in Sunday school, the Sunday morning service, the Sunday evening service, and the mid-week meeting. We rarely, if ever, hold a service in which preaching is not the central point. Even our Christmas banquets and New Year's Eve parties contain preaching. Additionally, it is not unusual for us to drive to neighboring churches and hear preaching on other nights of the week.

If we have this great appetite for preaching – and it is undeniable that we do – then why is the subject of preaching also here in Book Two? Very simply for this reason: much of the preaching we hear is bad preaching.

I do not say that because it is boring preaching. God forbid that our preaching should be labeled boring! Such would be the ultimate insult, if not downright crime in our circles. No, our platforms are filled to bursting with men who know how to shell the corn and how to rare back and preach. It is my contention, however, that

182

much of that preaching – while wildly entertaining – is empty of real value and devoid of actual content.

Nutrition is a funny thing. You can obtain calories from any of a number of sources, but it is an established fact that a salad is a better choice for those calories than a bag of cheese puffs. The foundational instruction in the New Testament on preaching is Jesus' repeated instructions to Peter in *John 21.16* and *17, ...Feed my sheep*. Peter clearly got the point, for he later instructed pastors to *Feed the flock of God which is among you, taking the oversight thereof, not by constraint, but willingly; not for filthy lucre, but of a ready mind. (I Peter 5.2)* To this, Paul also paid his respects in his last words offered to the pastors of the churches around Ephesus, *Take heed therefore unto yourselves, and to all the flock, over the which the Holy Ghost hath made you overseers, to feed the church of God, which he hath purchased with his own blood. (Acts 20.28)* Cheese puffs may be more fun to eat than a salad, but in the long run, the best nutrition builds the healthiest people.

Philosophizing

I see three primary mistakes often made in our movement in relation to preaching. The first is the tendency to substitute the preacher's opinion for the authoritative words of God. I call this kind of preaching philosophizing. Often, other than a token verse, the sermon consists of nothing more than the personal philosophy of the preacher.

Let us take, for example, the subject of relationships. This would include such vital life areas as husband and wife, parent and child, employer and employee, friend and friend, etc. These occupy large percentages of our time and focus. In fact, one could easily say that life is a matter of relationships. And the Bible speaks much to these relationships. There is much practical instruction in the Word of God in relation to each of these. And preaching upon such subjects is necessary and wise, provided said preaching consists of giving out God's instructions and explaining them. Instead and all too often, such sermons contain a list of things that are necessary in the mind of the preacher while none of the list is directly supported by Scripture. Such sermons, often driven by the preacher's personal observation and experience, contain some level or other of common sense but little, if any, of God's sense.

In actuality, this is hardly different than you would find from a life coach, a self-help book, or a daytime television show. And lives built on man's wisdom are built on sinking sand. Twenty years ago, I found such philosophizing very profound and intellectually stimulating. Now I find it all empty. I find myself wanting the substance of the Word of God and what God thinks about the matter under discussion. All too often, however, all I actually hear is what Bro. So-and-so thinks about the matter under discussion.

Lives built on man's wisdom are built on sinking sand.

Our personal philosophy has in entirely too many cases replaced the Word of God as the authority. And that is a preaching tragedy.

Spiritualizing

Worse yet is the tendency to take a text and interpret and apply it in some other way than it was plainly intended. This spiritualizing was exemplified to me in a sermon I heard shortly after my arrival in Chicago. Bro. So-and-so, an evangelist and Bible college professor, had brought a music group to an area church. I attended along with some of my church people. After enjoying the music, Bro. So-and-So got up to preach and took as his text *Acts 26.2*. In this passage, Paul, addressing Agrippa, says, *I think myself happy.* Paul goes on to say contextually that he is pleased with the opportunity to personally explain himself at length to Agrippa. However, Bro. So-and-so simply took those four words *I think myself happy* and proceeded to preach a very entertaining sermon on how we are to – in the midst of difficult circumstances – think positive thoughts and thus be happy in spite of our circumstances. That concept has perhaps some merit, but that clearly was not what Paul was conveying with the phrase *I think myself happy*. In essence then, an independent Baptist college professor acting in his official capacity as a representative of the college simply ripped four words out of a verse and said with them something completely foreign to their intended contextual meaning. And nobody blinked an eye. Imagine my horror, the following year, to take my people again to the exact same church to hear another music group only to watch a different representative of the same college get up and preach the identical sermon point for point! He had ripped it off Bro. So-and-so. Completely unaware that Bro. So-and-so had preached it there the preceding year, he thought he would try out what he deemed a good sermon.

I have heard sermons from *Ezekiel 47* that likened the millennial river to a time of trouble we must endure. Yet there is nothing in the text anywhere that indicates such is a valid application of Ezekiel's prophecy. He was speaking about an actual physical river. I have heard sermons from *Mark 8* on the blind man's statement, *I see men as trees walking,* and equated it to our need to view people as just waiting to be awakened by the warmth of our compassion. Yet there is nothing in the text anywhere that indicates such is a valid application of the blind man's statement. I could repeat such examples as these practically without end.

To spiritualize something is to assert that it has a secondary meaning, one lying below or beside the literal meaning. As a reader or student of a book, I have no right to lay claim to such an interpretation; the author alone has the right to say that his words carry more than one meaning. Are there places in Scripture that carry such double meaning? Yes. How do we know? We know when the Author tells us they do. But if the Author of Scripture does not tell us there is a spiritualized meaning, we then have no right to interpret and apply one.

I use these illustrations because they reveal the inbred and worsening systemic approach taken so often of a careless handling of the Word of God. The sad truth is the above stories are not isolated events. They are but examples of a pattern of sloppy preaching which has become the norm in some circles.

Our critics say this careless handling of the Word of God is par for the course with topical preaching and that the only (and required) solution to such an error is expository preaching. I like expository preaching. In fact, about two thirds of my preaching is expository preaching. My first book, *The Greatest Sermon Ever Preached,* about the Sermon on the Mount sprang from a long expository sermon series. But I completely reject the demand that we cease topical sermons and simply go verse-by-verse from Genesis to Revelation. The truth is there is not a single expository sermon in the New Testament. Such are not even modeled, let alone commanded. No, topical preaching in and of itself is not wrong; rather, non-textual topical preaching is wrong.

The great error of spiritualizing is that it makes the preacher the authority. The only limit to his power over the audience is the limit of his imagination. The scriptural truth ought be the exact opposite. The Word of God is to be the authority and the preacher's creative imagination must at all costs remain constrained within God's original or expressly delineated intent.

Non-Textual Preaching

In one sense it should not surprise me that such non-textual preaching is so popular in the independent Baptist movement. It is certainly easy to prepare. It allows the preacher to mold the church in his own image, forming them around his opinions and philosophy. It makes the preacher appear spiritually deep to his people. In essence, he impresses them with the stuff he finds in the Bible that they have never heard before – primarily because it is not actually in there. It allows the preacher a shortcut to passionate preaching since he can dwell at length on what moves him. Such passionate preaching is always entertaining.

Any time the preacher's opinions become the authority, the genuine authority of the Word of God is minimized.

Popular it is, certainly, but just as certainly, it is dangerous. After all, anything unscriptural is dangerous. Any time the preacher's opinions become the authority, the genuine authority of the Word of God is minimized. Such preaching showcases the preacher rather than the Word of God and creates just one more door through which the foot of pride may enter into his heart.

In addition to all of this, non-textual preaching inevitably produces malnourished Christians over the long term. A good friend of mine whose circles overlap the independent Baptist movement with some conservative evangelical movements was discussing the KJV double inspiration dust-up with one of his preacher friends on the conservative evangelical side. This man told my friend, "Your movement is a mile wide and an inch deep." Sadly, he was largely accurate in that assessment. In my view, we became that way at least partially via decades of giving and listening to non-textual messages.

Furthermore, such preaching is corporately dangerous to a church because it allows the preacher to go off the reservation without being called on it. I have heard men preach sermons that were not just wrong but blasphemously wrong. Yet they thought enough of their chosen sermon to present it at a national meeting. How can preachers get to a place where blasphemous preaching is acceptable? Perhaps it happens because their churches have become immune to any concept of scriptural preaching. Their own preacher has been the authority for so long that the Bible has ceased to have much influence at all. And when a preacher goes off the scriptural reservation without being called on it, his sermons will only get progressively worse.

This kind of non-textual preaching has developed for several reasons. First, we have de-emphasized hermeneutics. In retrospect, I find it appalling that I could get a Bachelor's degree in theology without a class on hermeneutics. In fact, it was not until eight years into my ministry while attending a continuing education class (in an entirely different wing of the independent Baptist movement) that I came to appreciate the importance of hermeneutics. I am glad my alma mater requires an entire course in it at this point, but hundreds

I find it appalling that I could get a Bachelor's degree in theology without a class on hermeneutics.

of men went into the ministry without any grasp of the importance of sound hermeneutics.

Secondly, we have over-emphasized theatrics. A good sermon has come to be defined as one in which the preacher put on a good show rather than one in which he accurately explained and applied God's words. Does he roam from one end of the platform to another? Does he wave a handkerchief? Better yet, does he jump a pew or two? Well then, the chatter in the car on the way home from the meeting is what an excellent sermon everyone just heard. Meanwhile, the sermon of the man who just stood behind the pulpit and spoke is often overlooked.

Lastly, non-textual preaching is the kind of preaching my generation of preachers was soaked in during their formative years. One influential independent Baptist leader often said at the very beginning of a sermon, "Close your Bibles and look up here at me." Now I do not for one moment think every time he said that he was taking his text out of context. But I do know that such statements lead impressionable young preacher boys to devalue the text and to overvalue the preacher's own opinions and philosophy.

Brethren, we must firmly reject such philosophizing and spiritualizing. We must turn from non-textual preaching. The test of a sermon cannot be how loud the preacher is, how much we were moved to laughter and tears, or how many microphone stands were kicked over. We must embrace the fact that the test of a preacher is his doctrine, his manner of life, and how closely his sermons bring out the simple and precious Word of God.

> *The test of a preacher is his doctrine, his manner of life, and how closely his sermons bring out the simple and precious Word of God.*

What is so ironic about this weakness is that no other religious group in America so elevates the Bible as our crowd. We carry it openly. We place great emphasis on having the correct version. We call on our people to read it regularly. Yet the truth is we have gradually removed it as the centerpiece of our sermons and replaced it with ourselves. As one preacher friend of mine said to me recently, "What a shame for people who clamor so loudly for the authority of the Bible to turn around and squander the divine authority of the Word for their own fallen presuppositions, soap boxes, and hobby-horses."

Where are we wrong? In the very area in which we think we are so right: we love bad preaching.

Study?

He is inspired, and yet he wants books! He has seen the Lord, and yet he wants books! He has had wider experience than most men, and yet he wants books! He had been caught up in the third heaven, and had heard things unlawful for a man to utter, yet he wants books! He has written a major part of the New Testament, and yet he wants books! The apostle says to Timothy and so he says to every Christian, "Give thyself to reading." The man who never reads will never be read; he who never quotes will never be quoted. He who will not use the thoughts of other men's brains proves he has no brains of his own.
-C. H. Spurgeon, *Paul – His Cloak and His Books*

The independent Baptist movement is one of those religious phenomena that largely sprang from men of action rather than men of thought. By that, I do not mean to imply that our forefathers were ignorant but rather that their lives and ministries were marked more by the churches they built than the commentaries they authored. Our faction has ever been one of movement. We are not currents in the deep. We are rapids foaming over the rocks.

In many respects, this is a good thing. When Joseph's Pharaoh, a wise man, delegated the care of his herds and flocks, he looked for *men of activity. (Genesis 47.6)* Such men are builders and doers, generally speaking, rather than thinkers. The organizations which they tend, as gardens do, often flourish. Under their care, mission boards thrive, ministries grow, and churches prosper.

It is largely in this mold that our movement has been built. What do pastors do upon arrival at a new church? They launch a bus route, add missionaries, start new Sunday school classes, etc. When our churches are struggling, we pound the pavement, knock more doors, and visit more absentees. As our people begin to grow in grace – and sometimes even before they do – we plug them into a place of service. "Here, drive this van, set up this classroom, pass out these tracts, do something for the cause of Christ."

I often use the illustration of a road with a ditch on either side. In this context, the ditch on one side of the road is an overemphasis on activity. The ditch on the other side of the road is an overemphasis on study. Independent Baptists, as a group, veer much closer to the ditch of activity than the ditch of erudition.

In a sense, it is easy to see why. Our practical approach to theology and our emphasis on evangelism lends itself to activity. Additionally, many of the men who so influenced the independent Baptist movement in the mid-twentieth century had experienced a resistance to their emphasis on evangelism. Much of this resistance was led by professors who sat in ivory towers pooh-poohing the fullness of the Holy Spirit and the chosen means of evangelism. Under the guise of Calvinism, hyper-dispensationalism, and lordship salvation they savaged the activity of the leading churches in the independent Baptist movement. Others embraced a dead theology that only found life on the dusty shelves of an academic library but had not preached a sermon in the power of the Spirit for decades.

The problem herein lies not with our emphasis on activity but in our attack on intellectualism. We long ago lurched away from the ditch on the left side of the road, rushed completely past a balanced position, and plunged into the ditch on the other side of the road. Earlier generations that were wary of a dead intellectualism produced in the next generation a scholarly apathy. A generation of apathy, in turn, produced its worse second cousin, antipathy. In the space of fifty years, we have gone from an arguably healthy skepticism of cerebral leaders to a downright aversion to them.

We have come so far in the wrong direction that ignorance is now celebrated. Commentaries are criticized. Never mind the fact that the independent Baptist pastor criticizing commentaries wants people to listen to his sermon – which is a commentary. (In the immortal words of Spurgeon, "It seems odd, that certain men who talk so much of what the Holy Spirit reveals to themselves, should think so little of what he has revealed to others.") The study of the original languages in which Scripture was written has somehow been twisted to become a thing nefariously unorthodox. *Exegete* and *expository* are terms of insult. The science of hermeneutics is neglected to the point of near death in many pulpits. The pastor's study where he laboriously dug out his sermons long ago transitioned to an office from which he exercises his prerogatives as chief executive officer.

We have come so far in the wrong direction that ignorance is now celebrated.

This now ingrained animosity to intellectual pursuits is aggravated by an increasing tendency to tell people what they are supposed to do and be without telling them why. Our pulpits thunder with denunciations of the wrong crowd, the wrong music, and the wrong standards with little to no explanation underlying it. I have reluctantly been forced to come to the conclusion that many an independent Baptist preacher not only does not have any underlying foundation of why but he actually does not want to bother his people with one either. He simply wants them to obey him.

In the short term, this works beautifully. Families line up with the right clothes, the right haircut, and the right music on their MP3 players. In the long term, this tyrannical insistence on "my way or the highway" embitters the next generation and sends them running for the contemporary evangelical churches by the boatload.

In *Proverbs*, Solomon constantly reiterates three main concepts: knowledge, wisdom, and understanding. Knowledge scripturally defined is *what*. This is illustrated in the question, "What do you know?" Knowledge is what you know. Twenty-one times Scripture uses the phrase *know what*. For instance, *The lips of the righteous know what is acceptable... (Proverbs 10:32)* What do they know? They know what is acceptable speech and what is not. Knowledge is what.

Wisdom scripturally defined is *how*, or perhaps I should say *know how*. Wisdom combines the *what* of knowledge with the proper *how* of how to use that knowledge. *Exodus 35* and *36* speaks of Bezaleel's significant contribution to the construction of Moses' Tabernacle. God *...filled him with the spirit of God, in wisdom, in understanding, and in knowledge....* Consequently, he was able to *devise curious works, to work in gold, and in silver, and in brass, And in cutting of stones, to set them, and in carving of wood...* Not only that but he could teach others how to do these things as well. As a result, *Then wrought Bezaleel and Aholiab, and every wise hearted man, in whom the LORD put wisdom and understanding to know how to work all manner of work for the service of the sanctuary...* Bezaleel knew how to get the job done. He was a wise man. *The LORD by wisdom hath founded the earth;... (Proverbs 3.19)* How did He do that? Exactly.

Since wisdom is about how to use the knowledge you possess, wisdom is all about making the correct decision. For instance, my wife is a knowledgeable and wise homemaker. She knows (knowledge) that the tomato is a fruit not a vegetable, but she is wise enough not to use it in a fruit salad. She knows how and when and where to use it properly.

Both of these – wisdom and knowledge – are found in decent amounts in the independent Baptist movement. What does God want us to do? How are we supposed to do that? Our pulpits and conferences and periodicals are filled to bursting with this kind of information. What is staggeringly absent in most of these discussions is the underlying reasons why.

The third concept Solomon goes to such great lengths to highlight is understanding. Scripturally defined understanding is *why*. The very first of the 346 times the Bible uses the term is found in *Genesis 11.7. Go to, let us go down, and there confound their language, that they may not understand one another's speech.* God took away their ability to grasp the meaning behind what was said. Philip asked the Ethiopian eunuch in *Acts 8.30, ...Understandest thou what thou readest?* "Do you grasp the meaning of that which you are reading?" Paul wanted the Philippian church to understand the meaning behind why he had been imprisoned. *But I would ye should understand, brethren, that the things which happened unto me have fallen out rather unto the furtherance of the gospel. (Philippians 1.12)*

It is in Paul's sense that it is used most often in Scripture i.e. why something should be done, why something should not be done, why something is true, or why something is not true. The biblical term *understanding* places a foundation that makes sense underneath or behind a truth or instruction. Job's three friends had the knowledge of what God had done to Job, but as Elihu pointed out, they had no idea why. *Great men are not always wise: neither do the aged understand judgment. (Job 32.9)*

Such a lack of understanding is a verifiable tragedy. *Proverbs* instructs us repeatedly to prioritize the acquisition of understanding. *(Proverbs 4.5, 4.7, 7.4, 9.6, 16.16, 23.23)* Solomon explained that obtaining understanding was one of the primary reasons *Proverbs* was penned *(Proverbs 1.2)*, and that in so doing, one acquires distinct advantages. *(Proverbs 2.11, 3.13, 16.22, 19.8)*

If understanding is so valuable, why is it so neglected? Very simply, obtaining it takes incredibly hard work. *I have more understanding than all my teachers: for thy testimonies are my meditation. (Psalm 119.99)* Such meditation is laborious. In another context, the Apostle Paul would phrase it this way: *Study to shew thyself approved unto God, a workman that needed not to be ashamed, rightly dividing the word of truth.* To study well takes a workman for *...of making of books there is no end; and much study is a weariness of the flesh. (Ecclesiastes 12.12)*

We are more comfortable telling people what to do and how to do it than we are with telling them why they should do it that way.

As you can see, all of this brings us back full circle to the word that titles this chapter. We are more comfortable telling people what to do and how to do it than we are with telling them why they should do it that way. We constantly fall back on the construct of ministerial authority or statistics of success as the end-all to most questions. This tendency is aggravated by our own internal inertias biased toward pragmatism and rules. But these are shallow supports when the thinking young person or church member begins to ask *why*. Why do we go back to church on Sunday night? Why is preaching the biggest part of every service? Why are we fundamentalists? Why do we go soul winning? Why are we different in our understanding and application of grace? Why do we hold these standards? Why is it wrong to drink? Why is it wrong to listen to the world's music? Why are we supposed to tithe? Why are the Mormons wrong? And on and on and on it goes.

Can you answer those questions? Can you explain why we believe in the imminent return of Christ? Do you understand why we as Christians embrace Israel? Do we grasp the fallacy of evolution on a logical level? Why do we still do Sunday school instead of small groups? Why do we say divorce is wrong? Is it wrong? Why do we reject contemporary Christian music? Why did God create you? Why are we still Baptist when so many are dropping the label? Why do we use the King James Version? Why do we refuse to read after the popular preachers of the day? Why does a good God allow evil? Why is Jesus God? Why is the Bible the Word of God? Why do we hold that Jesus actually performed miracles? Why is the Resurrection logical? Are we dispensational or covenant in our theological approach? Is Calvinism really all that bad?

The Bible is a gold mine. By definition then, said gold must be brought to the surface. Do you have a good understanding of the arc of the life of Christ? Is the Sermon on the Mount for our generation? What is faith? What is holiness? What is Heaven like? What character traits would God have us internalize? What are the primary subjects in systematic theology? What does the Bible say about marriage, money, parenting, aging, and amusing ourselves?

How does one mine that gold? What are the essential points of biblical interpretation? How does one approach the poetry or prophecy of the Bible? What portions are to be taken literally and what portions figuratively? How do you establish the deeper meaning of the words in the original language without falling into the trap of correcting the Bible?

The average independent Baptist pastor's sermons are often nothing more than a release of his own pent-up emotion. Do not misunderstand me. I am for emotion in teaching, preaching, and in listening to them both. But if there is no substance behind that emotion, if there is no explanation of and application of actual Scripture, the results produced will never last over the long term.

The average independent Baptist pastor's sermons are often nothing more than a release of his own pent-up emotion.

The problem is that the truths of Scripture do not generally lie on the surface. An infinite God authored an infinite Bible. What a shame it is to putter along the edge of the unmeasurable vastness that is the content of the Scriptures, being happy to simply play in the shallows. Is there truth at the edge? Yes, for it is all truth. But, oh, so much more truth lies further out! It is not a matter of being forced to choose between the false dichotomy of being a good preacher or a dull theologian. It is a matter of finding and delivering more of the truth that God wants His people to have.

Could you write a book if you needed to do so? I am not trying to be unreasonable here, but honestly consider the question. Is there any spiritual subject which you have studied out so thoroughly that you could actually write a book about it? One of the great indications of our movement's weakness is that not only the desire to write is missing but also the ability to write substantive tomes is spotty at best.

One of the great indications of our movement's weakness is that not only the desire to write is missing but also the ability to write substantive tomes is spotty at best.

The lack of writing is not only an indication of our problem but also a contributing factor. If our people want to read about grace or study the life of Christ or learn

Show me who you read, and I will show you where your church and ministry are going.

about holiness or discover the depth of the Pauline epistles, they must pick up an evangelical book to do so. Is it any wonder that independent, fundamental, Baptist churches are transitioning into contemporary evangelical ones by the dozen?

Show me who you read, and I will show you where your church and ministry are going. But how can our people read independent Baptist material if independent Baptists are not writing substantive books?

A dear friend of mine recently informed the world via social media that he had just read one of more well-known evangelical books of the last decade and that it was very good. He said, "This is one of the most powerful and challenging books that I've read in a long time. I don't know much about the author, but this book will move you."

As it turns out, the author does not use the KJV, embraces contemporary worship, co-writes books with the most egregious religious pragmatists of our day, and embraces a charismatic approach to spiritual gifts. Incredulous at his naiveté, I responded, "Leadership is influence. This book influenced you by your own admission. Why would you choose to follow a leader without first carefully establishing where he is, where he is going, and where he will influence you to go?"

His answer revealed the effect of the long term consequences that have come to our movement as a result of an under-emphasis on study. He said, "I partly agree. However, if I only read books by people in our circles, then I'd starve." He had apparently forgotten the vast wealth of previous generations but such is common in our historically ignorant day. And whether he should have read and recommended the particular book in question is not the point. The point is that he felt he had to read it if he was going to get anything of substance. It is illogical to expect younger preachers to remain deeply committed to a movement that produces very little worth reading to hold them.

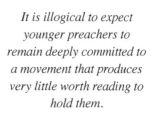

It is illogical to expect younger preachers to remain deeply committed to a movement that produces very little worth reading to hold them.

Holding people to the spiritually conservative traditions we cherish without the substance which comes only via the hard work of study is problematic at best. But entire wings of our movement attempt it, nonetheless. Thus it is that we so often fall back on the old support of hollering louder in the pulpit. Our young people abandon what they are taught, and our young preachers abandon the faith they were delivered. The only way we know to deal with that is to preach louder at them. Why? We have no why to give them. Why? We have not studied it out. In fact, we have preached suspicion of those who do. We have forgotten Paul's admonition to young Timothy, *The cloak that I left at Troas with Carpus, when thou comest, bring with thee, and the books, but especially the parchments. (II Timothy 4.13)*

Where are we wrong? In this, beloved: when our forefathers rushed away from the ditch of dead intellectualism, they propelled us toward the ditch of pragmatic activity. Now we think there is actually something unhealthy about a preacher who studies. Consequently, our movement is loud, wide, and active but has little depth of which to speak. And we are reaping the bitter fruit that has sprung from such ignorant seeds.

I Am of Paul

How can I act consistently, unless I receive and love all the
children of God, whom I esteem to be such,
of whatever denomination they may be?
-George Whitefield, letter to Mr. Thomas N, February 26, 1742

The church at Corinth was the most carnal church in the Bible.
In the two epistles Paul dedicates to straightening them out,
we plainly see they had a number of very serious issues. One of
those problems was their isolating tendency to group themselves in
ever-increasing fragments around one personality or another. *For
it hath been declared unto me of you, my brethren, by them which
are of the house of Chloe, that there are contentions among you.
Now this I say, that every one of you saith, I am of Paul; and I of
Apollos; and I of Cephas; and I of Christ. Is Christ divided? was
Paul crucified for you? or were ye baptized in the name of Paul?
(I Corinthians 1.11-13) For while one saith, I am of Paul; and
another, I am of Apollos; are ye not carnal? (I Corinthians 3.4)*

I gladly confess the Bible teaches ecclesiastical separation. I
realize *Amos* said, *Can two walk together, except they be agreed.*
But the same Scripture also says, *A new commandment I give unto
you, That ye love one another; as I have loved you, that ye also love
one another. By this shall all men know that ye are my disciples, if
ye have love one to another. (John 13.34-35)* To Jesus' admonition
in *John* is added Paul's in *Romans 12.10. Be kindly affectioned one
to another in brotherly love;…* Peter likewise chimes in. *Seeing ye
have purified your souls in obeying the truth through the Spirit unto*

unfeigned love of the brethren, see that ye love one another with a pure heart fervently. (I Peter 1.22) Not to be outdone Christianity's elder statesman, John, said, *For this is the message that ye heard from the beginning, that we should love one another. (I John 3.11)*

In wide segments of the independent Baptist movement, there is an elitism of fellowship. It insists that the only appropriate company for me and mine are those who believe exactly as I do. In word, such a position is denied; but in practice, it is vigorously embraced.

In a sense, I get it. I really do. We are separatists. It is in our DNA. As Fundamentalists, we long ago chose to take the path that others label as schismatic. But as with so many others of our weaknesses, this one also arises out of our own overreaction to others' errors. By definition, our forefathers separated over the fundamentals. Several generations later, we self-segregate over alma maters, national ministries, order of the Sunday morning service, and whether a man has pews or chairs in his auditorium. Separation for good reasons has become isolation for bad ones.

Separation for good reasons has become isolation for bad ones.

I believe Scripture teaches that I should choose my friends carefully. *He that walketh with wise men shall be wise: but a companion of fools shall be destroyed. (Proverbs 13.20)* But I do not necessarily have to develop a close friendship with any man in order to respect him, speak well of him, and view him as a brother in Christ.

Some men and ministries operate as if there were only two choices available: completely agree with me or you are the enemy. The truth is there are grades or levels of fellowship just as there are levels of friendship. A man of my acquaintance is not automatically either my best friend or my mortal enemy. He may be a good friend. He may be a friend I enjoy from time to time. He may be someone with whom I have limited interaction. He may be someone I respect from a distance, and I know that I must keep that distance in order to maintain that respect.

Somewhere along the line, we have gotten our concept of the enemy mixed up. The enemy has become the man who disagrees with me about some relatively minor aspect of doctrine and practice. The truth is our enemy is the devil and his minions. In theological terms, our enemies would be those who deny the deity of Christ, reject the atonement, water down the Word of God, doubt the Resurrection, and embrace a universal belief that all men go to Heaven. Such men reject ...*the faith which was once delivered unto the saints (Jude 3)* and have earned my contention. But if a man preaches the true doctrine of Christ according to the Bible, that man is my brother, not my enemy. *What then? notwithstanding, every way, whether in pretence, or in truth, Christ is preached; and I therein do rejoice, yea, and will rejoice. (Philippians 1.18)* He and I may differ on an issue or two or three, but that does not mean I must of necessity launch an all-out war against him. It means we keep a bit of distance, treat each other with respect, and go on about our business.

Our enemy is the devil and his minions.

Our tendency to go camping is yet another in a long line of visible evidences of our pride. It is as if we murmur to ourselves, "I am right, and you are wrong. Because you are wrong, I will attack you. Because I am right and only a few of us are smart, wise, and spiritual enough to perceive this right, my fellowship is severely limited." Of course, this is aggravated when every difference of opinion on doctrine and practice is interpreted as an attack on integrity and the entire course of a ministry. Oft times, balance in handling disagreement is sorely lacking on both sides of the exchange, and that touchiness has one root – pride.

After pastoring for nineteen years, I have unfortunately come to the sad conclusion that a number of men are independent Baptists not because they believe in the doctrines which underlie our position but simply because they disagree with everybody else. They are independent not out of conviction but out of sheer cussed stubbornness and arrogance.

For fifteen years or more, I have been active on various fundamentalist internet forums. My original purpose revolved around speaking up for the truths I believed in when it appeared that no one else would. Over time my involvement morphed into a genuinely respectful give and take with various members of the internet community who disagree with me on any number of important issues. I have found it helpful to have pushback against my understanding rather than just the near constant approval my church kindly offers me. After all, you cannot truly establish what you believe until those beliefs have been challenged.

I vividly recall one conversation or rather one statement in a conversation about a year ago. In that conversation, I expressed to the man on the other side of the screen that he and I were just on opposite sides of the aisle. In response he said, "When the persecution comes to America, I think you will discover we are actually on the same side."

He was completely right. God's family is full of men and women with whom I disagree on any number of issues, but they are still God's family. I will still share Heaven with them someday. They are still blood-bought children of God despite whatever else they may be wrong about. When the persecution comes to American Christianity, it will not be the independent Baptists alone standing up for truth, let alone the Baptists I allow inside my circle of fellowship.

Such facts compel me to offer our brethren in Christ my love and respect regardless of whether they dot my *i*'s or cross my *t*'s. There ought to be in God's people a largeness of spirit and a ready extension of charity and grace to all who hold the fundamental truths of Scripture.

Where are we wrong? In turning separatism into isolationism, in distorting contending for the faith into being contentious with others who preach the Gospel, and in allowing only two choices – best friend or full-blown enemy.

Irresponsible Evangelism

Let the servant of the Lord Jesus in this thing follow his Master,
and plough deep with a sharp ploughshare, which will not be
baulked by the hardest clods. This we must school ourselves to do.
If we really love the souls of men, let us prove it by honest speech.
The hard heart must be broken, or it will still refuse the Saviour
who was sent to bind up the broken-hearted. There are some things
which men may or may not have, and yet may be saved; but those
things which go with the ploughing of the heart are indispensable;
there must be a holy fear and a humble trembling before God,
there must be an acknowledgment of guilt and a penitent petition
for mercy; there must, in a word, be a thorough ploughing of the
soul before we can expect the seed to bring forth fruit.
-C. H. Spurgeon

Witnessing is a wonderful thing. It is obedience in work
clothes. It is an evidence of a genuine compassion for the
lost. It carries with it the potential to rescue a soul from hell and to
completely change the earthly, as well as the eternal destiny of a life.
But witnessing that is poorly done is hurtful to the cause of Christ.

Twenty-nine years ago, I went to my father and asked him to
teach me how to witness to the lost. I have been soul winning on
a regular basis for the entirety of the three decades since. In that
time, I have seen countless people join the soul-winning ranks
for a time only to leave them a little while later. Some quit soul
winning because they discover that it is hard work. Some quit
because they never learn how to conquer their fear. Others give

up in discouragement. Still others become backslidden, spiritual casualties. But many of the people who initially began to witness with great enthusiasm and zeal drop out because they became disenchanted with the sloppy soul winning they saw around them.

The overreaction of a man who stops soul winning because he thinks others do it poorly is not right. It does, however, happen and happen often. Irresponsible evangelism not only badly damages the sinner, but it also damages the cause so dear to the soul winner's heart – personal evangelism.

I do not question the boldness of irresponsible soul winners. Indeed, their aggressive take-no-prisoners approach has much to recommend it. As Paul, I covet your prayers so *...that utterance may be given unto me, that I may open my mouth boldly, to make known the mystery of the gospel. (Ephesians 6.19)* But boldness alone is not enough to overcome the errors of irresponsible evangelism.

Acts 18 tells us the story of a bold and eloquent man named Apollos. *And a certain Jew named Apollos, born at Alexandria, an eloquent man, and mighty in the scriptures, came to Ephesus. This man was instructed in the way of the Lord; and being fervent in the spirit, he spake and taught diligently the things of the Lord, knowing only the baptism of John. And he began to speak boldly in the synagogue: whom when Aquila and Priscilla had heard, they took him unto them, and expounded unto him the way of God more perfectly. And when he was disposed to pass into Achaia, the brethren wrote, exhorting the disciples to receive him: who, when he was come, helped them much which had believed through grace: For he mightily convinced the Jews, and that publickly, shewing by the scriptures that Jesus was Christ.* Apollos was bold, but boldness without careful and thorough accuracy is damaging.

> Boldness without careful and thorough accuracy is damaging.

In this sense, Apollos reminds me of the pharisaic Judaizers Paul dealt with in *Romans 10. Brethren, my heart's desire and prayer to God for Israel is, that they might be saved. For I bear them record that they have a zeal for God, but not according to knowledge.*

Like those Jews, Apollos had great zeal and boldness. I am sure his motivations were only the best. But his applied zeal was pointing people toward the wrong solution. In this case, Apollos referenced John the Baptist, who directed Israel toward faith in a generic coming messiah, but not to Jesus as that Messiah specifically. In so doing, Apollos was not helping people nearly as much as he thought he was nor was he helping his own cause. In a very real sense, by pointing people to John's concept, he ran the risk of inoculating them from being willing to transition that general faith in a coming messiah into a specific faith in Jesus as the Christ. Apollos was also weakening the church, in general; for a church must be built specifically and pointedly around Jesus Christ Himself.

I like bold soul winners. However, I do not like bold soul winners who witness without careful attention to detail and without a painstaking commitment to a thorough explanation of the Gospel.

Likewise, I do not generally question the motive of careless soul winners, either. Such people entertain an overwhelming desire to get people out of Hell. Others want to see their chosen ministry or church expand. Oh, I am sure some are motivated by pride, by a desire to be seen as a master soul winner, et al, but such immaturity is rather uncommon in the average church. Yet even those with exclusively good motivations for witnessing are not protected from wreaking spiritual havoc. Peter had a wonderful motivation when he pulled out his sword in the Garden of Gethsemane but his methods left much to be desired.

Just because you are bold in your witness does not mean you are correct. Just because you are motivated scripturally in your witness does not mean you are on target. Zeal without knowledge makes grievous mistakes.

For example, consider those who use salesmanship to manipulate people into a profession of faith. I have some acquaintance with that vocation, having made my living at various times selling knives, cemetery property, insurance, and cars. I held the importance of keeping a positive mental attitude. I set goals and hit them. I am familiar with the Socratic Method. I bought into the idea that "no" really means "I need some more information." I know how to talk a man into a decision and out of his money even when it is not in his best interests. But high pressure tactics in the spiritual realm usually produce nothing more than statistics.

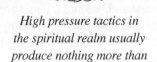

High pressure tactics in the spiritual realm usually produce nothing more than statistics.

One of the churches I attended years ago decided to try to replicate the day of Pentecost. As you know, three thousand people were saved and baptized on that day. Our church decided to do the same. My little part in this mission was to take an empty bus to the worst projects in town. I was to fill it up and drive to the church with fifty or so unsaved young people. I was to deliver these young people tbo a rented sports arena where the preacher would give a salvation message. Before returning the kids to the bus and thus to home, we were instructed to ensure that all of these young people were baptized after the invitation had been given.

Imagine for a moment the scene. Thousands of people unused to church were crammed into a building not acoustically designed for church. The average worker to rider ratio was about one to thirty. The service stayed just this side of pandemonium only with the help of frequent promises of cash prizes. At the invitation, all the people were instructed to repeat the sinner's prayer after the preacher. From the pulpit, instructions were given to the workers to herd their charges toward the swimming pools for baptism. I duly tried for thirty minutes before giving up and taking my increasingly restive group back to the projects.

Later that evening after all the activities of the day were over, the pastor of the church solemnly opened an envelope. To a cacophony of cheering and shouting, he told us that we had baptized more than three thousand people that day. Then turning to a guest speaker on the platform he said, "And all of these people were dealt with one on one out of an open Bible."

I sat there stunned in my seat. I was not stunned by the number but by the assertion that all of this was done carefully. The pastor was either lying or ignorant of how it really went down. I choose to believe the latter. Did those people – whom I never saw before and would never see again – hear the Gospel? Yes. The preaching was plain and clear. But the service was mass chaos, there was zero actual conversational give-and-take to ensure understanding, and the mass assent was primed and impersonal.

I have literally seen soul winners place their feet inside a door so as to prevent the homeowner from closing it. I have seen others simply read a tract word for word with no effort to ensure an adequate understanding. I have heard soul winners flail around their New Testament hunting for the next verse with no plan or apparent organized method behind their madness. I have heard soul winners complain that it took the ungodly sum of fifteen minutes in order to get a crowd of teenagers to pray.

Is it any wonder that independent Baptists are routinely attacked for these things?

"Where are they all?"

"You're just pluckin' green fruit."

"Oh, that's just easy believism."

"Numbers are all you guys are after."

"That's just 1-2-3-pray-after-me nonsense."

I have heard all of these criticisms more times than I care to count. Such criticisms are essentially incorrect. Each of them has a valid answer. None of these criticisms are valid reasons to give up on personal evangelism. But can we blame those who hurl them at us? We are so often guilty of dealing carelessly and hastily with the never dying souls in front of us. May God forgive us!

In so doing, not only have we damaged those whom we have dealt with in such a negligent manner, but we have also damaged the very concept of evangelism itself. Evangelism is or at least ought to be the heartbeat of the church. But many a Christian and many a church has looked at such methods as I have described and said, "Well, if that's evangelism, I want no part of it." In their self-righteous overreaction, they throw the baby out with the bathwater and embrace some hollow excuse for their own lack of witnessing. All the while, they are blaming us.

Four years after the special evangelism day I described above, we were tasked with doing something similar again. This time I had a little more pull. I set up my own system so as to ensure the results would be entirely different. Yes, I filled up an empty bus in the projects. But I recruited many more workers so our ratio was about one to three instead of one to thirty. On the way to church I had those workers carefully rotate through the seats. Their job was first to ensure that these people had not already made a profession of faith. I had no interest in "saving" people twice in order to drive up my numbers. Following that, they carefully went through the plan of salvation in very small groups. They were instructed to ask for understanding after each step. They were instructed to ask questions at the end to verify comprehension. Lastly, they were told to emphasize that repeating a prayer would get no one into Heaven if there was no heart belief behind the verbal profession. Following all of this, the service – which was in a much smaller venue with a much larger worker base – was almost an anticlimax. I personally talked to each person that rode my bus who made a profession of faith, verifying their understanding along with their willingness to be baptized. I do not remember how many people were saved and baptized on that occasion, but God gave us a wonderful day.

Fast forward with me twenty years. An independent Baptist pastor friend of mine in Iowa has completely rejected confrontational evangelism. In fact, he openly speaks out against it. Not coincidentally, he was in attendance on the first day I described above. On the other hand, an independent Baptist pastor friend of mine in New Mexico promotes personal evangelism. He has led his church to be a soul-winning church. He was also in attendance on the first day I described above, but in addition, he was in attendance on the second day, as well. I remember he came up to me afterward and asked for a word in private. He shared with me how much he was dreading the day due to his previous experiences and how blessed he was to see the day done conscientiously and well.

I could repeat these two pastoral examples with hundreds of names. So many people who used to embrace the wonderful independent Baptist emphasis on personal evangelism have walked away from it. And it is our own fault.

Beloved, let us prepare carefully. Let us take our time – all the time that is needed and more. Let us reject the easy temptation of manipulation, and seek instead the convicting presence of the Holy Spirit. Let us beware the canned speech reeled off with nary a response. Let us seek an actual conversation and a clear understanding. Let us not minimize the plan of salvation but rather maximize it. Let us not chase professions but heart belief. For the sake of their souls, for the sake of impressionable soul winners who look up to us, for the sake of the cause of evangelism, and for the sake of our Saviour Who shed His blood on that cross, let us do these things the right way.

As a teenager I was privy to an unusual conversation between another young soul winner and a very old preacher. The young soul winner, breathless with excitement, rushed up and said, "I just led a guy to the Lord, and he didn't even know it!" The old preacher looked down over his bifocals and simply said, "No you didn't, son."

I do not believe Scripture teaches one must undergo a month's worth of Bible studies before there can be an understanding of salvation. The thief on the cross, the woman at the well, and Nicodemus were all won to Christ during a single conversation. But I do believe there must be a solid grasp of the negative and positive truths of the Gospel message. Such must be established with painstaking care.

One of my college professors earned my undying affection for many reasons but one was this: he taught us to deal with everyone like we would want someone to deal with our own child. Twenty years later as the parent of three children who have all made a profession of faith under my own guidance, I feel the truth of that thought most keenly. Would to God it would be felt more widely.

Where are we wrong? In this: our inexcusably irresponsible evangelism.

We Call Young Men to Preach

If you can do anything else, then do it.
-C. H. Spurgeon

If you have not yet thrown this book against the wall in anger, this chapter just may drive you to it. Before you do, let me ask you a question. Who calls men into the ministry? God does, you say? Then why do not we let Him do it?

Let me tell you my story. I grew up in a pastor's home. Two months before I was born, my father became the pastor of an independent Baptist church in the Midwest. He remained at that church for nearly eighteen years before moving on to another church in a neighboring state for a further twenty years of ministry. I early learned to understand the PK (preacher's kid) label with all the good and bad that came with it.

One of the things on the negative side of this is the constant question a pastor's male children face: "Tommy, are you going to grow up and be a preacher like your dad?" I do not remember how old I was when I first heard that question, but it had to be earlier than first grade, I suppose. And it recurred with alarming frequency. They meant well, but the practical result in my heart was a determination not to be one if I could help it. Part of that was the natural pushback against pressure that every real man understands even at a young age. No one likes to be backed into a corner. Part of it was that as I grew up, I did not view my father as being very successful. (What an ignorantly ill-informed opinion I had then!) Part of it was my own natural inclination to move slowly and cautiously.

210

Not only did I face this question from the people around me at church, but I soon faced it from well-intentioned preachers as well. I began attending pastors' conferences with my father when I was about ten or eleven. It was common to hear, "Strike a match to your dreams and come down this aisle and surrender your life to the ministry." Conferences and youth rallies were considered a success based upon the number of young men who stood to be counted as called to preach. Preacher boy, as they were called, was about the highest position a young man could have in an independent Baptist youth group.

To my parent's everlasting credit I never faced any pressure from them. Not one time did my father ever ask me if I would consider being a preacher. Other churches had preacher boys clubs, but ours did not. The temptation for them must have been present. Years before, my mother (after four consecutive daughters) asked the Lord to send her a son and to make him a preacher, to boot. But she never whispered a word of that to me until I was practically a Bible college graduate.

The upshot of all of this – constant questions as to whether I was called to preach combined with my own natural inclination to push back – was a deliberate and very private consideration over a period of some years of whether I ought to be a preacher or not. I mulled it over in my mind as I strolled along delivering my afternoon papers. I contemplated it while watching the evening sun stream through the windows at church. I thought about it in detail during every invitation at every conference and youth rally I attended.

The summer before I entered high school I attended a Christian camp in southern Ohio. A group of several different churches had gone in together to rent the facility and put on a week of activity and preaching for their young people. My church was not one of them, but many of my Christian school friends were going. I wanted to go as well. Although my family was actually on summer vacation at the time, my father consented to go out of his way to drop me off on Monday and to return late Friday night to pick me up.

I enjoyed myself immensely. The food was good; the games were fun; the skits were entertaining; the girls were pretty; the fellowship was great; the preaching was highly entertaining. The boys sat on the left side of the tabernacle, and I early claimed ownership of the seat closest to the pulpit on the very front row.

Friday night came all too soon. I expected some sort of special invitation for young men to surrender to preach, but I had no idea just how unusual it would be. After a normal service and the beginning of a normal invitation, a commotion arose in the back of the tabernacle. A group of men dressed in fatigues with hoods over their faces burst into the back and began firing weapons. The song leader was blown away. A youth pastor jumped up to defend his preacher only to share the same fate. In mere moments, all of the preachers were lying in a tangle of limbs on the platform. I can still see in my mind's eye one particular teenage girl unknown to me, tears flowing, mouth open in a horrific scream.

At this point, the lead terrorist walked to the pulpit, took his hood off, and revealed himself to be one of the youth pastors. One by one, the supposedly dead preachers rose up to stand with him. Standing on the front row, surrounded by men in fatigues with the smell of gunpowder blanks still on the air, the real invitation was held. America was going to hell. If we boys did not surrender to the ministry, the Communists would surely take over, and this scenario would become an actual one. If the girls did not surrender to be preacher's wives, their doom would inevitably come.

I write this now from a vantage point nearly thirty years removed. In my mind, I am still seated on the front row watching as dozens of boys stream past me – most in tears – vowing to be the preachers necessary to save America from destruction. I distinctly remember sitting in my front row seat closest to the pulpit and thinking to myself, "Do they understand what they are doing? Do they realize the commitment they are making? Do they realize how this decision must change everything?"

Long into the invitation, only a few boys remained seated. I was one of them. As was my custom, I was interrogating myself to see if this was really what I wanted in life. Yes, I yielded to the Lord's call that night. When most of the boys had exited the altar and platform that night, my dad found me on my knees in tears. I gave in. I surrendered. I made the decision to become a preacher.

Some of you who read this are horrified. Others of you are thinking, "What's the big deal then? You surrendered, didn't you? And here you are years later preaching the Gospel. It all works." The pragmatism and spiritual immaturity of the second response is alarming. It does not work at all. The reasons I am still preaching thirty years later have nothing at all to do with the effectiveness of that invitation that night. It has much more to do with my mother's prayers, my father's respectful treatment of me, and my own deliberate consideration of the question and its consequences over a lengthy period. In other words, God's call and its effective outworking on my life had nothing to do with that invitation.

In a context that has direct bearing on this discussion, Jesus stood before a massive crowd of people, asked, *For which of you, intending to build a tower, sitteth not down first, and counteth the cost, whether he have sufficient to finish it? (Luke 14.28)* The independent Baptist movement for decades ignored that passage to our peril.

Six years after that summer, I was driving back to my dormitory room after an afternoon shift at the steel mill. For some reason, my mind turned to those days. I began to reckon the position of those young men who shared that altar with me that night. I knew so many of them so very well. Gradually, it dawned on me that the only one of the boys out of the forty or so that surrendered that night who was still preaching was me. Just six years later, the medium term *effectiveness* (if you can call it that) of the invitation that night was two and a half percent.

I do not generally measure things by their practical result. There are more reasons to be against such manipulation than just the eventual outcome. But even just using that weak measuring stick, the aftermath is brutal. Independent Baptist Bible colleges in America are filled with young men preparing for the ministry who are no more called to it than my lawn chair is, and then we wonder why the spirit is bad, the rules are flouted, and the work of learning the ministry is not taken seriously at all. Meanwhile, back in their home church, the guy who surrendered as a teenager but did not even make it to Bible college has most likely dropped out of church entirely. He feels like a failure. He has no desire to preach, but he knows he faces the constant scrutiny of his church if he shows no inclination to do so. In response, he just quits on God altogether. Still others persevere all the way through to the ministry out of sheer character only to quit when difficulties arise. In their wake, they leave a raft of the floating wreckage of disappointed churches, hurt teenagers, despairing wives, and confused children.

That is not all. If I have gotten anything across to you in this book at all, it is our tendency to overreact, to swing from the ditch on one side of the road to the ditch on the other. Increasingly, parents in our generation are resisting the entire idea of their children entering into ministry at all. In some entire sections of American Christianity, there are few, if any, young people surrendering to ministry. In a very real sense, this is a backlash against the manipulative tactics the parents endured as teenagers growing up in our movement. A forest properly managed will yield wood for generations. If you clear cut it, your initial results will be staggering; but nothing of any substance will ever grow there again. Youth groups all across America that were clear cut by manipulative preachers in the last generation no longer yield any young people for ministry.

Youth groups all across America that were clear cut by manipulative preachers in the last generation no longer yield any young people for ministry.

On my very first day of my very first class of my very first year of Bible college, my professor asked the entire class to stand. He then went through the class, counting carefully, and asked three fourths of us to sit down. He then informed the class that the ones standing would be the ones to graduate. Following this sober wakeup call, he counted carefully again and asked others to sit down at a ratio of ten to one. It looked like a corn field after harvest with only the stray stalk vertical here and there. Looking out at us, he calmly informed us that these would be the ones left in the ministry ten years after graduation. Two decades after my own college commencement, I agree with his percentages.

Beloved, there is something deeply amiss in a movement when only one in ten of the men and women who enter our Bible colleges in order to train expressly for the ministry are actually still in it at the age of thirty. A ninety percent casualty rate will lose the war every single time.

I believe in the call to preach. Do not count me with the numbers who say there is no such thing in the New Testament. Paul said, *...it pleased God, who separated me from my mother's womb, and called me by his grace, To reveal his Son in me, that I might preach him among the heathen;... (Galatians 1.15-16)* God gifts men to His church to lead it. *(Ephesians 4.11)* But it is God that must do this calling, not men. *...he counted me faithful, putting me into the ministry;... (I Timothy 1.12)* I am not supposed to put myself into the ministry, nor am I to put any other man into the ministry. That is the Lord's work. *As they ministered to the Lord, and fasted, the Holy Ghost said, Separate me Barnabas and Saul for the work whereunto I have called them. (Acts 13.2)* The Holy Spirit does not work through an atmosphere of emotional manipulation. He works through a still, small voice.

Where are we wrong? In this, my friends: we call young men to preach when it is not our place to issue that call. It is only our place to ask each person to consider that call. It is His effectual work in the heart that moves a man to put his hand to the plow. Let Him do that work.

We Wrap Ourselves in the Flag

Some Christians worried about a faith that was so embracing as
to be meaningless, that exalted not the Almighty so much as the
American way of life. When civil religion bleached the
challenge from faith and left behind a watery patriotism,
there was room for concern.
-Nancy Gibbs; Michael Duffy, *The Preacher and the Presidents:*
Billy Graham in the White House

Patriotism is a good thing. Love for country was commended
by implication when Jesus healed the Roman centurion's servant in *Luke 7*. There is clearly a national aspect to New Testament
Christianity. The Christian is commanded in Scripture to pray for
his country's leadership *(I Timothy 2.2-3)*, and to be in submission to them. *(Romans 13.1-2)* We are also to honor them with the
respect due God's ministers. *(I Peter 2.17)*

By the same token, however, patriotism – while implied as
acceptable in Scripture – is clearly outweighed in our understanding by the stress the New Testament places upon our allegiance to Heaven. The simple truth is we do not belong here. As
the old song says so well:

> This world is not my home, I'm just a-passing through.
> My treasures are laid up somewhere beyond the blue.
> The angels beckon me from Heaven's open door.
> And I can't feel at home in this world anymore.

The great example of this in both the Old and New Testament is Abraham as told in *Hebrews 11*. *By faith he sojourned in the land of promise, as in a strange country,...* The Promised Land was strange to him, not because it was new but because he was homesick for Heaven. *For he looked for a city which hath foundations, whose builder and maker is God.* This Heaven-ward focus, this loyalty and longing toward Heaven, produced in Abraham the same feeling of rootlessness as our Pilgrim forefathers felt in Holland. *These all died in faith, not having received the promises, but having seen them afar off, and were persuaded of them, and embraced them, and confessed that they were strangers and pilgrims on earth.* Ur was no longer home, and even Canaan did not satisfy Abraham. *For they that say such things declare plainly that they seek a country.* What country? They seek the new Heaven and the new Earth. *But now they desire a better country, that is, an heavenly: wherefore God is not ashamed to be called their God: for he hath prepared for them a city.*

This concept – a loyalty outside of and greater than our allegiance to our native land – was passed on by Abraham and Sarah to their descendants. *...Jacob said unto Pharaoh, The days of the years of my pilgrimage are an hundred and thirty years. (Genesis 47.9)* A thousand years later, David grasped this essential truth as well. *Thy statutes have been my songs in the house of my pilgrimage. (Psalm 119.54)* Nor is such a theme limited to Old Testament examples. Peter plainly instructs God's people to hold the same worldview. *Dearly beloved, I beseech you as strangers and pilgrims,... (I Peter 2.11)*

What does it mean to be a pilgrim? The clearest answer is illustrated in the word "pilgrimage." One of the five pillars of Islam is that each Muslim must undertake a religious journey to Saudi Arabia at least once in his lifetime. They refer to this as the Hajj, the pilgrimage to Mecca. This is the sense in which Scripture uses it. The idea is that we are not from here; we are only journeying through this life on our way to a much better life in our heavenly home.

Somewhere along the line, however, a large majority of the independent Baptist movement appeared to forget this entire truth.

Baptist fundamentalism with its strong Southern roots saw the old way of life threatened both within and without. On the outside were first the scary Communists and then the frightening terrorists. On the inside were the dirty liberals. To fight the external threat, we militantly embraced the Cold War and the war on terror. To fight the internal threat, we resisted the Civil Rights Act, busing, Roe v. Wade, the Equal Rights Amendment, and the growing influence of Hollywood, rock music, and the homosexual movement.

One entire wing of the independent Baptist movement lost its way entirely in its eagerness to put Ronald Reagan in the White House. A leading Baptist mega-church pastor formed a nationwide coalition bent on restoring decency and morality in America. A related yet different branch of independent Baptists rejected political activism but nonetheless explicitly embraced saving America as the goal. Young men must surrender to preach in order to save America. Young women must surrender to be pastor's wives in order to help those pastors save America. Churches must be started in order to save America. *II Chronicles 7.14* became the theme of the day. (Never mind the fact that it contextually relates only to national Israel. Certainly, it reveals principles of how God operates and honors prayer; but we cannot use it to claim that God will restore America to spiritual health.) Rallies and conferences were organized so that we might take America back. Enormous American flags dropped dramatically from the ceiling during invitations. We talked about Jesus, but we motivated people to respond not with the Holy Spirit but with the saccharine substitute of patriotism.

We talked about Jesus, but we motivated people to respond not with the Holy Spirit but with the saccharine substitute of patriotism.

Beloved, I beg of you not to misunderstand me. I am grieved that the America I knew as a boy is dead. On a recent family vacation to Washington D.C., I felt all week like I was whistling past a graveyard of the bones and monuments of an America that used to be. I stand when someone sings the Star-Spangled Banner. An American flag graces the platform of my independent Baptist church. Another flag flutters from the flagpole out front. I have voted in every election since I became eligible at the age of eighteen. Our church supports a Christian legal ministry that fights to preserve what is left of our freedom. I take my children to the cemetery for the Memorial Day observances. I happily recite the Pledge of Allegiance. For ten years, a picture of George Washington kneeling at Valley Forge graced the wall of my office until a pressing need for more bookshelves forced a rearrangement. Accompanying it were framed copies of the Constitution and the Declaration of Independence. I have walked the trenches of Yorktown where our country was born and the haunting fields at Gettysburg where it was saved. I have stood with spine-tingling respect in Independence Hall in Philadelphia. I know our history. I cherish our heritage, and I love our country.

Deeper than all of this, though, much deeper, lies my love for God and my loyalty to Heaven. My purpose in life is not to rescue America. I dare not lead my church to think this is their purpose, either. Neither can I motivate them to action by so doing. In a very real sense, I am to approach this life as if the place I am living – mine own, my native land – is simply a temporary stop on my pilgrimage toward home.

I love America more than I love any other country. I have the precious privilege of pastoring many first generation immigrants. Their love for America shines bright and fierce. But my theology forces me to admit that God does not love America more than any other country. There is zero scriptural indication that God is interested in saving America any more than He was interested in saving Carthage, Rome, or Genghis Khan's Mongolian empire. God has a special attachment to His people, the church. God has a special attachment to His people, Israel, and the land He long ago bequeathed to them. Beyond that, His great concern is His own glory and the never dying souls of men. *And they sung a new song, saying, Thou art worthy to take the book, and to open the seals thereof: for thou wast slain, and hast redeemed us to God by thy blood out of every kindred, and tongue, and people, and nation. (Revelation 5.9)* Americans, as people, are on this list; but so is every other ethnicity and nationality on the planet. The American culture and way of life are not.

God did not call me to live for America. He did not call me to sacrifice myself for America or for the restoration of what I think America ought to be. My Lord did not commission me to spend my life for my country. He called me to seek His kingdom first. Everything else – including my native land – must be viewed through this prism.

Where are we wrong? In this: we wrapped our movement in the American flag when we should have wrapped it in the Christian one. We pinned our hopes and dreams on national restoration. We motivated our young people to service with the Stars and Stripes. In so doing – as in all things unscriptural – we failed spectacularly. Let us not double down. Let us turn our focus toward Heaven. Yes, let there be a tear in our eye for what America used to be. Yes, let us be law-abiding citizens. Let us teach our children our history. Let us honor and pray for our leaders. Let us fight to retain what remains of our freedom. But more importantly, let us cultivate an attitude of pilgrimage.

America is not our home; Heaven is.

Pharisees Thrive

The folly of Israel lay in this, that they thought of only one
demon – him of idolatry – Beel-Zibbul, with all his foulness.
That was all very repulsive, and they had carefully removed it...
But this house, swept of the foulness of heathenism and adorned
with all the self-righteousness of Pharisaism, but empty of God,
would only become a more suitable and more secure habitation
of Satan; because, from its cleanness and beauty, his presence
and rule there as an evil spirit would not be suspected...and thus
the last state – Israel without the foulness of gross idolatry and
garnished with all the adornments of Pharisaic devotion to the
study and practice of the Law – was really worse than had been
the first with all its open repulsiveness.
-Alfred Edersheim, *Life and Times of Jesus the Messiah*

In one sense, it is completely unfair to label any independent Baptist a Pharisee. Theologically speaking, the modern
day equivalent is orthodox Judaism. The arc of the life of Christ
can accurately be viewed as a struggle between Him and the
Pharisees for the soul of the Jewish people. Both wanted to be
Israel's shepherd. Both offered compelling and influential arguments. Both could not succeed. When the Sanhedrin (the corporate representation of national Israel) formally chose to assassinate
Christ, God's people went along with their decision. In so doing,
national Israel unknowingly committed suicide. In the century after
Christ's Resurrection, great destruction came upon Israel via the
Roman Empire. When her Temple – the center of Jewish life – was

destroyed, she ceased to exist as a national entity; and her people were scattered. The broken fragments that were left largely chose to continue to follow the Pharisees in their long and wandering exile, and Judaism was born. And even the most doctrinally challenged and practically foolish independent Baptists I know are poles apart from orthodox Judaism.

That being said, it is also true that there is often a wretched application amongst independent Baptists of the Pharisees' philosophies, emphases, and practices. Let me sketch some of these pharisaical mistakes for you. As I do, see if some independent Baptist practices come to your mind as well.

Perhaps the best passage in the entire Bible that sums up Jesus' abhorrence of the Pharisees is *Luke 11.37-54*. Jesus and His Apostles are on a preaching trip through Judea in the months immediately prior to His crucifixion. Along the way, in some village, He was invited to eat at a local Pharisee's house. This sounds strange, but hospitality was ingrained in their culture. From the Pharisee's perspective, Jesus would be on the Pharisee's turf. It would give him an opportunity to berate Jesus at worst or to convince Him of the error of His ways at best. In so doing, said Pharisee got much more than what he bargained for on this occasion.

What is so remarkable about *Luke 11.37-54* is the utter vehemence with which Jesus tore into the Pharisees. It is matched or exceeded on only one other occasion in His entire ministry. It seems on the surface to be completely disproportionate. The Pharisees reprove Him for His lack of ritual washing before the meal, and His response is a veritable tirade of accusation and judgment that goes on for the rest of the chapter. If you did not know better, you would think Jesus was having a bad day and lost His temper. Of course, that is not the case but something clearly set Jesus off here; therefore, it behooves us to look at this a little more closely.

For years now, the Pharisees have been not only antagonistic to Jesus personally but taking the Jewish people that He loved so much in the absolute wrong direction religiously. They viewed Moses' Law with such reverence that they referred to it as the garden of the Torah. In their view, the best way to protect such a garden from being violated was to erect a tall and sturdy fence of extra-biblical instructions outside of that garden. In other words, to protect Israel from violating the Torah, they instituted a complex system of precepts designed to keep God's people well short of failing to obey the actual Law itself. Their desire to erect an extra-biblical fence around the garden of the Torah had resulted in a religion that was full of an astounding number of rules and a religion that tore the heart out of the people's obedience to the Lord.

On the occasion of *Luke 11.37-54* – that of a meal – it will better help us to understand them if we learn their approach. The psalmist said, *The earth is the Lord's and the fulness thereof. (Psalm 24.1)* Thus in their view, if you ate without thanking the Lord for the food, you were stealing. So far so good. But they then muddied the waters by seeking to ascertain if a separate blessing was needed over each item. Or did just the principle item need to be blessed? If it is just the principle item, how do you determine that? Does this perhaps depend on the dish and the ingredients in the dish? Now we have classes of items which we have ranked in order of importance so we can know when to bless which one. Unfortunately, each ingredient and each class also brings with it the opportunity for tremendous theological argument. Which blessing should be used for which ingredient when?

This sounds silly to us, but to the rabbis of Jesus' day, this was prime debating territory. For instance, the schools of Hillel and Shammai had a terrific row about whether the blessing should be said over the berries or the leaves of the caper plant. And this was just about the blessing before the meal! There were similar kinds of pharisaic theological arguments over who should sit where and who ought to wash in what way, in what order, and at what times. It was all a useless preoccupation with completely superfluous details, and it was further set within the context of a religious group that totally missed the main points of the Law.

The Pharisees had chosen to spend an exhaustive amount of time and energy debating and establishing arcane rules for items of minute importance. Meanwhile, they had completely neglected the matters of primary importance in the Scripture. On this day in that Judean Pharisees' home, Jesus has had enough. He is driven to a sudden, justifiable, righteous anger at their whole religious system. In the process, He reveals several specific areas of pharisaic failure.

Placing a Premium on the External
to the Neglect of the Internal

The first error with which Christ reproached the Pharisees was that of placing a premium on the external to the neglect of the internal. *And the Lord said unto him, Now do ye Pharisees make clean the outside of the cup and the platter; but your inward part is full of ravening and wickedness. Ye fools, did not he that made that which is without make that which is within also? (Luke 11.39-40).*

This is exceptionally strong language even for Christ, but He was plainly justified in His choice of words. How foolish it is to painstakingly ensure the outside of a dirty cup is carefully washed while all the while ignoring the filth on the inside! Certainly, I want any dish I pick up to be clean on both the outside and the inside; but of the two, the inside is the more important.

In this we see the same theme that has come up so often in His ministry, and that is the importance of the heart. In my book on the Sermon on the Mount, *The Greatest Sermon Ever Preached,* I bring this out in great detail. In a sense, it is the very core of that most famous of sermons. But Jesus must needs repeatedly emphasize this, not because Jesus did not care about the external but because the Pharisees did not care about the internal. What we see so often in American Christianity is the unbalanced mistake of being in a ditch on one side of the road or the other. Contrarily, what we see so often in Scripture is a balanced approach, one which takes into account the importance of both the inside and the outside.

Let us take the thorny example of women's dress, for instance. Take a walk through any mall in America, and you will see attractive women parading around in all sorts of short, tight, low, high, or revealing attire. Worse than that, however, is that you can see similar attire on almost any contemporary church youth group activity. Woe betide any preacher who dares to address the subject. He is quickly shouted down with references to legalism, liberty, grace, and "nunya business" as if the Bible is completely silent about the subject of how women ought to dress.

The simple truth is that the Bible does address it. *In like manner also, that women adorn themselves in modest apparel,... (I Timothy 2.9)* We may disagree over where to draw the line in relation to modest apparel, but we cannot disagree that there is a line and that God's Word explicitly commands women to dress modestly.

However, by the same token, there are independent Baptists in my experience who take great care to ensure that their women dot all the *i*'s and cross all the *t*'s when it comes to modesty. Yet these same independent Baptists sadly and completely fail to emphasize much at all the importance of the heart. Woe betide the preacher who dares to address that subject. In turn, he is also quickly shouted down with references to weakening standards, greasy grace, and neo-evangelicalism as if the Bible is completely silent about the condition of a woman's heart.

The simple truth is that the Bible does address it. *Whose adorning let it not be that of outward adorning of plaiting the hair, and of wearing of gold, or of putting on of apparel; But let it be the hidden man of the heart, in that which is not corruptible, even the ornament of a meek and quiet spirit, which is in the sight of God of great price. (I Peter 3.3-4)* We may disagree over what exactly a meek and quiet spirit means and what are the evidences and foundations of an incorruptible heart, but we cannot disagree that these are an absolute necessity and that God's Word explicitly commands women to cultivate them.

I do not think God's people ought to ink themselves with gang tattoos, wear clothing with swear words, or run around half naked. There is an emphasis on modesty and propriety and a clean-cut exterior in the Word of God that is sorely lacking in today's culture, both secular and Christian. But you can dress up your exterior to a modest and Christian fare-thee-well and still be as wicked as the devil inside.

The Pharisees were foolish in Jesus' view, not because they emphasized an external cleanliness but because they did so while completely ignoring the inward *hidden man of the heart*. The solution to this great pharisaic error is not to abandon any teaching or correction in relation to the visible part of life but to place, without fail, a tremendous emphasis on the invisible part of life.

Holiness is being like Christ. That does not come natural to humanity. We are greatly blessed in that He has furnished us with the Holy Spirit-enabled grace to do what is unnatural in order to progress in holiness. But a holiness that is never seen by others is not a genuine holiness. A holiness that is only tacked up like a false front is not a genuine holiness, either.

Let us make clean the outside of the cup, but let us also at the same time make clean the inside of the cup.

When we as strict standard enforcing independent Baptists only talk about the outside we are as foolish as the Pharisees were.

> *A holiness that is never seen by others is not a genuine holiness. A holiness that is only tacked up like a false front is not a genuine holiness, either.*

Majoring on the Minors

The second error with which Christ reproached the Pharisees was that of majoring on the minors. *But woe unto you, Pharisees! For ye tithe mint and rue and all manner of herbs, and pass over judgment and the love of God: these ought ye to have done, and not to leave the other undone. (Luke 11.42)*

My small city garden is going gangbusters this year. It includes two kinds of peppers, green beans, zucchini, tomatoes, and, yes, mint. In fact, I just had a tremendous helping of green beans and a slice of zucchini bread for lunch today courtesy of this little garden. Now that I am thinking about it, I just may make myself some mint iced tea after a while. But what I probably will not do is count all my mint leaves and make sure one out of every ten ends up in the offering plate next Sunday.

The Pharisees though were keen on exactly this kind of persnickety adherence to the letter of the Torah's admonitions regarding tithing. Interestingly enough, Jesus does not condemn them for it saying, *these ought ye to have done.* But He does fervently condemn them because while they counted and tithed their garden produce, they completely failed to emphasize the love of

God. And in the big scheme of things, the love of God is a much bigger part of the Scripture than is tithing your garden produce. The Pharisees had made the classic mistake of majoring on something relatively unimportant while at the same time ignoring that which should have been highlighted.

Years ago in our little country church in rural Pennsylvania, a young couple visited and then came back several more times. They were immediately noticeable because the wife wore a head covering. My wife and I invited them over to our home, and we spent some time with them in an effort to welcome them into our church. At first, things went swimmingly until I discovered that even though both of them had been saved since they were children, neither one had yet been baptized. Knowing full well that this is the very first step of obedience for the new Christian and is repeatedly mentioned in the New Testament, I began to try to convince them to accept baptism. Curiously enough, although they acknowledged the validity of baptism, they refused to submit to it. Instead, they contented themselves with a Christianity that consisted of visiting a round of local churches in order to enjoy the singing and occasional fellowship they found. And, of course, wearing a head covering was enjoyed also.

It is true that Paul instructs women in *I Corinthians 11.5* to pray with their head covered. I happen to believe that this head covering consists of a women's long hair *(I Corinthians 11.15)*, but if a woman of my acquaintance believes differently and wears a head covering, I am not going to quarrel with her about it. What I do find to be utterly backwards is a woman who insists on obeying this relatively minor instruction – mentioned only one time in Scripture – at all costs. At the same time, she rebelliously refuses to obey the very first command God gives Christians; it is a command emphasized dozens of times in the New Testament.

Years ago, I heard Clarence Sexton, pastor of the Temple Baptist Church in Knoxville, Tennessee, say that we ought to place the emphasis in our ministry where God places the emphasis. That statement rang true with me, and I set about seeking to discover what God emphasizes the most. What I have since learned I seek to replicate in my life and in my church. It has been a wonderful study and application. While I am not at all sure I have succeeded in it, I am sure that I am trying.

Rabbit trails and hobbyhorses make for entertaining preaching, but they also make for shallow movements and weak Christians, a phrase which all too often describes entire sections of the independent Baptist movement. I meet them all the time. They carry the biggest King James Bible you have ever seen. They proudly wave it around to all and sundry, but their families are a colossal disaster spiritually. There is no love, grace, or wisdom exhibited in their lives. They can and do vigorously debate the finer points of the *Textus Receptus,* but they have not fed a hungry person in years. They eschew vanity in their outward apparel with exactitude, but their mouth regularly dispenses razor sharp gossip that slices to pieces those around them. They well up with tears at the Southern Gospel concert as the group sings about Heaven, but they have not cried over their own or anybody else's sins at an invitation altar in decades.

> We ought to place the emphasis in our ministry where God places the emphasis.
> -Clarence Sexton

Such an unbalanced faith never moves one to spiritual maturity. Beloved, let us beware of this tremendous pharisaic mistake. We cannot afford to turn spiritual molehills into mountains nor mountains into molehills. Let us place the emphasis where God places the emphasis. Let us not ignore any aspect of Scripture, but let us endeavor to lay it before other people and live it out in our lives with the same sense of proportion with which God gave it to us. It is the only way we can truly be biblical Christians.

An Untenable Religious System

Another error with which Christ reproached the Pharisees was that of having an untenable religious system. In other words, their approach produced in practice an unworkable religion. *And he said, Woe unto you also, ye lawyers! for ye lade men with burdens*

grievous to be borne, and ye yourselves touch not the burdens with one of your fingers. (Luke 11.46)
The Pharisees originated with sincere intentions. Some good men in the centuries before Christ saw Hellenization taking over their unique Torah-based culture and fought back by emphasizing a strict interpretation and application of the Law. In their view of the Law as a garden that contained wonderful flowers, they believed it needed protection from the encroaching Greek and Roman cultures. They well remembered the deep flaws of their great grandparents in the days before the Babylonian Captivity which saw Jewish monotheism under incredible assault from idolatry. They remembered the mixed multitude of Nehemiah's day and admired the great lengths to which he went to maintain the religious and moral purity of the Jewish people.

In the minds of these early Pharisees, it thus made great sense to put their unbreakable fence of various detailed rules and regulations around the lovely garden of the Torah so as to protect it and, by default, the Jewish people's loyalty to it. Somehow, they found a way to the erection of this fence via an oral Torah which the first rabbi, Moses, had supposedly issued alongside that of the written Torah when he came down from Mount Sinai. In one fell, albeit gradual swoop, the Pharisees thus became the self-appointed custodian for the religious, cultural, moral, and ethnic soul of Israel.

One of the great problems with the system they produced, however, was the very justification which produced it. If a fence that kept you six feet away, metaphorically speaking, from violating the garden of the Torah was good, then one that kept you twelve feet away was even better. If a five foot high fence was good, then a ten foot high fence was better. There was a foundational rationale for producing an ever more complex and minute series of instructions designed to ensure that people did not violate the Law of Moses.

The result by Jesus' day was a system that was practically impossible to actually obey. For instance, examine briefly the Pharisees approach to keeping the Sabbath. It was absolutely incredible. It is certainly true that the Torah forbids working on the Sabbath. *Remember the sabbath day; to keep it holy. Six days shalt thou labour, and do all thy work: But the seventh day is the sabbath of the LORD thy God: in it thou shalt not do any work, thou, nor thy son, nor thy daughter, thy manservant, nor thy maidservant, nor thy cattle, nor thy stranger that is within thy gates. (Exodus 20.8-10)* But the Pharisees had taken this relatively straightforward commandment and fenced it in with numerous regulations so as to make it absolutely ridiculous.

J. W. Shepard, a twentieth century Southern Baptist missionary and professor said it this way in his book *The Christ of the Gospels*: "There was no institution among the Jews regarded with more veneration and scrupulosity than that of the Sabbath. It was a divinely ordained and beneficent part of the Mosaic economy, designed for the rest of man and for his worship and service to God... Beginning with sunset on Friday, announced by three trumpet blasts from the Temple and synagogue, it ended at sunset on Saturday. All food must be prepared, all vessels washed, all lights kindled, and all tools laid aside. There were restrictions laid down in the Mosaic law; but the Rabbis had elaborated from these a vast array of injunctions and prohibitions, making of the Sabbath law a veritable bondage. Moses said: "Thou shalt not do any work." The Rabbis made out a system of thirty-nine works, which done rendered the offender subject to death by stoning. Derived from these "father-works" were numerous "descendant-works." One of the "father-works" was ploughing: a son of this was "digging." Wearing false teeth was a "descendant" of "carrying a burden." Among the descendants of "reaping" were the "plucking of a head of wheat" or the "pulling out of a grey hair" from one's head. Lengthy rules were formulated about what kind of knots one might tie on the Sabbath. The camel-driver's and sailor's knots might not be tied or unloosed. Two letters of the alphabet might not be written together. To kindle or extinguish a fire was a great desecration, not being justified even in case of the emergency of sickness. The Sabbath had become a grievous burden by the thousands of restrictions and rules too numerous to mention."

To this, Edersheim adds in his classic *Life and Times of Jesus the Messiah*: "For example, it was forbidden to draw a chair along the ground lest it should make a rut; and although it was permissible to spit on a pavement and rub the expectoration with the foot,

it was debated whether it were permissible to perform the operation on the earth, inasmuch as the foot would scratch the surface...
To walk on a crutch or a wooden leg was permissible; but to go on
stilts was forbidden, since it was not the stilts that carried the man
but the man that carried the stilts...A tailor must not go abroad with
his needle nor a scribe with his pen toward sunset on Friday, lest the
Sabbath should begin ere his return and find him abroad with his
burden... An ordinary Sabbath day's journey extended 2000 cubits
beyond one's dwelling. But if at the boundary of that "journey" a
man deposited on the Friday food for two meals, he thereby consti-
tuted it his dwelling, and hence might go for another 2000 cubits...
Supposing a traveler to arrive in a place just as the Sabbath com-
menced, he must only take from his beast of burden such objects as
are allowed to be handled on the Sabbath. As for the rest, he may
loosen the ropes and let them fall down of themselves."

There were twenty-four entire chapters of the Talmud devoted
to the specific rules related to what you could and could not do
on the Sabbath. For instance, you could not carry a burden, and a
burden was defined as the weight of a fig. But if you divided the
fig in half and carried it twice, it was legal on the Sabbath. If water
fell on a dress you could shake it, but you do could not wring it out.
Chapter after chapter is dedicated to such nonsensical specificity,
and the Talmud itself speaks approvingly of one particular rabbi
who spent two-and-a-half years studying just one of these chapters.

If we take the time to look at the specifics, we discover a veritable mountain of instructional data. If a woman was handling or
cooking grain on the Sabbath and she rolled it to remove the husk,
it was considered sifting or working. If she rubbed the head, it was
considered threshing or working. If she bruised the ear, it was considered grinding or working. If she tossed the kernel in her hand,
it was considered winnowing or working. If she dropped a stalk of
grain, she was not allowed to bend over and pick it up. That was –
you guessed it – considered working. However, the learned scribes
had determined that if she then dropped a spoon on top of the
stalk of grain she had already dropped and since she was allowed
to carry a spoon on the Sabbath, she could bend over, pick up the
spoon, and pick up the grain with the spoon at the same time. Was

not it thoughtful of them to provide such a creative outlet for getting around their own draconian rules?

We can see in this just how much Rabbinism had produced a system in which an incredible amount of study was done in order to make sure one really obeyed God. At the same time, an incredible amount of ingenuity was contrived in order to get around all the rules with which they had tied themselves up in knots. *For they bind heavy burdens and grievous to be borne, and lay them on men's shoulders';...(Matthew 23.4)*

I realize I did not grow up with such a system from my youth, but I do not see for the life of me how in the world one could possibly make sure they kept every single one of those rules perfectly! The burden – for such it was and a great one – that rabbinic pharisaism placed on the back of the people of Israel was impossible to carry.

> *In our zealousness to preserve for God a people separated from the world unto Him, we have cultured a tendency to produce an ever-growing list of extra-biblical rules – spoken and unspoken – that must be followed.*

What does this have to do with the independent Baptist movement? Namely this: in our zealousness to preserve for God a people separated from the world unto Him, we have cultured a tendency to produce an ever-growing list of extra-biblical rules – spoken and unspoken – that must be followed if someone is to be right with God. Women must wear hose in public. Men must wear suits and ties to church services. The only acceptable color for dress shirts is white. Haircuts must be tapered in the back rather than blocked. Facial hair of any sort is forbidden on a preacher. Sideburns must not extend below the middle of the ear. Music in church services must flow instead of rock. However, even music that flows instead of rocks is not acceptable if it was written by someone or popularized by someone who once sang with someone who once sang with someone who once sang with someone who was a charismatic. Ecclesiastical separation is no longer enough; now we must separate from the one who did not separate from the one who was not ecclesiastically separated. Divorced men cannot preach. Strike that, they can on a bus somewhere, but no divorced man should ever grace a platform of a church. In fact, you cannot even preach in the same program with a brother who is divorced even if you are preaching on Friday, and he is preaching on Tuesday. Preaching must never be replaced by a choir cantata in any service, even for Easter. And God forbid you allow a choir to sing a cantata on Good Friday. That is the Roman Catholic holiday, and an independent Baptist church that does a cantata on such a day is under the double whammy of God's judgment. A church without a bus ministry is a fake church because it is evident that it has no compassion for the lost. If the church is small and broke, a van ministry is acceptable but only if the attendance is less than fifty. Anything beyond that demands an actual bus. Soul winning must be done door-to-door. No door may be skipped on your side of town. Speaking of sides of town, no other independent Baptist church should locate on your side of town without your express permission. Television? Forget about it. Cable or satellite is not acceptable. Free television is acceptable, provided you only watch the news and football. Attendance at movie theaters is forbidden, but video streaming services are acceptable. On second thought, the only thing that you can watch via video streaming is documentaries.

I could probably continue to add to the above paragraph – some of which has a root in scriptural principle and some which does not – almost indefinitely. Therein lies one of the great tragedies of our movement. We have been so concerned to produce a generation not influenced by the world that we have legislated a thousand and one different things to protect them. We are exactly like the Pharisees. We may not call our rules a fence around the garden of the Torah, but the intent and result is rather symmetrically equivalent in my view.

God is after your heart, not necessarily how big of a fig you carry around your house on Saturday. Are you living holy? Are you loving your wife? Are you raising your

God is after your heart, not necessarily how big of a fig you carry around your house on Saturday.

children to love and serve God? Are you involved in some ministry helping people? Are you telling others about Christ? Are you honoring the Lord with your money? Are you looking for His return? Do you pray? Do you praise Him? Are you pursuing wisdom? Do you soak your mind and life in the Word of God? Is church a priority with you? Are you honest in your business dealings? Do you keep your word? Are you living a life of faith, mercy, and compassion? Is your life marked by worldliness and vanity? Are you covetous or grateful? Are you forgiving or bitter? Are you faithful to Him in the midst of trial and testing? Are you growing in grace? Are you closer to the Lord this year than last year? Do you love the Lord with all your heart, soul, strength, and mind? These are the questions, beloved, that we should be seeking to answer rather than whether some brother across town keeps a long list of unwritten extra-biblical rules.

God never intended for our religion to be burdensome. *My yoke is easy, and burden is light (Matthew 11.30),* Jesus said. Now that can certainly be misapplied and has been by all manner of antinomians in every century of church history, but that does not make the statement invalid. There is a simplicity to our religion, or at least there ought to be. *(II Corinthians 1.12, II Corinthians 11.3)*

We must be careful here. No, our theology is not anywhere near as unscriptural or complicated as rabbinic pharisaism, but we live in an unashamed pursuit of religious purity. That wonderful, godly desire has a natural human tendency to breed rules. Those rules have a natural human tendency to become increasingly large, complex, burdensome, and unwieldy. We must guard against these natural human tendencies and against the foundational errors of pharisaism. We must constantly seek to ensure that our people are free to focus on the Lord and on the actual condition of their own heart before Him. Certainly, this can be done without abandoning our desire for or pursuit of religious purity, or else that very freedom becomes lawlessness and bondage in turn. But it must be done regardless.

Ask Me No Questions

Yet another error with which Christ reproaches the Pharisees is murder. *Woe unto you! for ye build the sepulchres of the prophets, and your fathers killed them. Truly ye bear witness that ye allow the deeds of your fathers: for they indeed killed them, and ye build their sepulchres. Therefore also said the wisdom of God, I will send them prophets and apostles, and some of them they shall slay and persecute: That the blood of all the prophets, which was shed from the foundation of the world, may be required of this generation; From the blood of Abel unto the blood of Zacharias, which perished between the altar and the temple: verily I say unto you, It shall be required of this generation. (Luke 11.47-51)*

Without any shadow of a doubt, when your system arrives at the place that it kills people in order to perpetuate itself, your system is rotten to the core. Politically speaking, we saw this revealed in the bloodiest of centuries, the twentieth, in the systems of Communism and Fascism. Religiously speaking, we saw it revealed in the Dark Ages via the Roman Catholic Church with the Inquisition, and we are seeing it revealed again in the modern day with Islam.

I have little doubt that any Christian reading along would agree with this proposition. Thus, I am more concerned to address with you what produces this and to discover the underlying causes which generate years down the line a system which murders people in order to perpetuate itself. If we can realistically spot such causes, we can identify beforehand which systems are already rotten.

A religion that is bold enough to kill in the name of its god is one which is dogmatically convinced that it alone is right. But surely it has to be more than that. The leaders of that religion have to be convinced that only their interpretation of the divine is accurate. Such a rigidity produces a black and white world, not ethnically but morally, in which there are no shades of gray. I do not mean about the big issues; I mean about all issues. Thus it is that a difference of opinion about any matter, ever so slight though it may be, becomes interpreted as an attack on the authority and veracity of that human leader, and thus on the very religion itself. Ergo, it becomes my sacred, religious duty to my god to exterminate any heretical belief by assassinating the proponent of said belief.

Take the Roman Catholic doctrine of papal infallibility, for instance. Such a position holds that not only is the Roman church the only correct church but that its human leader is right about absolutely everything he formally says and does in relation to the church. It is true that this doctrine was not officially established until the First Vatican Council in 1870, but you can find specific historical support for it as far back as 1087. Thus it was that the Roman church had the supposed authority to slaughter thousands of religious nonconformists during the Dark Ages.

Let us back up even further, for again, I do not believe that any of the Christians who would read this book would believe in the infallibility of any of their religious leaders. What is it that brings men to believe they are right about everything? The answer to that is pride, of course, indisputably. What reveals that condition – a pride-built, internal infallibility – to the outside world? I think it is this: a refusal to be questioned.

> *A religious system that is led by a person who refuses to be questioned has already within it the seeds of its own rotten destruction.*

If you are still following me, then let me say it plainly: a religious system that is led by a person who refuses to be questioned has already within it the seeds of its own rotten destruction. Now with that statement, I think I have backed this error of the Pharisees up to the place where we can see hints of it in our own religious world; and I do not think I have strained at a gnat and swallowed a camel to do so.

Have you ever known an independent Baptist preacher who refused to be questioned? Have you ever known a preacher who believed he was right about everything? Have you ever known a preacher who believed that the only possible correct interpretation of Scripture was his own? You are thinking of somebody right now, are you not? And it did not end well, did it? No, of course not. Such an arrogant attitude is not only unscriptural but additionally carries within itself the seeds of its own systemic destruction.

Although there was vigorous debate within the pharisaic structure, it was a veritable monolith when compared with the differences Jesus Christ had with it. And it refused to admit its error about anything. No matter what Jesus brought up, the Pharisees insisted their interpretation was right; and Jesus' was wrong. There was in them not a hint, not an iota, of humility and grace. The proof of this, and the ultimate proof of the rottenness of their system, was the blood of Christ running in rivulets down the old, rugged cross.

Let us hold the truth firmly, but let us do so in charity. Let us argue the rightness of our positions unashamedly, but let us do so with grace. We are not right about everything. Let us view no mortal man as infallible or as an oracle of God. Let us not shrink from questions, but rather let us welcome them. After all, if we have the truth, it can stand a vigorous examination in the full light of day. And if we do not, well, then we need to know that, too.

Lies

The last error with which Christ reproaches the Pharisees is hiding the truth from people. *Woe unto you, lawyers! for ye have taken away the key of knowledge: ye entered not in yourselves, and them that were entering in ye hindered. (Luke 11.52)*

We must never forget that the devil is a liar and the father of it. *(John 8.44)* He is, in every respect, the opposite of Jesus Christ, Who is the Truth. *(John 14.6)* The religious systems which hide from the truth and propagate lies are an anathema to God and ought to be an anathema to people. The same is true of the religious leaders who lead those systems and the followers who fill them.

Granted, it is certainly true that some people will refuse to see the truth as truth when you display it or will insist either sincerely or insincerely in misunderstanding the truth. These, too, are all human failings. But speaking broadly, we have nothing to fear when holding and displaying the truth; we have everything to gain.

I could point my finger at any number of religions, but this is a book about the independent Baptist movement. Let me hew close to our own crowd here. I have known soul winners who lied about their soul-winning results. I have known bus workers who promised promotions that they knew were not going to happen. I have known preachers whose sermons were replete with fake illustrations. I have known Bible college students who lied about their homework. Certainly, every human being has lied at one point or another, but when we lie in the process of serving God or about what we are doing for God, it is abominable. We are not only hurting ourselves but also those around us. We are hiding the knowledge of the truth from them, and no matter how sincere or good our motives may be, the result will eventually be damage rather than edification.

> *Winston Churchill once said that truth in a time of war was so precious she needed to be protected by a bodyguard of lies. Sometimes I think Churchill was an independent Baptist.*

Winston Churchill once said that truth in a time of war was so precious she needed to be protected by a bodyguard of lies. Sometimes I think Churchill was an independent Baptist. We lie about our attendance, our offerings, our salvations, our baptisms, and our missionary support. We sell it to ourselves and each other as being necessary for "the good of the ministry." After all, we must keep up morale. We represent that everything is going wonderfully well so that people will not be discouraged in their service for the Lord. Meanwhile, we justify such shady tactics by telling ourselves what we say is mostly true or used to be true or might be true next week.

That great prophet of righteousness Isaiah thundered against just such lousy justifications. To him, truth was such a rare and precious jewel it was worth guarding with nothing other than truth. *For our transgressions are multiplied before thee, and our sins testify against us: for our transgressions are with us; and as for our iniquities, we know them; In transgressing and lying against the LORD, and departing away from our God, speaking oppression and revolt, conceiving and uttering from the heart words of falsehood. And judgment is turned away backward, and justice standeth afar off: for truth is fallen in the street, and equity cannot enter. Yea, truth faileth; and he that departeth from evil maketh himself*

a prey: and the LORD saw it, and it displeased him that there was no judgment. (Isaiah 59.12-15)
Tell the truth to your wife. Tell the truth to your children. Tell the truth to your coworkers. Tell the truth to your boss. Tell the truth to your customers. Tell the truth to your pastor. Tell the truth to your members. Tell the truth to each other. Tell the truth to your friends. Tell the truth to yourself. Tell the truth to God. Plus nothing, minus nothing. Just tell the truth.

Where are we wrong? In this: we have built a system that fosters the same philosophies and practices of the Pharisees. It is noxious in the eyes of God and increasingly in the eyes of thoughtful people everywhere.

The Lingering Taint
of an Old Racism

...and what's his reason? I am a Jew. Hath not a Jew eyes? Hath not a Jew hands, organs, dimensions, senses, affections, passions? Fed with the same food, hurt with the same weapons, subject to the same diseases, healed by the same means, warmed and cooled by the same winter and summer as a Christian is? If you prick us, do we not bleed? If you tickle us; do we not laugh? If you poison us, do we not die? And if you wrong us, shall we not revenge? If we are like you in the rest, we will resemble you in that. If a Jew wrong a Christian, what is his humility? Revenge.

If a Christian wrong a Jew, what should his sufferance be by Christian example? Why, revenge! The villainy you teach me I will execute, and it shall go hard but I will better the instruction.
-William Shakespeare, *The Merchant of Venice*

Fundamentalism was not originally an independent Baptist movement. When Fundamentalism was born, there were few, if any, independent Baptists as we understand the term today. But the Baptists quickly became the leaders of the infant movement by virtue of the numerical plethora of their members and churches, as well as the stature and heft of their influential leaders.

That influential fundamentalist leadership – in both the South and the North, at first interdenominational and later increasingly Baptistic – was deeply marked by a racism that was sometimes virulent, sometimes subdued but almost always present. For instance, in 1933 the *Hebrew Christian Alliance Quarterly* claimed that notable Fundamentalists were tolerating anti-Semitism. The source of their charge was the broad fundamentalist embrace of *The Protocols of the Elders of Zion*. This widely disseminated document purported to represent the minutes of a meeting of late nineteenth century Jewish leaders. This meeting allegedly discussed a plan for a global Jewish confederation that would be brought about by Jewish control of the media and the economy and a gradual undermining of morality. This fake document – wholeheartedly embraced by men of the times as varied as Adolf Hitler and Henry Ford – was likewise viewed with respect by leading pastors, seminary presidents, professors, and editors of a fledgling fundamentalist movement.

In and of itself, such a mistake is almost understandable in the sense that men everywhere generally share the prejudices of their age. It ceases to be understandable, however, when *The Protocols* were clearly seen as a forgery, and the most influential northern Baptist pastor refused to admit it. Indeed, he doubled down on his anti-Semitism by publishing a book in 1934 that insisted *The Protocols* were authentic and that Jewish conspirators were out to get him. Quoting Hitler positively and at length, the book reeks of the nauseating philosophies that underpinned the Nazis. His sermons of the time continued to blame the Jews for America's economic crisis, her entrance into World War I, and the decline of the Democratic Party. Thankfully, he received much pushback from other influential Fundamentalists in the North, but the stubborn fact of his intransigent racism remains. Other leading fundamentalist publications viewed Henry Ford's retraction of support for *The Protocols* as simply more evidence of a worldwide Jewish conspiracy.

Of course, the more conservative sections of the United States embraced a brand of Europe's anti-Semitism in the decades between the world wars, as well. The Ku Klux Klan would see its highest membership during these years. At its peak in the mid-1920s, it claimed five million on its rolls, approximately fifteen percent of the adult white population in America. The traditional – read here sometimes reactionary – movement that was Fundamentalism all too often saw similar goals when it eyed the Klan. The father of the greatest independent Baptist writer and editor of the twentieth century was a Baptist preacher and a Klansman. This editor's sermons during the period between the wars, while not marked with the virulent anti-Semitism of other fundamentalist leaders, are visibly marked by what they do not say as much as in what they do.

For example, in May 1930 Sherman, Texas, experienced an ugly race riot. A black man named George Hughes was accused of raping a white woman. At his trial, an angry mob of five thousand white men surrounded the courthouse and fought their way through the Texas Rangers and National Guard assigned to protect him. After setting fire to the courthouse, the mob dragged Hughes's body behind a car, pulling to a stop at the front of the drugstore in the black section of town. After hanging him on a tree in front of this drugstore, the lynch mob built a fire with the store furnishings so they could simultaneously roast and hang the already dead Hughes. By morning, most of the town's black business district lay in ashes.

Exactly one year later, the Baptist preacher and Klan member's son conducted a city-wide crusade in Sherman. He managed to find the courage to call out by name and preach against both the doctors and druggists who prescribed whiskey and the local Baptist pastor who sponsored mixed swimming parties. Somehow, though, he could not find the courage to utter one word of condemnation for the anarchy, mob violence, lynching, and general mayhem wreaked upon the town's black population. He did not speak for it, but neither did he speak out against it.

Yet another leading Baptist pastor of the era – this one pastored two large churches in different states simultaneously – thundered loud and long against anything he perceived as a threat to white racial purity. Preaching about interracial marriage he roared, "I can name to you a people south of the Mason-Dixon Line that if a Negro should take a white girl's hand in marriage that girl would be without a Negro husband before the sun arose the next morning." He then cheerfully offered to conduct the funeral.

One of his prominent allies in the ministry was an independent Baptist evangelist of national reputation. Preaching at the seventh annual British Israel World Federation in 1926 this evangelist opined, "I know of no truth today that can so restore confidence as this Anglo Israel Truth, because in my country, in the southland of America, you find the old Anglo-Saxon Puritan blood in the ascendancy." In 1928, this pastor of two churches joined with his evangelist friend and another friend (who had recently opened a southern Bible college) to rally the country against the Catholic candidacy of New York's governor, Al Smith. At one Texas rally he snarled, "What a conglomeration, Tammany Hall, Roman Catholicism, bootleggers, carpetbag politicians, and negroes. What will the white people of Texas do?" At another rally held in Alabama he groused, "Al Smith believes in social equality. He approves of miscegenation, the intermarriage of negroes with whites. He associates with negroes. He stoops to social equality to get negro votes. He ran for the New York Assembly on the same ticket with negroes. He has negro members of his legislature. He has taken the negro away from the Republican Party. He has made the negro believe that he will be welcome in the White House when he is elected. If he is elected, it will be because the negro and foreign-born vote enables him to carry the east while the South remains solid."

While it is true that such unpleasant facts mark our history, it is also true that good men – even some of the men I just discussed – gradually came to see the error of their ways. By the late 1940's the independent Baptist editor I referenced earlier had moved from the South to the North, and a corresponding shift became evident in his writing. He now openly denounced the Klan even though his father had been a member. When a local ice cream parlor refused to serve his family because a black gospel singer was with their party, he indignantly walked out never to return. Like the rest of the independent Baptist movement, he was on a slow and painful journey out of prejudice.

Painful is the right word, however. The American societal transformation of the 1940s and 1950s that produced the Civil Rights Act and actions of the 1960s did not come easy to either the country or Christian Fundamentalism. One of the leading Fundamentalists of the mid-twentieth century, the evangelist and college president I referenced earlier, saw fit to launch a diatribe in favor of segregation with his Easter Sunday morning message in 1960. He took for his text *Acts 17.26*. *And hath made of one blood all nations of men for to dwell on all the face of the earth, and hath determined the times before appointed, and the bounds of their habitation.* The sermon that followed managed to entirely ignore the first half of the verse and the many New Testament passages that urge the church to racial color blindness. Instead, he asserted that the last half of the verse indicated black people should have stayed in Africa where God put them. (Somehow he also completely missed the fact that such logic would have compelled the white man to stay in Europe where God had put them.) In his mind, the proper solution to ethnic strife was sending the black man back to Africa. Failing that, it was for the black man to keep to himself in his own churches, his own cafeterias, and his own schools. Again and again he referred in his sermon to "the established order" by which he meant the rule of black people by white people. This stomach-turning excuse of a sermon asserts the civil rights movement was a tool of the theological liberal, the communist agitator, and the anti-Christ. In the same breath, it refuses to be called prejudiced but then turns around and says that though black Christians are our spiritual brethren, that spiritual family relationship can never be allowed to apply to marriage, education, or church.

Not coincidentally, the Bible college he founded would go on to lose its tax exemption due to its refusal to admit black students. Again and again, it has been driven through the muck of media exposés that have brought great harm to the cause of Christ. It continued to hold staunchly to its racist roots into the twenty- first century before finally giving them up.

Do not misunderstand me. I am a Fundamentalist with a capital F. I am with Athanasius who on being told the whole world was against him during the Arian heresy controversy calmly replied, "Then I am against the whole world." But to maintain such a bull-headed stubbornness on a position the Bible clearly and repeatedly condemns is incredibly damaging to the cause of Christ in general and the fundamentalist movement in particular.

The Southern heritage of our movement handed us many wonderful things, but in the treasury was some lead along with the gold. Even my own Northern ministry training was visibly marked by the remnants of racism. At the age of twenty, I heard one preacher proclaim with scorn during his sermon, "Black people don't have no souls." I was routinely forbidden to have a black attendance larger than five percent of the total on my bus route. Just this week I talked to two independent Baptist pastors who informed me they have peers in the ministry and people in their congregation who believe – in the infamous words of George Wallace – in segregation today, segregation tomorrow, and segregation forever. In other words, black people should have their own church; Hispanic people should have their own church; white people should have their own church.

What is so heartbreaking about this is the absolute clarity with which Scripture speaks to exactly this subjcct. The Jews of Jesus' day were incredibly racist. Not coincidentally, the Jewish roots of the organization He founded – the church – clashed again and again in those early decades with the God-given mandate to take the Gospel to the whole world. Jesus fought the battle with His own Apostles. On several different occasions, He conspicuously ministered to Gentiles. Along the way, He plainly revealed that the plan of God was free of any and all ethnic prejudice.

At His birth, Simeon prophesied He would be ...*a light to lighten the Gentiles... (Luke 2.32)* It was Gentiles from the East who first worshipped Him as a babe in Bethlehem. John the Baptist saw beyond the nationally limited Jewish messianic desires of the day to announce, ...*Behold the Lamb of God which taketh away the sin of the world. (John 1.29)* Jesus saw greater faith in a Gentile centurion than He ever did in any of His own people. *(Matthew 8.10)* In the same story, He explicitly told His Apostles that Gentiles would sit at the same table with the Jews in His coming kingdom. *And I say unto you, That many shall come from the east and west, and shall sit down with Abraham, and Isaac, and Jacob, in the kingdom of heaven. (Matthew 8.11)* No one was more esteemed in the Jewish mind than the patriarchs, and Jesus – to a crowd of Jews in a Jewish city – explicitly placed Gentiles on the same level as the fathers. Perhaps the clearest witnessing example in the Bible is Jesus' conversation with the Gentile Samaritan woman at the well in *John 4.* On His last tour of Judea prior to His crucifixion, He again referenced the Gentiles equivalence to Abraham, Isaac, and Jacob in the kingdom. *(Luke 13.28)*

The Apostle Peter, when faced with the dilemma of whether to minister to the Gentile Cornelius is plainly instructed, ...*What God hath cleansed, that call not thou common. (Acts 10.15)* That the Gentiles had an equal place in Christianity was clearly understood in its own time as a message to the Jews. *And they of the circumcision which believed were astonished, as many as came with Peter, because that on the Gentiles also was poured out the gift of the Holy Ghost. (Acts 10.45)*

Paul dwells at length upon this very subject in his epistle to the Ephesians. Again and again, the union of Jews and Gentiles in the early churches was a cause for strife. Under the inspiration of the Holy Spirit, Paul spoke up not just for equality but for true unity. *Wherefore remember, that ye being in time past Gentiles in the flesh, who are called Uncircumcision by that which is called the Circumcision in the flesh made by hands; That at that time ye were without Christ, being aliens from the commonwealth of Israel, and strangers from the covenants of promise, having no hope, and without God in the world: But now in Christ Jesus ye who sometimes were far off are made nigh by the blood of Christ. For he is our peace, who hath made both one, and hath broken down the middle wall of partition between us; Having abolished in his flesh the enmity, even the law of commandments contained in ordinances; for to make in himself of twain one new man, so making peace; And that he might reconcile both unto God in one body by the cross, having slain the enmity thereby: And came and preached peace to you which were afar off, and to them that were nigh. For through him we both have access by one Spirit unto the Father. Now therefore ye are no more strangers and foreigners, but fellowcitizens with the saints, and of the household of God. (Ephesians 2.11-19)* If the church

> *If the church is the body of Christ – and it is (Colossians 1.24) – then to segregate the church on an ethnic basis is anathema to God.*

is the body of Christ – and it is *(Colossians 1.24)* – then to segregate the church on an ethnic basis is anathema to God.

President Theodore Roosevelt, speaking before an Irish cultural
group in 1915 said, "There is no room in this country for hyphenated
Americanism. When I refer to hyphenated Americans, I do not refer
to naturalized Americans. Some of the very best Americans I have
ever known were naturalized Americans, Americans born abroad.
But a hyphenated American is not an American at all. The one absolutely certain way of bringing this nation to ruin, of preventing all
possibility of its continuing to be a nation at all, would be to permit
it to become a tangle of squabbling nationalities, an intricate knot of
German-Americans, Irish-Americans, English-Americans, French-
Americans, Scandinavian-Americans or Italian-Americans, each
preserving its separate nationality, each at heart feeling more sympathy with Europeans of that nationality, than with the other citizens
of the American Republic. There is no such thing as a hyphenated
American who is a good American. The only man who is a good
American is the man who is an American and nothing else."

So it is or at least ought to be
with God's people. Separate but
equal is a concept long ago rejected
in jurisprudence – and rightly so.
Would to God it would be rejected
by the independent Baptist movement, as well.

> *Separate but equal is a
> concept long ago rejected
> in jurisprudence – and
> rightly so. Would to God
> it would be rejected by the
> independent Baptist
> movement, as well.*

I do not care if you are a native-
born citizen of the United States, a
naturalized American, a legal visa
holder, or an illegal immigrant; the ground is level at the foot of the
cross. I do not care if you are Caucasian, Latino, Asian, African,
Polish, Assyrian, Pinoy, Indian, Italian, German, Romanian, or
Irish; the ground is level at the foot of the cross. I do not care if
your 401k is maxed out for the year already or if all your cash is
tied up in debt; the ground is level at the foot of the cross. I do not
care if you have so many degrees behind your name that you could
be a thermometer or if you spent the best three years of your life in
the eighth grade; the ground is level at the foot of the cross. I do not

care if you are tall or short, light or dark, rich or poor, educated or ignorant, respected or neglected, a dreamboat or a shipwreck; the ground is level at the foot of the cross. We will all get to Heaven the same way, and that is through the shed blood of Jesus Christ. We will all sing in the greatest choir in history, assembled with the millions on that glassy sea, facing that emerald rainbow-encircled throne. We will all walk the streets of gold and kneel prostrate at His feet. The ground is level at the foot of the cross.

No less an authority than our Saviour Himself called for the church to be ethnically blind and completely united. *And other sheep I have, which are not of this fold: them also I must bring, and they shall hear my voice; and there shall be one fold, and one shepherd. (John 10.16)*

I have the rare privilege of having pastored two very different churches thus far in my life. The first was in rural Pennsylvania. The region around was almost exclusively white. The second is in inner-city Chicago. The neighborhood around is predominantly Hispanic and Polish. Along the way, I have learned a thing or two about myself, about God's people, and about the truth. Although we strive to see all things biblically, we cannot help but so often partake of the prejudicial worldviews of those around us.

For example, I used to subscribe to the notion that immigrants – legal and illegal – were often criminal, largely lazy, and ruinous to our Judeo-Christian culture. The truth is my position was but a thinly veiled racism. Now for twelve years, I have walked among them. I shop at their stores. I eat at their restaurants. Their children play with mine. I pastor them by the score, legal and illegal. And my heart is broken at my former ignorance and the callow blindness of so many of God's people in white America.

> *My heart is broken at my former ignorance and the callow blindness of so many of God's people in white America.*

Not only do I see this in my own past but I see it or at least the lingering effect of it nationally amongst independent Baptists. It is common for some brochure to show up in the mail advertising some conference or other around the country.

With sadness I say that in almost every case, every man on the speaking schedule is white. I do not think that is because of conscious racism on the part of the men planning and leading such conferences. I think it has never actually occurred to them that there might be something unseemly about it.

Think with me for a moment. I want to reach the many Hispanic people in my neighborhood. How does it look to a Hispanic visitor if he walks in the front door of our church and finds that the greeter is white, the nursery worker is white, the ushers are white, the song leader is white, every choir member is white, and the pastor is white? I can verbally assure him that he and his family are welcome, but that verbal assurance will be lost in a sea of Caucasian faces. Could I not somewhere find someone who looks like him to stand up in front of our people in some capacity so as to make him feel welcome? Of course I can. It may take some ingenuity and effort on my part at the beginning, but it can and should be done.

I am not calling for an independent Baptist version of affirmative action. But are there no qualified black men, qualified Hispanic men, or qualified Asian men available to preach in these conferences? Are there none available to teach in our Bible colleges? Surely such would not be difficult to find if the leadership would actually place a priority upon it.

The sad truth is we are all for people of other ethnicities to come to Christ as long as they do not come to our country. White independent Baptist churches by the hundreds fled America's inner cities in the 1970s, and the result was a horrendous vacuum of sound doctrine and religion in those cities. Say what you will, you cannot adequately reach an inner city by running buses into it on a Sunday morning and segregate the resulting crowd into a second class Sunday school, well insulated from the drive-in, middle-class, white crowd. Twelve years of hard won experience in the inner city has proven that to me. The American independent Baptist movement is demographically doomed by its own rural and increasingly aged lily-white statistics. The only solution is to return to the cities; go back to the ethnic neighborhoods from which we fled, and plant indigenous churches by the hundreds. Not only is that the demographic solution but it is just as clearly the scriptural solution. God did not die for the white Anglo-Saxon Protestant American male; He died for every man – red and yellow, black and white.

Where are we wrong, beloved? In this: we have whitewashed the racism of our past. Worse yet, we have allowed its lingering taint to continue on, unrebuked in the calls for segregation and hostile attitudes toward ethnic immigration. The resulting movement may be pure in doctrine and practice, but it is rightly doomed if it does not change. Let us turn again to the ethnic neighborhoods close to our churches, and bring them in. Let us turn again to the claustrophobic great American inner cities. Let us embrace, once again, the whole of the world within our bosom; and love them with a great love.

In short, let us be like Jesus.

Book Three-Strengthen the Things Which Remain

This life therefore is not righteousness, but growth in righteousness, not health, but healing, not being but becoming, not rest but exercise. We are not yet what we shall be, but we are growing toward it, the process is not yet finished, but it is going on, this is not the end, but it is the road. All does not yet gleam in glory, but all is being purified.
-Martin Luther

The Cure

Imagine there was a cure, but finding it would cost you everything. It would completely ruin your life. What would you do?
-Marissa Meyer, *Cinder*

A diagnosis without a cure is cruelty. It simply leaves the patient in a worse condition, for now he knows he is badly sick. He thinks there is nothing he can do to fix it. To his list of maladies he must now add that of a pessimistic discouragement and a depressed spirit that weighs down his attempts to grow healthy again.

I have several great fears in writing this book. Most assuredly, one of them is that it will produce nothing more than disillusionment. I have sought to balance this by emphasizing not only what we do that is right but also by pointing out how to fix that which is wrong. In John's letter to the church at Sardis, Jesus takes a similar tack. ...*I know thy works, that thou hast a name that thou livest, and art dead. Be watchful, and strengthen the things which remain, that are ready to die: for I have not found thy works perfect before God. (Revelation 3.1-2)* In Jesus' view and in mine, the solution to a deeply flawed church system is not to let it die; it is rather to work vigorously at raising it back up to health and strength.

In that spirit, I offer for your consideration this last section. It will not be long, for the careful reader has already gleaned much along the way. It also bears repeating that I do not believe I alone have the answers or that I have all the answers or that all of my answers are correct. Indeed, one of my great hopes for this book is that it will provoke a conversation – amongst friends, online, or at least in your own heart – about what is both right and wrong with our movement and how to fix it. In that vein, I would willingly hear from you the sum and substance of your own perspective. But in advance of that, let me offer for your consideration several closing thoughts. I have discussed at length where we are and how we got here. Let me now address to you some brief thoughts about how to get to where we ought to be.

Repentance

Repentance is a change of mind that leads to a change of actions. Our actions may change under the motivation of any number of short term or temporary motivations, but systemic permanent change only comes via repentance. I must come to view my current situation as unacceptable. I must hold my reasoning up unhesitatingly to the light of day and see it for the flawed creature that it is. I must then lay aside my previous prejudices, my long held opinions, and my errant certainties. If I reach into the cupboard for a glass and discover it has a long crack running down the side of it, I must repent. I must make the decision to set that glass aside and to reach for one that is still sound.

So many of the fallacies I have discussed in the second section of this book are like that cracked glass. It may be my favorite glass. It may be one I have used for many years. It may be one that fits my hand well. It may be one that keeps my preferred beverage at the right temperature. But if it is shown undeniably to be flawed, I must lay it aside, sentiment notwithstanding.

Many years ago, as a young man I spent two summers traveling with a much older evangelist. In nearly fifty years on the road, he had encountered almost everything it was possible to experience in ministry. Experience is often the teacher that produces wisdom within us. Not surprisingly, this man had much wisdom. One of the dictums he uttered time and again was that every pastor thinks he is right about everything. Each pastor thinks his methods are the best methods; his approach is the correct approach; his highly refined opinions are superior to the brother across town.

Such a dictum is only logical. After all, why would the pastor do something, promote something, practice something, or believe something he thought was incorrect? Obviously, he makes his decisions and puts them into effect because he believes he is right. The point, then, of the dictum is that leaders resist change. Most of the time, they will only risk change when highly pressured, borderline desperate, or dragged into it kicking and screaming.

Beloved, we must change. We simply cannot continue to hold unscriptural positions and practice unbiblical behaviors. And that change must begin with repentance. It must begin with the admission that we have been incorrect. What we used to view as right must now be viewed as wrong if it is actually wrong.

Job was a good man. God paid him a tremendous compliment when He informed the devil *...that there is none like him in the earth, a perfect and an upright man, one that feareth God, and escheweth evil. (Job 1.8)* Yet even such a man as Job was not sinless. He was not right about everything. He was not completely correct in his thinking, speech, or actions as revealed in *Job*. After a long and painful process of contemplative self-examination, he could not help but say *...I abhor myself, and repent in dust and ashes. (Job 42.6)*

Good men, religious men, or men who have given their lives in service for God are often the most resistant to repentance. On the day before His death, our Saviour said to a group of Israel's religious leaders, *For John came unto you in the way of righteousness, and ye believed him not: but the publicans and the harlots believed him: and ye, when ye had seen it, repented not afterward... (Matthew 21.32)* Those most visibly stained with the excrement of sin are usually the first to admit it. But those who see in themselves none of the filth of the world – à la Job – take forty chapters of combined hectoring and justification before they will repent.

Beloved, repentance cannot be a doctrine for others yet not for us. Is there nothing of which I should be ashamed? Are there no thoughts, no actions, or no words of mine that are wrong? Is there no perspective, no chain of reasoning, or no emotional reaction of my own that needs abandoned? Surely that cannot be the case. I dare not allow it to be. A teacher who is no longer teachable has lost his right to teach. A leader who refuses to follow is not worth following himself. An authority figure who will not yield to other authorities in his life is a poor excuse of an authority figure himself.

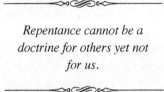

Repentance cannot be a doctrine for others yet not for us.

The question then facing us here at the end of this book cannot be, "Should I repent?" but rather "Where should I repent?" If my ninety one thousand words have not caused you to examine yourself in some way, to rethink something, or to double check something, then we have both wasted our time. I dare you to walk along with the sweet psalmist of Israel. *Search me, O God, and know my heart: try me, and know my thoughts: And see if there be any wicked way in me... (Psalm 139.23-24)* Both you and I are human. Some glass we are holding is cracked. Let us repent. Let us set it aside and reach for one that is whole. Let us cease justifying our every word, action, and attitude. Let us change our mind and thus our actions.

When God calls you and I to account for our generation and the ones we influenced that succeeded us, what will He say? Will He clear us? Only if we repent. *For godly sorrow worketh repentance to salvation not to be repented of: but the sorrow of the world worketh death. For behold this selfsame thing, that ye sorrowed after a godly sort, what carefulness it wrought in you, yea, what clearing of yourselves, yea, what indignation, yea, what fear, yea, what vehement desire, yea, what zeal, yea, what revenge! In all things ye have approved yourselves to be clear in this matter. (II Corinthians 7.10-11)*

Do Not Throw the Baby Out with the Bathwater

Having just sought to persuade you to change, let me now take the other tack and encourage you not to change too much. To the uninformed mind, it may seem as if I am arguing with myself. To the contrary, I am seeking to strengthen the things which remain, not to eliminate them.

The contemporary American expressions of Christianity are littered with the self-appointed drop-outs of the independent Baptist movement. They haunt online forums and clutter social media newsfeeds. They might as well have the word "overreact" tattooed to their forehead. They have seen that which is wrong – and that is all. They have unerringly focused in on our flaws – and that is all. They have cried shame upon us – and that is all. Nary an "Amen" ever passes their lips for what we do that is right. There is in them no thoughtful expression of a carefully wrought Christianity. There is only the harshness of criticism and the abandonment of flight.

Several years ago, after a particularly disastrous black eye for the independent Baptist movement, I was talking with one of our missionaries. She was expressing her disgust for some of the same deep flaws that I have sought to portray in this book. Along the way, she said something I have heard more times than I care to count: "I don't know that I even want to be an independent, fundamental Baptist anymore."

Emotionally, I could see her point. Maintaining her belief system in the face of enemy and friendly fire had brought her spirit to the place of deep weariness. At some point, even salmon get tired of constantly swimming upstream especially when the resistance begins to come from its own doubting heart. Maybe I am in the wrong stream? After all, if we were really right, would not God be blessing us?

As I listened to her speak those words (though I sympathized), I found I could not let them pass unchallenged. In response I said, "I believe in the doctrines that drive our belief system as Baptists. I believe in the doctrines that drive our belief system as Fundamentalists. I believe in the doctrines that drive our belief system as independents. None of those have changed. Thus, I am an independent, fundamental Baptist regardless of who has done what or will do what."

My heart hurts for those whom our movement has hurt. Some we have hurt intentionally. We have sliced them to ribbons with our tongues. We have preached them out. We have taken advantage where none ought to be taken. We have belittled, abused, maligned, scorned, and mauled many a child of God in the name of standing firm for the faith.

Others we have hurt unintentionally. We have pursued our secret sins, careless of the awful destruction we were bringing down on our heads. In an effort to promote the right, we have lied, cheated, and deceived. We have ruined lives. We have pushed men to the breaking point and then attacked them when they broke. All too often, we have left in our ministries a thoughtless trail of imploded churches, broken marriages, bitter children, and disillusioned saints.

Should it surprise us when those broken pieces cut? Should it shock us when they hurl invective, reproach, and damnation at every independent Baptist within shouting distance? It should not. They are our creation. We built these fire ships and then launched them directly at our own navy.

We built these fire ships and then launched them directly at our own navy.

While our hearts should be filled with compassion, what we cannot do is listen to them. What we cannot do is believe their – and I say this kindly – warped perspective. If we do, we will become them. And under the guise of correction, the result will eventually be a wholesale abandonment of truth and right.

Others have changed. This change was not as a result of being influenced by the loud voices of those who claim victimhood but as a result of their own desire to thrive. They have looked on with envy at the growing branches of American Christianity so long they eventually found the necessary justification to transfer. They have shifted their families and their churches, sometimes quickly, sometimes slowly but always sadly. Our movement built the desert in which they found themselves, and they ran for the

Our movement built the desert in which they found themselves, and they ran for the shimmering oasis of contemporary Christianity they saw on the horizon. I am convinced they have run pell-mell toward a mirage.

shimmering oasis of contemporary Christianity they saw on the horizon. I am convinced they have run pell-mell toward a mirage.

Between these three groups – the victims, those the victims have influenced, and the pragmatists – more independent Baptists than I care to count have thrown away their heritage. Some have tossed their heritage away because of sin, some because of insincerity, some because of envy but all because of overreaction. They have thrown the baby out with the bathwater.

Do we need to grow? Do we need to change? Do we need to improve? Does that involve the hard choice of repentance and renewal? Are some of those changes substantial? Yes. But we do not need to jettison our core belief and practice. It is absolutely scriptural to be an independent, fundamental Baptist.

Prayer

When I glance back over the areas in which I believe we have been wrong, some common things jump out at me. There are some similar threads through the ugly part of the weave of our crowd. Desire is one of those threads. So much of what drives our errors is a misguided effort to build something or reach someone. Although they are errors, they are often errors of effort. In a way, we often simply try too hard. We want so badly to reach the world or at least the part of the world we see around us. Apathy is not our sin; lethargy is not our crime.

Solomon said, *Through desire a man, having separated himself, seeketh and intermeddleth with all wisdom. (Proverbs 18.1)* In this our error is not found in the fact we have a great desire to see God work; it is rather in that we so often turn to what we ourselves can do rather than waiting upon the Lord.

Do not misunderstand me. I do not believe God blesses the laziness of inertia. Again and again in the Scripture we find calls to work, to serve, to be about our Father's business. At the same time, however, it is also true that there is a great emphasis placed in the Word of God on beseeching God to do the work. As with so many other things in the Christian life, there is a maturity to be found in the balance between our work for Him and our prayer to

Him. In my view, one of the reasons we have developed a number of serious errors is because we have sought to humanly force a spiritual result. We have so longed for God to work that when He did not seem to be doing so quick enough or big enough for our satisfaction, we took matters into our own hands.

The fault is not a new one. Four thousand years ago, Abraham, eager to realize God's wonderful promise of numerous descendants, forced a solution via Hagar. More than five centuries later, an overconfident Moses, impatient to see the deliverance of God's people, killed an Egyptian overseer in an effort to jumpstart a slave rebellion. Another millennium would grant us the sad picture of a nervous Saul, staring down a massive Philistine invasion with no apparent help from Samuel, rashly deciding to take it upon himself to offer the necessary sacrifices. The result in all these cases and numerous others was the same – disaster.

Why do we so often manipulate people into praying a sinner's prayer, badger young people into walking an aisle to yield their life to Christ, arrogantly tell people we know God's will for their life, and incorporate scripturally suspect methods to build our church? For the same reasons Abraham, Moses, and Saul ran ahead of God.

Prayer is the hand that moves the hand of God. If God's hand is not moving, the answer does not lie in questionable methods or actions of doubtful provenance. The answer lies where it has always lain – in prayer. F. B. Meyer, the English Baptist pastor and author said it this way in his book on the life of Moses: "Oh for grace to wait and watch with God, though a horror of great darkness falls on us, and sleep steals up into our eyes, and the head becomes thickly sown with the gray hair of age! One blow struck when time is fulfilled is worth a thousand struck in premature eagerness. It is not for thee, O my soul, to know the times and seasons which the Father hath put in His own power; wait thou only upon God; let thy expectation be from Him; wait at the gates of thy Jericho for yet seven days; utter not a sound until He says, Shout: but when He gives the signal, with the glad cry of victory thou shalt pass over the fallen wall into the city."

Our great error is not that we do not work; it is that we do not work at prayer nearly as much as we work at ministry. We do not avail ourselves of the great power of our omnipotent and gracious Heavenly Father. Our pulpits are filled with arrogance, and our prayer closets are empty of humility. We devour the latest "how-to manual" from the business world while the weeds of neglect grow in our garden of prayer. We plead with men when we ought to be supplicating with God. We push and prod and force and drive to see our vision realized when we ought rather to pour out our souls at the throne of grace. We have not *James* tells us

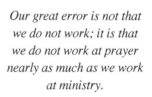

Our great error is not that we do not work; it is that we do not work at prayer nearly as much as we work at ministry.

quite plainly not because our methods need updating but because we ask not. We fail at prayer while succeeding in the worst way possible at accomplishing our godly desires. Zeal? We have it in spades. Intercession? What is that?

I have probably twenty-five books on prayer in my office. Of them all the most convicting ones have to be those by the nineteenth century Methodist minister E. M. Bounds. One particular statement of his has been ringing in my mind as I write. "The Church is looking for better methods; God is looking for better men. What the Church needs to-day is not more machinery or better, not new organizations or more and novel methods, but men whom the Holy Ghost can use — men of prayer, men mighty in prayer. The Holy Ghost does not flow through methods, but through men. He does not come on machinery, but on men. He does not anoint plans, but men — men of prayer."

Earlier I spoke of a desert, a wasteland caused by our own errors. *Isaiah* speaks eloquently of a desert that is transformed into a lush garden. ...*For in the wilderness shall waters break out, and streams in the desert. And the parched ground shall become a pool, and the thirsty land springs of water: in the habitation of dragons, where each lay, shall be grass with reeds and rushes. (Isaiah 35.6-7)* God is able, so able, to cause our barren wilderness to blossom as a rose. But the answer is in Him. It is in feeling after Him and in seeking His face. It is not in us. It is not in the self-help aisle at the bookstore. It is not in our ability to produce, inspire, cajole, shame, or push. Without Him, all we have produced is statistics and empty ones at that. But with Him, ah, beloved, with Him we can still change the world.

Paul told Timothy, *...First of all, supplications, prayers, intercessions, and giving of thanks... (I Timothy 2.1)*

First of all, last of all, most of all, let us pray.

A Grace-Filled Firmness

Twenty-seven times God put the words *mercy* and *truth* into the same verse. It is a key principle in relation to how He operates and how He desires us to operate. In this sense, it is not enough to have mercy upon somebody: to be kind, forgiving, charitable, understanding, and supportive. By the same token, taking the opposite tack is not enough, either: to be hard, nay harsh, to emphasize alone the strict demands of truth. Only when they are combined are we like God. *For the LORD is good; his mercy is everlasting; and his truth endureth to all generations. (Psalm 100.5)* Only when they are combined are we effective in relationship and leadership. *...Mercy and truth preserve the king:... (Proverbs 20.28)*

Mercy and truth, which I have attempted to describe with the phrase "a grace-filled firmness," are essential to the independent Baptist movement going forward in two ways. First, it is vitally necessary in relation to the rest of American Christianity. The independent Baptist movement is not nearly as dead as some folks like to make it out to be. Thousands and thousands of our churches serve millions of our people. But though that is true, it is also true that our movement represents a small minority in America's larger religious community. Even when we set aside the growing cults such as the Latter Day Saints and the gigantic Roman Catholic Church (both of which are egregiously heretical), we are still but a meager minority.

The majority – even of the genuine family of God in the United States – is going in a different direction than we are. In my view, it is a more worldly and less scriptural direction. I would not necessarily call it a stampede, but I would unhesitatingly say the herd is generally going in a direction we do not want to go. We must somehow find the backbone necessary via the grace of God to permanently resist that constant pressure. I suspect that should include a more diligent explanation to the younger men; using the Word of God, we must define the reasons for our stand. This must be paired with a genuinely mature example by the older men.

Even so, this firmness must not be held harshly; for that very harshness will undermine the succeeding generation's willingness to follow. Even worse, it will continue to engender not only harshness toward one another but also an increasing tendency to splinter and attack other good men and churches with whom we differ only slightly. Instead, let us hold firmly to whom we are and what we believe, but let us do so with grace and charity.

Let us hold firmly to whom we are and what we believe, but let us do so with grace and charity.

Secondly, this grace-filled firmness is essential as we face the growing paganism of secular America. Isaac Watts said three centuries agone that this vile world is not a friend to grace to help us on to God, and it has not improved at all in the meantime. In fact, the world is waxing worse and worse *(II Timothy 3.13)*, and the speed at which it is regressing is picking up. It does not take a crystal ball to anticipate more government interference, less freedom of religion in the public square, increased demonic opposition, and a higher ratio of negative publicity in the media in the coming years. Additionally, fewer and fewer people will be raised in a traditional home with traditional understandings of gender roles and without a basic background in the stories of the Bible. Sin will be flaunted as never before. As America becomes increasingly urban and ethnically diverse, adherence to eastern religions will continue to rise. In fact, I expect to see in coming days the slow restoration of the ancient pagan religions of Native America, Britain, Scandinavia, Rome, Greece, and Egypt. *But as the days of Noe were, so shall also the coming of the Son of man be. (Matthew 24.37)*

The previous paragraph may well depress some. It does not depress me. The grace of God that was sufficient for our grandfathers in their generation will be sufficient for our grandchildren in theirs, as well. None of this wickedness will surprise God, let alone intimidate Him. It ought not to intimidate us either. ...*Greater is he that is in you, than he that is in the world. (I John 4.4)* We must and can continue to stand firmly against all the pressure Satan, through the world's system, can bring to bear on us. Along the way, we dare not become bitter, angry, vengeful, shrill, vindictive, or petty. His entire world rejoiced as it crucified Christ on the cross, yet still in His last hours, He spoke with grace and love. Beloved, as in all things, let us be like Him in this, too.

Hermeneutics

The high calling of the pastor and teacher in the local church environment, of the professor in the institutional environment, and of the editor in the media environment is to *preach the word. (II Timothy 4.2)* That word is not or ought not be their own word; it is to be His Word.

Ezekiel, the captivity prophet who ministered to the Jewish nation in Babylon, paid his respects to a number of spiritual flaws amongst the people. Adding to that mix was the egregious error of prophets who claimed to be speaking for God when they actually were not. In so doing, he gives us a vivid illustration. *And her prophets have daubed them with untempered morter, seeing vanity, and divining lies unto them, saying, Thus saith the Lord GOD, when the LORD hath not spoken. (Ezekiel 22.28)* Mortar is what holds the bricks of an edifice together. Untempered mortar is mortar that will not set or harden properly. Thus, the rising structure cannot bear its own weight, and the resulting construction must be either redone or abandoned.

This is not the only time Ezekiel used the phrase *untempered morter* in the context of prophets speaking words that are not actually God's words. He also used it four times in *Ezekiel 13.10-16.* I believe it is fair to say then that this phrase as used by him speaks of those who attempt to give legitimacy to what they are proclaiming. They are asserting it is of God when actually it is anything but.

In my opinion, there are two kinds of untempered mortar. There is deliberately untempered mortar as represented by the blatant false teachers of the cults, the prosperity gospel, et al. Then there is the carelessly untempered mortar of the sincere but unscriptural preacher. I seriously doubt that any person reading this book would willingly and deliberately falsify the Word of God in order to advance their own purposes. But if the Scriptures are handled carelessly, the effect and devastation is exactly the same – untempered mortar and an unstable edifice. Paul speaks of those ...*which corrupt the word of God... (II Corinthians 2.17) ...handling the word of God deceitfully... (II Corinthians 4.2)* We must endeavor rather to be those who have simply ...*spoken unto you the word of God... (Hebrews 13.7)*

There is a great need to do this for several reasons. First, we are handling the Word of God. His Word is pure. There is no error mixed in that needs weeded out by the preacher or teacher. His Word is powerful. Our words have little influence to construct men or launch movements. Neither does our personality, wit, or oratorical ability, at least not in the long run. The power to change men, to move them to become like Christ is not found in our words; it is only found in His Word. As well, His Word is perfect. It cannot be improved upon by some verbal gymnastics or philosophical meanderings on my part. Nothing I add in substance is going to make anything better; it will only make it worse.

The Book is not our word; it is His Word. We are bound to tell men and women and boys and girls what He has said rather than what we would say. *Now then we are ambassadors for Christ, as though God did beseech you by us: we pray you in Christ's stead, be ye reconciled unto God. (II Corinthians 5.20)* We are not to teach a compendium of man's opinion; we are to teach the pure, powerful, and perfect Word of Almighty God.

> *The Book is not our word; it is His Word. We are bound to tell men and women and boys and girls what He has said rather than what we would say.*

Secondly, we must realize we are teaching never dying souls. We are not building cars, houses, appliances, soda cans, furnace ducts, or streetlights. We are not designing landscaping, electrical schematics, or computer programs. We are seeking to edify, to build up a never dying soul in the way of truth and for the glory of God.

If we make a mistake in designing a soda can, someone gets sticky. If we make a mistake in guiding a never dying soul, the result is troubled people *(Acts 15.24)*, deceived people *(II Peter 1.4)*, and eventually destroyed people *(Ezekiel 22.27)*. What we ought to be doing is delivering these souls – *A true witness delivereth souls: but a deceitful witness speaketh lies (Proverbs 14.25)* – from hell, from punishment, from the consequences of mistakes, from trust in us, and from trust in themselves. A Sunday school teacher, a professor, a youth director, an evangelist, a pastor, et al – none of these are dealing with recyclable materials that can be scrapped and then reused. We are dealing with the completely unique and pricelessly valued souls of men. We must deal with them carefully.

Thirdly, we do not want to bring God's judgment down upon ourselves – and He always judges those who pervert His Words. *For I testify unto every man that heareth the words of the prophecy of this book, If any man shall add unto these things, God shall add unto him the plagues that are written in this book: And if any man shall take away from the words of the book of this prophecy, God shall take away his part out of the book of life, and out of the holy city, and from the things which are written in this book. (Revelation 22.18-19)*

All of which brings us full circle back to the subject of hermeneutics. It must become our passion as a movement not to preach entertaining sermons but to preach sound sermons. For far too long, too many of our leaders have neglected the study of the Word of God in favor of the study of church growth methods or the short-term satisfaction of using a sermon as a chance to get something off their chest. The questions we must ask ourselves are not how well did I preach, but rather how clearly did I convey God's meaning?

What is God saying in this book and chapter and verse? What are the great themes of Scripture? How does this thought tie into them? If I teach this, am I being true to the intent of the Author in this passage? What was He saying before? What did He say afterward? Why did He say it? Who did He say it too? In what kind of language did He say it? Is it Law? Is it a parable? Is it prophecy? Is it poetry? Does it deal with Israel or the church?

I must learn to study individual words and solitary phrases. I must grasp the flow of thought in its grammatical context. I must place this accurately into the context of the passage, of the book, of similar books, and of this theme in the Bible. Then I must place all of that within the context of all that God has said in the entirety of Scripture.

Undeniably this will take work. We cannot rightly teach the Word of God to others without it first involving a painstaking process on our part. We must abandon throwing something together. We dare not slap some mortar on the wall as we fumble for another brick. We must temper it diligently.

Beloved, we dare not speak authoritatively from our own opinion, philosophy, experience, sensed need, or emotions. We must not base our teaching on stories from *Chicken Soup for the Soul* or the latest and greatest fad book being mass produced by the Christian publishing industry. Let us cling to the simple yet pure, powerful, and perfect Word of God. *That which was from the beginning, which we have heard, which we have seen with our eyes, which we have looked upon, and our hands have handled, of the Word of life; ...That which we have seen and heard declare we unto you. (I John 1.1, 3)*

Strong churches are not the reflections of strong men; they are the reflections of a long and diligent and careful application of the simple Word of God. Our movement will not remain and grow by producing more effective leaders, smarter leaders, kinder leaders, or more relevant leaders. It is not new methods, new music, new lighting, new buildings, new locations, or new ideas that we most need. Spiritual edification requires tempered mortar – the simple application of the pure Word of God.

Strong churches are not the reflections of strong men; they are the reflections of a long and diligent and careful application of the simple Word of God.

We must return to it with passion, and remain in it with dedication. All else may produce an impressive edifice in the short term, but in the long term, it will come crashing down.

Take the Long View

Psalm 37 and *Psalm 73* both take for their theme a similar concept, namely, that the Christian must be patient when things look good for the wicked man in the short term. Instead, God's people are to keep in mind the end. They are to live and love and lead and labor not with the short-term result in mind but with the long-term outcome uppermost. This pairs well with the contrast of the wicked man and the righteous man in *Proverbs*. The wicked man thinks of what he can gain immediately, while the righteous man looks far down the road to see what the end will be of such an action.

I cannot count the number of times I have ground my teeth in frustration at a short-term decision made by an independent Baptist leader of my acquaintance. I would criticize no man openly in this book, but I have a fair amount of experience at picking up the rubble of structures that once looked imposing but were built with little long-term care. Entirely too many churches and pastors have asked themselves, "How many can we have next Sunday?" instead of asking themselves, "How many can I have in ten years?" Or better yet, they ask "How many can I develop into holiness? How far along are they? How close is my church to being like Christ?"

This philosophical bias toward hasty action reveals itself financially, numerically, and spiritually. It shows up in the shattered marriages and health and spirit of middle-age pastors. It shows up in wild swings of attendance from one decade to the next. It shows up in the glorification of "Big Days" and the neglect of prayer meetings. It shows up in the fullness of our stats and the emptiness of our bookshelves. It shows up in the volume of our sermons and the spiritual hunger of our people. It shows up literally in everything. No, it may not show up immediately, but it always shows up. Time always tells the truth.

New England's nineteenth century treasure Henry Wadsworth Longfellow said it this way:

> For the structure that we raise,
> Time is with materials filled;
> Our to-days and yesterdays

Are the blocks with which we build.

Truly shape and fashion these;
Leave no yawning gaps between;
Think not, because no man sees,
Such things will remain unseen.

In the elder days of Art,
Builders wrought with greatest care
Each minute and unseen part;
For the Gods see everywhere.

Let us do our work as well,
Both the unseen and the seen;
Make the house where Gods may dwell,
Beautiful, entire, and clean.

Else our lives are incomplete,
Standing in these walls of Time,
Broken stairways where the feet
Stumble as they seek to climb.

I do not want to build children who only serve God while I am
breathing down their neck. With all my heart and more than I want
anything else in my life, I want them to grow up to love and serve
God for a lifetime. That is my great purpose in parenting. I could
not care less if my parenting makes a short-term, good impression
on Bro. So-and-so. The long term is what I am after.

I do not want to build a church that will collapse if I am hit
by a bus tomorrow. I do not want to build an empty shell, known
in reputation but hollow doctrinally, numerically, and spiritually
at its core. I want to build a church that will hold to the Word of
God regardless of what storms may come and one that will passionately pursue the sinners that overflow the sidewalks and shops
and homes in this neighborhood. I want them to continue to do
that decade after decade. If that means I have to sacrifice financially, then that is what it means. If that means I have to sacrifice

reputationally, then that is what it means. If that means I have to grind it out, to lever the pick of the Holy Spirit through the hard-packed soil of the American inner city piece by piece, sweating as I grub out a work for God, then that is what it means. Next month in my church does not concern me much; the next five decades do. The long term is what I am after.

I spend hundreds of hours a year writing. I do not write in response to the latest fad. I rarely respond to the most recent theological argument. I seldom comment in a formal way on the current preoccupations. Whether anyone reads my books or not, I want them to be worth reading in seventy-five years. Whether I get thousands of hits on my blog this week or not is not my concern. I would rather write something that will change someone or help someone permanently than simply drive traffic and get attention.

In my view, entirely too many independent Baptist pastors do the exact opposite of what I just described. They push their people to the breaking point in order to get a crowd now. They stress giving with ferocious intensity so that they may construct a show piece of a building now. They move and act and run and jump and yell and scream and manipulate and extort and demand and insist with increasing vehemence. In the short term, it works beautifully. In the long term, what they build collapses into ruin shortly after their ministry is over.

When you build for the long term, you build carefully.

Contrarily, when you build for the long term, you build carefully. You take the time necessary, all the time that is needed, in order to solve problems permanently. You build people rather than crowds. You grow men rather than reputation. You develop your prayer life rather than your number of social media followers. You stay out of debt. You preach substance. You disciple and discipline and mentor and lead and follow and exemplify and assert with the long view.

Finally, and most importantly, you take the longest of views. Someday you will stand before God and give an account of your stewardship of that Sunday school class, of that youth group, of that bus route, of that class, of that church, of those children. Will you do it with joy or with grief? When your works are lit on fire, will they burn or remain? How will those whom you fashioned, led, taught, influenced, motivated, and constructed do on that Day? May God grant us leaders who keep eternity in view!

In this way, we will build faithfully and well. In this way, we will preserve and strengthen the things which remain. In this way, we will spend our lives well. In this way, we will hand to our children and grandchildren an active, vibrant, deep, and warm faith and practice. In this way, we will please God, be useful to His cause, advance His kingdom, edify His people, and bring glory to His name.

Return to the Simplicity of a Genuine Ministry

Some time ago I was idly leafing through a magazine that had come across my desk. I had not subscribed to it; it just shows up from time to time. It is a bi-monthly periodical of one of the fundamentalist organizations mentioned previously on these pages. On page eleven I ran across an article about the importance of the pastor's prayer life. The Holy Spirit graciously stirred my heart as I read it. Leaving my office, I walked up the steps into our church auditorium and prayed for a while. Some time later I returned to my office to find the magazine open to page thirteen. The article there, entitled "How To Make An Effective Preacher", was credited to an unknown author. I have since discovered it was penned by a Presbyterian pastor named Floyd Doud Shafer in 1961. From the very first word it arrested me as nothing I had read in years had. In short order I found my heart burning within me, and the tears flowed so swiftly down my face I could barely see the words. It spoke with an eloquent simplicity and a fiery passion about the things that must needs be present in the life of a pastor. I can think of no better words of my own with which to end my advice to the independent Baptist movement. So here it is. May God grant that it set your heart on fire like it did my own.

"There was a time, about three generations ago, when the minister was known as the parson. Parson, in those days, was not a nickname, but an honorific title, and it meant The Person. More often than not the parson was the best educated man in the community and he ranked with the physician and the pedagogue, and the lawyer in eminence. But our time has seen a complete switch in this situation. The minister is no longer a parson. The advent of a highly educated public has put the minister close to the bottom of the listings in educated persons. Our reaction to this turn of events should have been a determined and disciplined effort to regain and maintain superior excellence in the things which pertain to God. Instead, the clergy retreated in mad scramble behind the breastworks of administrative detail, ecclesiastical trivia, and community vagrancy. Whenever our conscience bothered us, we simply ran off to another meeting to make arrangements for succeeding meetings to flee to. We are no longer parsons, now we are 'good Joes' and in place of providing the Church with her needed 'Scholar teachers' who are equipped to bring God and man together in reasoned relation, we now find ourselves among those who need to be reached by the 'Scholar Teacher' and wise men of God. What is the resolution of this ridiculous farce?

The answer ought to be obvious. Actually, it is in the nature of a cabala. Here it is in taunting simplicity: Make him a minister of the Word! But what does that mean? What could be more esoteric? Very well, we will say it with more passionate bluntness. Fling him into his office, tear the office sign from the door and nail on the sign: 'Study.' Take him off the mailing list, lock him up with his books (get him all kinds of books) and his typewriter and his Bible. Slam him down on his knees before texts, broken hearts, and the flippant lives of a superficial flock, and the Holy God. Throw him into the ring to box with God till he learns how short his arms are: engage him to wrestle with God all the night through. Let him come out only when he is bruised and beaten into being a blessing. Set a time clock on him that will imprison him with thought and writing about God for 40 hours a week. Shut his garrulous mouth forever spouting 'remarks' and stop his tongue always tripping lightly over everything non-essential. Require him to have something to say before he dare break silence. Bend his knees in the lonesome valley, fire him from the PTA and cancel his country club membership: burn his eyes with weary study, wreck his emotional poise with worry for God, and make him exchange his pious stance for a humble walk with God and man. Make him spend and be spent for the glory of God.

Rip out his telephone, burn up his ecclesiastical success sheets, refuse his glad hand, and put water in the gas tank of his community buggy. Give him a Bible and tie him to his pulpit and make him preach the Word of the Living God. Test him, quiz him and examine him: humiliate him for his ignorance of things divine, and shame him for his glib comprehension of finances, batting averages, and political infighting. Laugh at his frustrated effort to play psychiatrist, scorn his insipid morality, refuse his supine intelligence, ignore his broadmindedness which is only flat headedness, and compel him to be a minister of the Word. If he wants to be gracious, challenge him rather to be a product of the rough grace of God. If he dotes on being pleasing, demand that he please God and not man. If he wants to be unctuous, ask him to make sounds with a tongue on which a Holy Flame has rested. If he wants to be a manager, insist rather that he be a manikin for God, a being who is illustrative of the purpose and will of God.

Form a choir and raise a chant and haunt him with it night and day: 'Sir, we wish to see Jesus.' When, at long last, he dares assay the pulpit, ask him if he has a word from God: if

Form a choir and raise a chant and haunt him with it night and day: "Sir, we wish to see Jesus."
-Floyd Doud Shafer

he does not, then dismiss him and tell him you can read the morning paper, digest the television commentaries, think through the day's superficial problems, manage the community's myriad drives, and bless assorted baked potatoes and green beans ad infinitum better than he can. Command him not to come back until he has read and re-read, written and re-written, until he can stand up, worn and forlorn, and say, 'Thus saith the Lord!' Break him across the board of his ill-gotten popularity, smack him hard with his own prestige, corner him with questions about God, and cover him with demands for celestial wisdom, and give him no escape until he is backed against the wall of the Word: then sit down before him and listen to the only word he has left: God's Word. Let him be totally ignorant of the down-street gossip, but give him a chapter and order him to walk around it, camp on it, suffer with it, and come at last to speak it backwards and forwards until all he says about it rings with the truth of eternity. Ask him to produce living credentials that he has been and is true father in his own home before you allow him license to play father to all and sundry. Demand to be shown that his love is deep, strong, and secure among those nearest and dearest to him before he is given contract to share the superfluity of his affability with all sorts and conditions of persons. Examine his manse whether it be a seminary of faith, hope, learning, and love or a closet of fretting, doubt, dogmatism, and temper; if it be the latter, then quarantine him in it for praying, crying, and conversion, and then let him go forth converted, to convert.

Mold him relentlessly into a man forever bowed but never cowed before the unconcealed truth which he has labored to reveal, and let him hang flung against the destiny of Almighty God; let his soul be stripped bare before the onrushing purposes of God, and let him be lost, doomed, and done that his God alone be all in all. Let him, in himself, be sign and symbol that everything human is lost, that Grace comes through loss; and make him the illustration that Grace alone is amazing, sufficient, and redemptive. Let him be transparent to God's grace, God himself. And when he is burned out by the flaming Word that coursed through him, when he is consumed at last by the fiery Grace blazing through him, and when he who was privileged to translate the truth of God to man is finally translated from earth to heaven, then bear him away gently, blow a muted trumpet and lay him down softly, place a two-edged sword on his coffin and raise a tune triumphant, for he was a brave soldier of the Word and e'er he died he had become spokesman of his God."

Epilogue

For the past year this book has lain heavy on my heart. More times than I care to remember the wee hours of the morning have found me wide awake, debating whether I ought to publish it or not. Frankly, I am afraid. I am afraid that it will mark me for the rest of my ministry as a malcontented critic. I am afraid it will limit future ministry opportunities for me. I am afraid I will be completely misunderstood. I am afraid that in later years I will look back and wonder why I just did not keep my mouth shut. Alongside my own fears I have fears for others. I fear my friends will be tarred by the same brush the critics will use to tar me. I am afraid I will hurt good men, that I will cause pain and puzzlement in their heart over something I have said. I am afraid our enemies will use these words as a rhetorical club against us.

...yet here it is anyway. As Jeremiah said, ...*his word was in mine heart as a burning fire shut up in my bones, And I was weary with forbearing, and I could not stay. (Jeremiah 20.9)* This book is all that is in my heart, and soul, and mind. Writing it has been in every sense of the word a labor. Paul told the Galatians, *My little children, of whom I travail in birth again until Christ be formed in you. (Galatians 4.19)* As God sees my heart that is the great cause behind my travail. I long to see the leaders, the churches, the pastors, and the people in the independent Baptist movement formed into the image of Christ. I likewise long to see that in my own life and ministry. If somehow in the process of this burden of my soul, this travail has hurt you I am sorry. If you believe me to be greatly in the wrong then pray greatly for me. I shall, in turn, pray for you as well, and look forward to the time in Heaven when no misunderstandings, misapprehensions, or mistakes will mar our perfect fellowship with God and with one another.

On the other hand, if you have found something or several somethings in this book to be helpful please share it. Pass your copy along to your friends. Quote selections from it on social media or in your blog. Recommend it to those you know who are struggling with what they believe, or wondering if they ought to remain independent Baptist. Copy a chapter or two and give it away. The truth is I will never make any money off of this book. In fact, I seriously doubt I will break even so do not let that bother you. My writing is a ministry. If you can think of some way to use it to minister to those around you whom you know to be in need do so. Nothing would please me more.

In closing, let me say that I welcome a conversation with you if you are so inclined. I may be reached on Facebook at Brennan's Pen, via email at brennanspen@gmail.com, at my website brennanspen.com, or on my blog at concerningjesus.blogspot.com. In the meantime, *The Lord bless thee, and keep thee: The Lord make his face shine upon thee, and be gracious unto thee: The Lord lift up his countenance upon thee, and give thee peace. (Numbers 6.24-26)*

Select Bibliography

Alfred Edersheim, *The Life and Times of Jesus the Messiah, Volumes I* and *II,* 1972, Grand Rapids, Michigan, Wm. B. Eerdmans Publishing Company, 1,523 pages total

Andrew Himes, *The Sword of the Lord, The Roots of Fundamentalism in an American Family,* 2010, Seattle, Washington, Chiara Press, 316 pages

C. H. Spurgeon, *C. H. Spurgeon's Autobiography, His Diary, Letters, and Records, Volumes I, II, III,* and *IV,* 1992, Pasadena, Texas, Pilgrim Publications, 1507 pages total

Cindy Hyles Schaap, *The Fundamental Man, Jack Frasure Hyles, A Biography,* 1998, Hammond, Indiana, Hyles Publications, 528 pages

Dan Lucarini, *Why I Left the Contemporary Christian Music Movement, Confessions of a Former Worship Leader,* 2004, Webster, New York, Evangelical Press, 141 pages

David Martyn Lloyd-Jones, *The Unsearchable Riches of Christ,* 1979, Ann Arbor, Michigan, Baker Book House, 315 pages

David O. Beale, *In Pursuit of Purity, American Fundamentalism Since 1850,* 1986, Greenville, South Carolina, Unusual Publications, 457 pages

Dennis Corle, *The Chemistry of Separation,* 1999, Claysburg, Pennsylvani, Revival Fires! Publishing, 554 pages

E. M. Bounds, *The Complete Works of E. M. Bounds on Prayer,* 1990, Grand Rapids, Michigan, Baker Books, 568 pages

Elmer L. Towns, *World's Largest Sunday School,* 1974, self-published, 189 pages

Ernest D. Pickering, *The Tragedy of Compromise, The Origin and Impact of New Evangelicalism,* 1994, Greenville, South Carolina, Bob Jones University Press, 184 pages

Ernest Pickering, *Biblical Separation, The Struggle for a Pure Church,* 2008, Schaumburg, Illinois, Regular Baptist Press, 318 pages

F. B. Meyer, *Moses, The Servant of God,* 2002, Fort Washington, Pennsylvania, CLC Publications, 233 pages

Fawn M. Brodie, *No Man Knows My History, The Life of Joseph Smith the Mormon Prophet,* 1979, New York, New York, Alfred A. Knopf, 499 pages

Frank Garlock, Kurt Woetzel, *Music in the Balance,* 1998, Greenville, South Carolina, Majesty Music, Incorporated, 204 pages

Fred Moritz, *Be Ye Holy, The Call to Christian Separation,* 1994, Greenville, South Carolina, BJU Press, 134 pages

G. Campbell Morgan, *The Crises of the Christ,* 1936, Old Tappan, New Jersey, Fleming H. Revell Company, 477 pages

J. C. Ryle, *Holiness,* no date given, Old Tappan, New Jersey, Fleming H. Revell Company, 333 pages

J. Dwight Pentecost, *The Words and Works of Jesus Christ, A Study of the Life of Christ,* 1981, Grand Rapids, Michigan, Zondervan Publishing House, 629 Pages

J. Gresham Machen, *Christianity and Liberalism,* 1923, Grand Rapids, Michigan, William B. Eerdmans Publishing Company, 189 pages

J. W. Shepard, *The Christ of the Gospels, An Exegetical Study,* 1939, Grand Rapids, Michigan, Wm. B. Eerdmans Publishing Company, 650 pages

James Stalker, *The Trial and Death of Jesus Christ, A Devotional History of our Lord's Passion,* 2007, Charleston, South Carolina, Bibliobazaar, 195 pages

James L. Snyder, *In Pursuit of God, The Life of A. W. Tozer,* 1991, Camp Hill, Pennsylvania, Christian Publications, Inc. 236 pages

James R. Beller, *America in Crimson Red, The Baptist History of America*, 2004, Arnold, Missouri, Prairie Fire Press, 606 pages

John M. Frame, *Contemporary Worship Music, A Biblical Defense*, 1997, Philipsburg, New Jersey, Presbyterian and Reformed Publishing Company, 212 pages

John Stalker, Dan Lucarini, *Can We Rock the Gospel? Rock Music's Impact on Worship and Evangelism*, 2006, Webster, New York, Evangelical Press, 267 pages

Karen Armstrong, *Muhammad, A Biography of the Prophet*, 1992, New York, New York, HarperSanFrancisco, 290 pages

Kevin Bauder, Robert Delnay, *One in Hope and Doctrine, Origins of Baptist Fundamentalism 1870-1950*, 2014. Schaumburg, Illinois, Regular Baptist Books, 387 pages

Kevin Bauder, Roy E. Beacham, *One Bible Only? Examining the Exclusive Claims for the King James Bible*, 2001, Grand Rapids, Michigan, Kregel Publications, 238 pages

Loraine Boettner, *Roman Catholicism*, 1962, Phillipsburg, New Jersey, The Presbyterian and Reformed Publishing Company, 466 pages

Marty Braemer, *This Little Light*, 1997, Claysburg, Pennsylvania, Revival Fires! Publishers, 73 pages

Michael Kerrigan, *A Dark History: The Roman Emperors, From Julius Caesar to the Fall of Rome*, 2011, New York, Metro Books, 255 pages

Ned B. Stonehouse, *J. Gresham Machen, A Biographical Memoir*, 2004, Willow Grove, Pennsylvania, The Committee for the Historian of the Orthodox Presbyterian Church, 470 pages

Phil Stringer, *Faithful Baptist Witness*, 1998, Haines City, Florida, Landmark Baptist Press, 267 pages

R. A. Torrey, A. C. Dixon and Others, *The Fundamentals, A Testimony to the Truth, Volumes 1, II, III,* and *IV*, 2000, Grand Rapids, Michigan, Baker Book House, 1470 pages total

Robert Duncan Culver, *The Life of Christ*, 1993, Grand Rapids, Michigan, Baker Book House, 304 pages

Roger Martin, *R. A. Torrey, Apostle of Certainty*, 1976, Murfreesboro, Tennessee, Sword of the Lord Publishers, 300 pages

Viola Walden, *John R. Rice, "The Captain of our Team"*, 1994, Murfreesboro, Tennessee, Sword of the Lord Publishers, 528 pages

William P. Grady, *Final Authority, A Christian's Guide to the King James Bible*, 1995, Schererville, Indiana, Grady Publications, 392 pages

About the author

Tom Brennan is the pastor of the Maplewood Bible Baptist Church in Chicago where he has served for the past twelve years. He and his lovely wife of sixteen years, Mandy, have three children. Tom is happiest at home, surrounded by his family, with a cup of tea to hand, and a large stack of books within easy reach.

For more detail see his author page, brennanspen.com.

Additionally, he can be found blogging quite regularly at concerningjesus.blogspot.com.

Also by Tom Brennan and available through Xulon Press...

THE GREATEST SERMON EVER PREACHED

TOM BRENNAN

Jesus was the greatest preacher who ever lived. His greatest sermon was given on a hill overlooking the Sea of Galilee toward the beginning of His ministry. Over the course of three chapters early in the New Testament it offers us both a connection to the Old Testament and an explicit appeal to a new kind of life. It balances inward calls to self-examination with eminently practical instructions relating to daily life.

This book is both an explanation of and an application of that great sermon. Over the course of thirty chapters the author walks through its sections and emphases. He lays before us the intent of Jesus' message by immersing us in His day while at the same time relating that message to our own. In the process he directly challenges us to live, inwardly and outwardly, the truths found in the greatest sermon ever preached.